Knowledge Shared

Knowledge Shared

Participatory Evaluation in
Development Cooperation

Edward T. Jackson and Yusuf Kassam
editors

This book is dedicated, with great hope, to the next generation of development workers and practitioners of participatory evaluation: may your senses be keen, your hearts joyful, and your solidarity with others permanent. We also dedicate this book to our children: Noah and Jacob, and Yassir and Omer.

Knowledge Shared: Participatory Evaluation in Development Cooperation.

Published 1998 in the United States of America by Kumarian Press, Inc., 14 Oakwood Avenue, West Hartford, Connecticut 06119-2127 USA.

Published 1998 in Canada by the International Development Research Centre, PO Box 8500, Ottawa, Canada K1G 3H9.

Production supervised by Jenna Dixon   Copyedited and proofread by Linda Lotz
Typeset by First Folio Resource Group, Inc.   Index by George Neumann
The text of this book is set in 10/13 Adobe Meridien.
The display type is Adobe Antique Olive.

Printed in Canada on acid-free paper by Transcontinental Printing and Graphics. Text printed with vegetable oil-based ink.

⊗ The paper used in this publication meets the minimum requirements of the American National Standard for Information Sciences—Permanence of Paper for Printed Library Materials, ANSI Z39.48-1984.

Library of Congress Cataloging-in-Publication Data
   Knowledge shared : participatory evaluation in development
     cooperation / Edward T. Jackson and Yusuf Kassam, editors.
       p.   cm.
   Includes bibliographical references and index.
   ISBN 1-56549-085-1 (pbk. : alk. paper)
   1. Evaluation research (Social action programs). 2. Rural development—
Evaluation. I. Jackson, Edward T., 1951–   . II. Kassam, Yusuf, 1943–
H62.K627   1998
300'.72—dc21   98-35799

Canadian Cataloging in Publication Data
Main entry under title :

Knowledge shared : participatory evaluation in development cooperation

Includes bibliographical references.
ISBN 0-88936-868-6

1. Economic development projects — Developing countries — Evaluation.
2. Sustainable development — Developing countries — Evaluation.
3. Community development — Developing countries — Evaluation.
I. Jackson, Edward T.
II. Kassam, Yusuf.
III. International Development Research Centre (Canada)

HC79.E44K46   1998   338.91   C98-980291-4

07 06 05 04 03 02 01 00 99 98   10 9 8 7 6 5 4 3 2 1   1st Printing 1998

Contents

Illustrations

Foreword

This is a most welcome addition to the growing world literature on participatory research and evaluation. It is welcome because there is a large and continuing interest in participatory evaluation on the world scene. Nongovernmental organizations, government social agencies, intergovernmental bodies, and social movement structures of many types have expressed a preference for participatory forms of evaluation. Indeed, unless an evaluation plan has some provision for participation by either intended beneficiaries or stakeholders, it is likely to be rejected in these times. This book provides readers with a variety of articles covering such critical themes as ethics, techniques, case studies, historic reflections, and invitations to action. Further, this anthology brings together some of the best-known specialists from many parts of the world. This is a book that has a global feel because it is an articulation of a global network of colleagues who in a variety of formal and informal ways follow and support one another's work.

This book is doubly important because it represents a collaboration between two senior international scholar-activist-practitioners. Yusuf Kassam and Edward T. Jackson have both been at the task of thinking about and doing participatory research for roughly twenty-five years each. Yusuf Kassam began working along these lines as a professor of adult education at Tanzania's University of Dar es Salaam and as director of the Institute of Adult Education in his birthplace of Tanzania. He was the first coordinator of the African Participatory Research Network, affiliated with the work of the International Council for Adult Education (ICAE), and subsequently worked at the ICAE Secretariat in Toronto, Canada, for many years. His pioneering work in participatory research and evaluation, particularly his giving audibility to the voices of rural literacy learners, is internationally respected.

Ted Jackson began his work in the evaluation of social action projects with Frontier College in Canada's Atlantic provinces in the early 1970s. He developed his thinking and practical skills further in collaboration with a number of indigenous colleagues, including Grace Hudson and Gerry McKay from Big Trout Lake in northern Ontario, as they worked on an evaluation of the environmental impact of water and sanitation options in that community. His comparative and international work began at that time as well, as he made his first links with Ghana via a Canadian government project on rural water supply in the northern region of that country. He has gone on to become, along with Yusuf Kassam, among the best-known and best-respected evaluation specialists internationally. And like Kassam, Jackson's life's work maintains a consistent subtext of social, economic, and environmental justice.

This volume, like the concept of participatory evaluation itself, contains and represents the full range of tensions that an applied practice in this world manifests. Who has the right to evaluate whom? If evaluation is, as Kamla Bhasin notes in this collection, "reflection on action," why is the literature of evaluation so monopolized by the writings of those who serve the dominant interests? Why does the evaluation literature so seldom reflect the direct concerns of the majority of the poor? What are the discursive forms of a social movement evaluation literature? Like the concept of research itself, is the very concept of evaluation an intellectual construct of knowledge and power, as Foucault notes, which limits the possibility of transforming power relations? In other words, do the language and forms of work that make up the discourse and practice of evaluation inevitably limit it as a transformative practice? Or can a social movement or civil society organization initiate processes of participatory evaluation that will in fact contribute to the strengthening of resistance and/or the modifying of power relations in specific contexts?

Covering oneself in a cloak of participatory evaluation is another tension raised by this volume. There are many evaluations that claim to be participatory but upon reflection are anything but. And in a global context, where the very word *development* has become a code for a form of economic and political relations that is ultimately destructive, the fact that so much of the evaluation literature grows from that financial base raises still more questions. Participation, when invited by the powerful of the less powerful, offers as many dangers as opportunities.

But at the same time, this volume provides readers with ideas about working in many new directions. Those of us who from time to time are engaged in evaluations might ask ourselves a series of questions provoked by these authors. To what extent are the voices of those who have been marginalized made audible through our work? What structures are in place to protect those whose voices are critical? To what degree does our work enhance the capacity to resist of women, racial minorities, the young, and those with different physical or mental abilities? How can real economic or related benefits for all those participating along with us be achieved? How can new paradigms for community, sustainability, deepened democratic life, or human rights be shared if and when they arise from work of this nature? And finally, how can social movements and civil society organizations themselves initiate effective evaluations of the institutions and forms of political and economic domination that most affect them?

One of my first publications was a chapter on evaluation for the 1972 *Handbook on Adult Education* published by the Institute of Adult Education in Dar es Salaam. The title of that chapter was "Evaluation: How Well Have We

Done?" Based on the spirit represented by this most valuable and internationally representative book, I would say that we have done very well indeed, but
there is still much to keep us busy for years to come.

Budd L. Hall
Chair, Department of Adult Education, Community Development and
Counselling Psychology, Ontario Institute for Studies in Education,
University of Toronto

Acknowledgments

We owe great thanks to the contributors of this volume, who responded enthusiastically and rapidly to our call for papers in late 1993. The "test runs" for this volume took place in Ottawa in 1993 at the annual conference of the Canadian Association for the Study of International Development and, with the assistance of the International Development Centre, in Vancouver in 1995 at the International Evaluation Conference. Both sessions were received very positively. Our day-to-day work in teaching and consulting further convinced us that there was a readership for the book, so we pressed on toward publication.

We would like to thank the First Folio Resource Group of Toronto for editorial assistance. Our colleagues at E.T. Jackson and Associates Ltd. have also been valuable allies in this project, particularly Huguette Labrosse, Janis Norris, and Nancy Peck. So too has Norean Shepherd of Carleton University's Centre for the Study of Training, Investment and Economic Restructuring. And we continue to draw great inspiration from leaders in the field of participatory evaluation and research around the globe. Among those special persons are Kamla Bhasin, Robert Chambers, Patricia Ellis, Orlando Fals-Borda, Marie-Thérèse Feuerstein, Paulo Freire, John Gaventa, Budd Hall, David Smith, Marja-Liisa Swantz, Rajesh Tandon, and Francisco Vio Grossi.

Finally, we wish to thank our partners, Magda Seydegart and Zubeda Kassam, for generously giving us the love, space, and support to complete this project and the many others in which we are privileged to be engaged.

INTRODUCTION

Edward T. Jackson and Yusuf Kassam

Knowledge shared equals results shared.

At the onset of the twenty-first century, the concept of sharing enjoys little currency among elites and the dominant media; our airwaves, newspapers, and websites are crammed with stories about the folly and the tragedy of domination, selfishness, and greed. Yet human beings have always shared with one another, and continue to do so. In every community on the planet, remarkable acts of solidarity and mutual aid enrich and enliven everyday life. Our species is oriented to sustaining the collectivity as well as to meeting our own individual needs.

Sharing is central to successful development cooperation. Within poor and disempowered areas, amid scarcity and want, resources must be pooled and channeled into common, achievable undertakings. In development cooperation, the most effective interventions are carried out by coalitions of interests in both the South and the North: villagers and barrio residents, local development workers, government officials, local nongovernmental organization (NGO) staff, Northern development specialists, and donor agency personnel. Sharing information, resources, and common objectives, such coalitions can influence, even drive, all phases of the intervention cycle: planning, implementation, and evaluation.

Evaluation involves the production of knowledge about the effectiveness and efficiency of development interventions. Traditionally, most evaluations have been donor driven and professionally controlled; they have been top-down exercises in which the sharing of knowledge has occurred too little and too late. However, many years of development practice have established beyond doubt that local citizens possess valuable information and analytical capacity to assess the achievements and constraints of development processes. Participatory evaluation strategies can help communities and development agencies mobilize and share local knowledge in combination with the expertise of outside specialists. The shared knowledge that emerges through this process is more accurate, more complex, and more useful than knowledge that is produced and deployed by professionals alone. It is precisely by sharing the different types of knowledge they bring to the evaluation process—and the new knowledge they create together—that citizens and professionals can generate analysis that will render interventions more capable of yielding significant and lasting results.

Shared knowledge is the essence of participatory evaluation. Shared knowledge better serves the interests of both the local beneficiaries and development agencies. By its very nature, participatory evaluation democratizes and enriches the assessment of development. At the same time, participatory evaluation enhances the capacity of interventions to achieve impacts that benefit the stakeholders engaged in the process. Drawing on experience from all parts of the world, this book examines the practice of participatory evaluation: its limits and its potential, what works and what doesn't work, the issues that frame and shape it, and the diversity of methods used to implement this approach to evaluation.

The Diverse Identities of Participatory Evaluation

Participatory evaluation has been given varied and multiple meanings by practitioners around the world. The profile of participatory evaluation takes on different forms, depending on the conceptual and methodological framework emerging out of a given context and a particular set of circumstances. Such a framework is determined by the varying degrees of emphasis or priority given to one or more of the following main characteristics of participatory evaluation. It is a process that:

- Supports and extends participatory models of development more generally;
- Empowers communities, organizations, and individuals to analyze and solve their own problems;
- Values the knowledge and experience of local citizens in analyzing their economic, political, social, and cultural reality;
- Uses learning and education to promote reflection and critical analysis by both project participants and development workers;
- Serves the purpose of improving the program and organization in a given development intervention, in the interests of the beneficiaries;
- Involves the active participation of project beneficiaries, who play a decisive role in the entire evaluation process;
- Promotes the beneficiaries' ownership of a development program;
- Uses participatory methods of obtaining data and generating knowledge, employing a wide range of predominantly qualitative methods, sometimes in combination with quantitative methods; and
- Is participatory and collective and that creates better, more in-depth, and more accurate knowledge of the performance and impacts of a development intervention.

After more than two decades of practice and reflection, participatory evaluation has now acquired four broad identities: as a development intervention in its own right, as a project management tool for sustainable development, as a source of obtaining qualitative data, and as a challenge to the conventional ways in which donor agencies undertake the evaluation of their development assistance. In relation to this last identity, some practitioners of participatory evaluation in recent years have been testing approaches to better serve the needs of both donor agencies and beneficiaries. This is important work.

For the purposes of this book, we propose the following working definition of our subject:

> Participatory evaluation is a process of self-assessment, collective knowledge production, and cooperative action in which the stakeholders in a development intervention participate substantively in the identification of the evaluation issues, the design of the evaluation, the collection and analysis of data, and the action taken as a result of the evaluation findings. By participating in this process, the stakeholders also build their own capacity and skills to undertake research and evaluation in other areas and to promote other forms of participatory development. Participatory evaluation seeks to give preferential treatment to the voices and decisions of the least powerful and most affected stakeholders—the local beneficiaries of the intervention. This approach to evaluation employs a wide range of data collection and analysis techniques, both qualitative and quantitative, involving fieldwork, workshops, and movement building.

This introductory chapter highlights the major critical issues and themes—development-related, epistemological, and methodological—as they have emerged in the evolution of the theory and practice of participatory evaluation over the past two decades.

Development Issues

Starting with Empowerment

The term *participatory evaluation* first appeared twenty years ago in development cooperation literature in the context of increasing interest in the paradigm of *participatory development*. Case studies and manuals for practitioners were published and circulated in the 1970s and 1980s by engaged scholars, development practitioners, and some policymakers in the large donor agencies. Participatory evaluation techniques were applied around the world, at the local level, through the various disciplinary or sectoral "lenses," including adult education, anthropology, sociology, primary health care, water supply and sanitation, and rural and community development. At the heart of all this work, and, in effect, what binds this literature together, lies the conviction that *evaluation should and can be used to empower the local citizens to analyze and solve their own problems.* In this sense, participatory evaluation has distinguished itself from conventional forms of aid evaluation. Conventional approaches have relied heavily on outside professional experts to "objectively" assess the technical and management effectiveness and efficiency of development interventions with reference to project plans, logical frameworks, and work breakdown structures. Conventional evaluation has not challenged power relations in the development process.

Advocates of participatory evaluation staked out their ground vigorously and often aggressively, arguing on many levels in favor of the right of local citizens to define and shape their world, and that such a process yields more accurate and more socially just and equitable development strategies. Northern and Southern practitioners alike were influenced by the work of Southern educators, intellectuals, and activists such as Paulo Freire and Orlando Fals-Borda and later by Kamla Bhasin, Rajesh Tandon, Anisur Rahman, Francisco Vio Grossi, and many others. Inspired by Southern practitioners and stimulated by the experience of working in the South, many Northern practitioners also began to articulate the theory and shape the practice of participatory evaluation (see Selener 1997). They included Marja-Liisa Swantz, Budd Hall, John Gaventa, Marie-Thérèse Feuerstein, and Robert Chambers. A host of nongovernmental and other organizations around the world adopted participatory research and evaluation as their modus operandi. These organizations included the International Council for Adult Education and its regional affiliates, CUSO in Asia, Oxfam-UK, the Dutch agency NOVIB in Latin America, and many units of UNICEF, to name only a few.

As participatory evaluation began to be used more widely in the 1980s, it was found that, in some instances, it degenerated into a narrowly conceived *technical* application of a "toolbox" of methods. Advocates cautioned that participatory evaluation is not merely a technical exercise. They reminded the development community that the central mission of participatory evaluation is to *empower* individuals and communities, not merely to mobilize their labor or ideas.

During the 1990s, the limitations of local participation have increasingly been recognized. Practitioners became aware that the participation process must be reconceptualized to include other stakeholders involved in development interventions. This did not mean abandoning preferential treatment for the participation of local citizens and, in particular, the poor. But it did call for greater recognition and precision in analyzing *whose* participation and how these various participations interrelate (Rebiens 1995). Consequently, the rhetoric of people's justice and revolution of the 1970s has been ratcheted down and, for better or worse, a more pragmatic strategy for involving all stakeholders is now more frequently built into participatory evaluation. We believe that this is for the better.

The 1990s have also seen a much greater priority and visibility accorded by the large donor agencies, particularly the World Bank and some bilaterals, to participatory development. This is ironic, because such institutions for the past two decades have aggressively promoted structural adjustment programs, the very antithesis of citizen participation. Perhaps the end of the cold war and the collapse of communism have made participation a "safer" endeavor. In any case, the participation theme has now been widely "bought," for at least a while, by some interests within the large donor agencies, and this circumstance has created new space for activism by advocates of participatory evaluation and other forms of participatory development.

From Empowerment to Stakeholder Interaction

Rebiens (1995) noted that often the rhetoric of empowerment in participatory evaluations far exceeds the reality achieved on the ground. This is an important and valid observation. He also observed that there is a danger that outside professionals can, in an expression of solidarity with local citizens, put words into the mouths of project participants. This, too, is a valid concern. How the outsider manages his or her own agenda in the participatory evaluation process has always been a challenge to practitioners and is much discussed in the literature.

In response to these concerns, Rebiens argues that participatory evaluation should incorporate more centrally the framework and methods of "fourth-generation" evaluation (Guba and Lincoln 1995). In this type of evaluation, "the issues to be looked into are defined by stakeholders and where the evaluation knowledge cannot be objective, but emerges out of interaction between evaluator and evaluee" (Rebiens 1995, 9). In this sense, the concept of participation is replaced by the concept of stakeholder interaction, which offers perhaps less rhetorical attraction but more methodological achievability.

Preferential Treatment for Decisive Stakeholders

However, in participatory evaluation, some stakeholders are created more equal than others. In a full-fledged participatory evaluation process, there are decisive and non-decisive participants. "Decisive participants are those who are central to the process that is being evaluated. These are the activists, the animators, the local people. The non-decisive participants are those who have stakes in the evaluation process but, are not central to it. These are the intermediary organizations, the donors and other stakeholders" (Chaudhary, Dhar, and Tandon 1989, 9).

In other words, a bias must be built into the participatory evaluation process in favor of the poorest interests and their allies. The powerful and elites can participate, but their voices cannot be permitted to dominate. This tests the will and skill of the outsiders involved in the evaluation, who are likely being contracted and paid by the powerful rather than by the less powerful.

This fundamental commitment to a bias in favor of the least powerful constituencies in the evaluation exercise sets participatory evaluation apart from other collaborative forms of assessment. Beneficiary assessment, for example, treats the perspectives and values of local program participants as but one component of a larger effort that includes detailed analysis of the views of program managers and executives in both the North and the South (see Casely and Kumar 1987; Salmen 1987; Kumar 1993; Valdez and Bamberger 1994). When local participants' views represent only one of a menu of perspectives, there is every likelihood that the proximity, persuasiveness, and power of the Northern aid professionals and/or Southern elites and professionals will exert a dispro-portionate degree of control over the evaluation's findings and conclusions. While they may well participate and mobilize for action, such participation and action may not be relevant, and may even be in contradiction, to the interests of the poor targeted by the development intervention under study.

Several of the chapters in the present volume illustrate the countervailing forces acting against the priorities, analyses, and solutions of what should be the decisive participants in the evaluation process (see Chapters 5, 10, and 13).

Participation at Different Points on the "Aid Chain"

Development cooperation is an international enterprise with many stake-holders spanning a range of nations, classes, and cultures. Social and organiza-tional relations in development interventions can be conceived of as a chain linking identifiable components. Among the various components of this "aid chain" are Northern taxpayers, Northern (government) donor agencies, Northern implementation agencies (private firms, educational institutions, NGOs), Southern governments, Southern implementation agencies (line min-istries, national NGOs, universities), local development organizations (village development committees, neighborhood development groups), and Southern citizens who are intended to benefit, ultimately, from the intervention. These various stakeholder groups possess different levels of wealth and power, differ-ent cultures, access to different information, and different missions. Their involvement in a development program or project requires that they form, in essence, a *coalition* for the purpose of achieving the common objectives of the intervention. Stakeholders interact continuously along the aid chain, held together by the project coalition.

In conventional aid evaluations, power and influence are typically concen-trated in the hands of the sponsors of the evaluation—the donor agencies—and their consultants. Donor accountability and management concerns are weighted heavily; the time and resources devoted to beneficiary involvement are typically minor.

In contrast, the participatory evaluation approach seeks to reverse this power relationship and devote extensive resources and time to local partici-pants as authentic stakeholders. To do otherwise, as Guba and Young (1989, cited in Rebiens 1995) argue, is unfair and discriminatory, since these stake-holders have much to risk in the evaluation. At the same time, however, the participatory evaluation process seeks to ensure that other stakeholders on the aid chain are able to participate fully, especially project field staff and regional project managers in the intervention area, as well as stakeholders at other points on the chain.

Participation Continuum or Cycle of Reflection and Action?

Most literature on participatory development in general and participatory evaluation in particular includes the concept of a continuum of participation. At one end of this continuum, project beneficiaries are passive recipients of inputs and activities. At the other end of the continuum is total self-management by the beneficiary group. In between, moving from less to more participation, the other stages are consultation, consensus building, decision making, sharing of responsibilities, risk sharing, and partnership. The continuum is sometimes depicted as consecutive steps in a ladder (Beaulieu and Manoukian 1994). In general, full participation is full power sharing among the major actors.

Still, some commentators express dissatisfaction with the continuum concept. The key to understanding participation, they argue, is the cycle of problem identification, information gathering, goal setting, choosing options, and taking action. "At the point of action, the process starts over again. Life in any community is made up of a great many sequences which interpenetrate to produce a pattern of life in the community" (Smith 1995, 64). In fact, both concepts are useful. The continuum sheds light of the nature of negotiations and transactions among stakeholders. The reflection-action cycle highlights the nature of the problem-solving process used by specific groups to assert their interests.

Epistemological Issues

Macro-Level Deconstructionism

Epistemology is the study of how knowledge is produced. At the macro level, that is, at the level of societies and of national political discourse and struggle, participatory evaluation is part of the tradition of deconstructionism.

The postmodernist critiques suggest important implications for participatory evaluation in the relationship of power and knowledge and in the politics of research and knowledge. Postmodernist writers, such as Foucault (1973, 1977) and Lyotard (1984), challenge the universal validity of the overarching explanatory theories or the "grand narratives" that have shaped the politics and guided social change in the modern period. Postmodernism, recognizing a multitude of perspectives and approaches, seeks to "deconstruct," or pull apart, the grand themes by engaging in an analysis of power relationships related to specific situations and social issues.

Viewed in the context of postmodernist critiques, participatory evaluation represents an attempt to deconstruct the dominant research and evaluation paradigms. In particular, participatory evaluation attempts to change the power relations in the creation and use of knowledge. At the same time, this reconception of power and power relations addresses the larger issues of poverty, inequality, and oppression.

Micro-Level Constructionism

At the same time, recent theoretical work has more clearly identified the epistemological parameters of participatory evaluation. In particular, at the micro level, participatory evaluation is now becoming associated with constructionist epistemology, in which various stakeholders bring their perceptions and analysis of reality "to the table" to create a negotiated reality, from which flow recommendations for action (Rebiens 1995, 5). This epistemological tradition is also associated with "fourth-generation" evaluation, which is defined as an interpretative approach to evaluation based on and guided by issues identified by all stakeholders (Guba and Lincoln 1995).

Research in the education sector indicates that the process of stakeholders socially constructing their reality through participatory evaluation enhances organizational learning significantly (Cousins and Earl 1992). This is consistent with the work of Senge (1990) and others on organizational learning in other sectors. In the field of education, research committees, advisory committees, work groups, and administrative councils have all been found to be effective vehicles for cooperative stakeholder inquiry (Cousins 1996).

The Continuing Rationalist-Objectivist Challenge

Notwithstanding the growing recognition that, at the micro level, participatory evaluation is part of the constructionist paradigm, there remains a serious challenge from the rationalist-objectivist tradition. Advocates of this tradition claim that in fact an objective reality does exist, can be measured accurately, and stands apart from the subjectivity of constructionism (Mathie 1995). One source of this challenge is the dominant discourse in the mainstream evaluation field in the North, which is rooted in a rationalist-objectivist epistemology. Another is the dominant discourse in the field of development cooperation, where concerns with accountability, value for money, and results have been heightened by budget cuts and public scrutiny.

Gender and Knowledge Production

There is also a gender dimension to how knowledge is produced. Leading practitioners such as Bhasin (1992, 1994), Maguire (1987, 1993), Waring (1990), and others have shown how women are systematically excluded in most societies from knowledge-production processes that are dominated by men—even ones that claim to be participatory. Further, they have shown that, overall, women's style of creating knowledge tends to be more holistic and collective than male-dominant forms.

Participatory evaluation has, very imperfectly, begun to confront the structural implications of gender relations. Sometimes special methods are used to engage the participation of women in the evaluation process. Over the past decade, an array of gender-sensitive approaches to evaluation and impact assessment has been developed in the North (Maguire 1987) and the South (Ellis 1997).

However, too frequently, even after many years of practice, women's voices are muted and their priorities remain invisible in participatory evaluations. "Women do not have the power necessary to represent personal concerns publicly and, by default, have to conform to the categories of concern given in advance," writes Mosse (1994, 515). Scholars and practitioners of participatory evaluation everywhere must work harder to overcome such barriers to a gender-equitable process of knowledge production.

Ecology and Knowledge Production

There is an ecological dimension to knowledge production in participatory evaluation, as well. Vio Grossi argues that an ecological society, in its ideal form, is a society in a permanent process of decentralizing and distributing power, rather than concentrating it in the hands of the privileged. An authentic ecological society, he writes, is characterized by an ethic of diversity and decentralization in all aspects of life: biological, economic, political, and cultural. In the sphere of education, an ecological society must ensure equitable distribution among the population to participate in the creation of knowledge, in the process of actively learning and generating a diversity of critical, heterogeneous, and imaginative ideas (Vio Grossi 1995). Among marginalized groups of people everywhere, women, in particular, have a special role in the ecological production of knowledge (Bhasin 1994).

Methodological Issues

Relationship to Other Forms of Critical, Collaborative Inquiry

Methodologically, participatory evaluation shares much in common with other forms of critical, collaborative inquiry. In particular, participatory evaluation is closely related to what is known as participatory research and participatory action research. Growing out of the work of Paulo Freire, Francisco Vio Grossi, Rajesh Tandon, Patricia Ellis, Kamla Bhasin, Marie-Thérèse Feuerstein, and the International Council for Adult Education, participatory research, like participatory evaluation, "links social investigation to education and action" (Hall, Etherington, and Jackson 1979, 5) and relies on committed, activist outside evaluators to promote the community's right to know and control the knowledge creation process (Fernandes and Tandon 1981; Chaudhary, Dhar, and Tandon 1989).

Participatory action research is closely associated with the work of Orlando Fals-Borda, Anisur Rahman, Susanta Tilakaranta, and many others and seeks to enable marginalized groups in society to construct countervailing power to that of their oppressors through the acquisition of serious and reliable knowledge. With its roots in sociology and anthropology, participatory action research pays special attention to methods that involve collective research, value folk culture, recover indigenous history, and produce and diffuse new knowledge (Fals-Borda and Rahman 1991).

A term that is currently receiving prominence in some evaluation literature is *empowerment evaluation*. According to Fetterman (1996, 4), empowerment evaluation "is the use of evaluation concepts, techniques and findings to foster improvement" among citizens and the programs intended to serve them. Emerging from community psychology and community development, this approach to evaluation is "attentive to empowering processes" (Fetterman 1996, 4) and uses self-evaluation and reflection by program participants to collectively help themselves and improve their programs. Outside evaluators act as coaches or facilitators in these processes, in which training, advocacy, and action all are essential elements. Although not as overtly or ambitiously political as participatory action research or participatory research, empowerment evaluation is clearly related to participatory evaluation as well.

Qualitative and Quantitative Methods

Participatory evaluation employs a wide range of qualitative and quantitative research techniques. The use of some of these techniques is demonstrated in the case studies presented in this book. Among the qualitative methods used in these processes are community evaluation committees, community workshops, self-directed focus groups, popular theater, community radio, transect walks, wealth ranking, and many others. Participatory evaluations may also make use of quantitative methods that rely on questionnaires, household interviews, and survey sampling techniques, as well as computerized statistical analysis. With today's powerful notebook computers, sophisticated quantitative data analysis can be carried out around the campfire at night in rural areas. In any case, the choice of methods used in any particular evaluation project will depend on local conditions and the comfort level, skills, and interests of various stakeholders. The ability to choose from a diversity of techniques, observes Tandon (1990, 100), is "important because some constituencies may feel more comfortable using stories, drawings, role-plays, theatre, puppetry, and similar other forms of data collection and analysis, while others may feel more familiar and comfortable with questionnaires, in-depth interviews, surveys and the like" (see also Marsden, Oakley, and Pratt 1994; Marsden and Oakley 1990; Feuerstein 1978, 1986, 1988).

Practitioners have begun to turn their attention to developing, in conjunction with communities, qualitative and quantitative indicators of effectiveness, efficiency, and impacts. Considerable emphasis in this work is placed on devising indicators or indices that measure the capacity of communities to manage the development process (see, for example, Chapter 4).

Partnership: Shared Values and Equality

Participatory evaluation can also be viewed in the context of the development paradigm of *partnership* in international development cooperation. Among other elements of a genuine partnership relationship between Northern and Southern development organizations, participatory evaluation contributes to building relationships based on the values of equality, sharing, mutual trust, and transparency. Seen from this perspective, participatory evaluation can be one of the key interventions that helps to overcome the donor-driven and control-oriented approaches that predominate the field of development cooperation (see Gariba, Kassam, and Thibault 1994).

In the context of the dynamics of a genuine partnership, and given sufficient will on the part of Northern donors to engage in a partnership relationship, participatory evaluation can both strengthen recipient ownership and accommodate donor accountability requirements. In addition, since the concept of partnership is integrally linked with the process of capacity building, participatory evaluation contributes to the building of research and evaluation capacities of the Southern partners.

In terms of relations between implementing agencies, there are good reasons for partnerships in participatory evaluations to be Southern led rather than, as is usually the case, being led by the North. Southern-led partnerships are guided by an in-country project team with the authority, knowledge, and skills to move the project ahead efficiently and effectively. Foreign resources should be mobilized only when necessary, set clearly within the context and priorities established by the Southern team. There are considerable cost savings to be accrued in view of the lower fee or salary structures of Southern as opposed to Northern development professionals and the fewer mistakes and less wasted time and resources resulting from the decisions of an on-site, knowledge-intensive team (Gariba and Jackson 1993).

The Importance of Facilitation Skills

Clearly, the facilitation skills of participatory evaluators are central to making the process work successfully. Whether they are Northern or Southern, outsiders or insiders, those coordinating the effort must create a process and an environment that permit each of the stakeholder representatives to speak freely and to learn productively. In particular, the facilitator must create a safe environment where stakeholders will not fear retribution and where the usual hierarchies are decisively leveled. The facilitator must understand in detail the political, cultural, gender, and organizational dynamics that may prevent representatives from speaking or that may permit them to register their views assertively and clearly.

Manuals and Tool Kits

The past decade especially has witnessed the production of an array of handbooks and "toolboxes" for practitioners in participatory evaluation. In the areas of health and social development, a seminal work in this regard was Marie-Thérèse Feuerstein's 1986 book *Partners in Evaluation*, as well as subsequent articles and reports by Feuerstein (1988). In water and sanitation, Deepa Narayan of the World Bank has been a leader (Narayan and Srinivasan 1995; Narayan 1993; Narayan-Parker 1991). In community forestry, the Food and Agriculture Organization has published practitioner guides on participatory evaluation (for example, Davis-Case 1990). A superb bibliography developed by the Institute of Development Studies at Sussex University and published by the International Institute for Environment and Development, based in London, abstracts manuals and tool kits produced by such Northern NGOs as Actionaid, World Vision International, the World Resources Institute, PACT, Enfants du Monde, and Save the Children U.K. (Gosling 1993); Southern NGOs such as the Bangladesh Rural Advancement Committee; and donor organizations, including the International Fund for Agriculture Development and the U.S. Agency for International Development (McPherson 1995). The United Nations Development Programme has published a new handbook on participatory evaluation, as well (UNDP 1997).

One of the issues highlighted by this and other bibliographies (see also Johnson 1994) is the richness of methods available in different traditions related to participatory evaluation, particularly participatory rapid appraisal (known in some quarters as participatory learning for action), NGO self-evaluation, beneficiary assessment, and so on. However, practitioners have begun to caution one another on the pitfalls of mixing potentially incompatible methods. This issue deserves closer scrutiny.

In any case, a productive dialogue on methods continues. There are many vehicles for this dialogue. *PRA/PLA Notes* is published regularly by the International Institute for Environment and Development. *Convergence*, the journal of the International Council for Adult Education, regularly publishes case studies of participatory research and evaluation, as do the *Community Development Journal*, the *Rural Extension Bulletin*, and *World Development*, among other journals concerned with development cooperation.

Challenges

Can the Powerful Change Their Behavior?

Participatory evaluation, in its fullest, most developed form, can take place only if the powerful change their behavior. They must, in Chambers's view, give things up. "For the rich to give up their wealth, without being forced by countervailing power, is difficult and improbable; but [for the powerful] to give up dominance at the personal level, putting respect in place of superiority, becoming a convenor, and provider of occasions, a facilitator and catalyst, a consultant and supporter, is less difficult; for these roles bring with them many satisfactions and non-material rewards" (Chambers 1995, 42). The task, and the opportunity, writes Chambers, is to enable large numbers of Northern aid executives and managers and senior government officials in the South to experience these satisfactions and rewards directly—personally.

The critical point here is that for less powerful interests to become authentically involved in participatory evaluations, the powerful must concede control of the process. They must place their trust in stakeholders further along on the aid chain. There is no natural contradiction between ensuring accountability and facilitating participation. In fact, as all the chapters in this book show, participation can *maximize* rather than limit results in development cooperation.

There is increasing clarity on the kinds of skills development officials require in order to help make participatory development happen. Rather than directing and controlling, project managers must learn to perform such new roles as initiating, facilitating, participating, sharing expertise, navigating, and nurturing the development process (World Bank 1996). These skills must be taught, *and rewarded.*

From Local Action to Global Change

But even if the powerful change their behavior, aren't participatory evaluations too "micro" in nature, too local, almost by definition, to exert a significant impact? Aren't the macro forces of globalization, transnational corporate strategy, and structural adjustment far more powerful? Certainly, individual participatory evaluation efforts on their own cannot change the macro context. It is essential, therefore, that networks of practitioners, scholars, agencies, and communities be established to exchange experience and aggregate lessons learned. It is also essential that communities and professionals engage in broader social movements and political activities that can build greater leverage to challenge the power of global forces and institutions.

Promoting Accountability and Results

Recent years have seen a major push among Northern donor agencies toward greater accountability and results in the delivery of development cooperation projects. Falling aid budgets and deficit-conscious legislatures have prompted calls for more value for money in development programming and have driven a move away from activity-based management regimes toward results-based management systems. Accordingly, the evaluation and monitoring functions in development cooperation—now more frequently referred to as performance review and measurement—are being "reengineered" to emphasize the assessment of outputs and impacts rather than, as in previous eras, of inputs and activities.

Can participatory evaluation promote accountability and results, or is it too "soft," too qualitative, and too process oriented? The answer is that participatory evaluation *can* advance accountability and results in international development. No one has a greater stake in optimizing results than project beneficiaries on the ground. This is precisely the group whose views and decisions can find strong expression in participatory evaluation. Furthermore, accountability and results are advanced when the broader network of stakeholders interacts, evaluating together the outputs and impacts of what has been accomplished, identifying obstacles to progress, and formulating joint action to improve the intervention. Accountability is an issue that involves more than Northern treasuries and auditors-general. A poor farmer or an illiterate microentrepreneur calling a central government official or a foreign project manager to account in a participatory evaluation workshop is an even more important type of accountability in a developmental sense.

Blending participatory evaluation with results-based management demands that local project participants, as well as other stakeholders, become engaged in a meaningful way in defining the results to be achieved by a project, as well as the indicators and methods to be used to assess performance. Because participatory evaluation will produce better knowledge than conventional forms of evaluation—that is, analysis that is more accurate and locally appropriate, often backed by a consensus among key stakeholders—it will also help produce better development results.

Confronting the Economics of Participation

One of the obstacles to widespread adoption of participatory evaluation is the perception that it is more costly and time-consuming than more conventional, expert-driven evaluation. In fact, at the *front end*, it is. Participatory evaluation processes take time while stakeholder groups engage in the process, define their positions, and revise those positions in dialogue with other parties. It takes time to listen, negotiate, and take action when a plurality of parties is involved in evaluation. It takes money, too.

Certainly, it is much faster and cheaper to ask a consultant to simply design and conduct a more conventional evaluation alone, managing his or her own views and schedule rather than those of others. The problem with this is that conventional approaches can result in self-centered, inaccurate analysis. Equally important, nonparticipatory evaluations do not engage the stakeholders in building a common plan of postevaluation action. Shared analysis and shared action can lower downstream program costs, and increase downstream benefits, of subsequent development interventions.

Those who favor participatory approaches in development cooperation often claim that participation is a process and, as such, cannot be quantified. This position is no longer tenable. Cost-aggressive managers in donor agencies, Southern governments, and NGOs frequently block participatory evaluation proposals with economic arguments. And such arguments can be refuted only with hard data.

Some relevant literature exists in this area. In particular, Isham, Narayan, and Pritchett (1996) transformed qualitative data on participation in 121 World Bank water projects into quantitative data suitable for statistical analysis. Based on earlier work by Narayan (1995), they reported "strong statistical findings that increasing participation directly causes better project outcomes"

(Isham et al. 1996, 196). Another study of World Bank projects revealed that participatory projects, overall, did not take more time to plan and implement than nonparticipatory projects (Rietbergen-McCracken 1996).

We need a new round of economic research on participation that involves professionals and citizens in all sectors of the development-cooperation enterprise. Taxpayers in the North and poor households in the South have much to gain from such an exercise if it is done with integrity and rigor and communicated to the general public in accessible and transparent form.

Spreading and Improving the Practice of Participatory Evaluation

As a process that promotes both development results and democracy, participatory evaluation deserves to be spread and applied more broadly worldwide in the future. For this purpose, an organized global network on participatory evaluation would be of great assistance.

But "spread" alone is not enough. Advancing the quality of participatory evaluation practice, promoting its continuous improvement, is an equal priority. Both spread and improvement must be encouraged at the same time.

Recent years have seen a number of organizations in the South and the North step forward to lead a global renewal of energy and activism in participatory evaluation. Among these organizations are Participatory Research in Asia (New Delhi), the International Institute of Rural Reconstruction (Quito), the Institute of Development Studies at Sussex University (Brighton), the Participatory Action Research Network at Cornell University (Ithaca), the International Development Research Centre (Ottawa), the United Nations Development Programme (New York), and the World Bank (Washington, D.C.), as well as many other NGOs and practitioner networks around the world (see the list of organizational resources and useful websites at the end of this book). A wide range of historical and methodological works (Selener 1997; Smith, Williams, and Johnson 1997), project assessments (Rietbergen-McCracken 1996; Narayan 1995), manuals (United Nations Development Programme 1997; World Bank 1996), and bibliographies (Mebrahtu 1997; McPherson 1995; Johnson 1994) has recently been added to the literature on participatory evaluation and development. Because of these efforts, the velocity of the spread and improvement of participatory evaluation is accelerating, and its application is expanding rapidly.

Organization of the Book

This book is intended to make a contribution in both spreading the practice of participatory evaluation and stimulating further work on improving the quality of participatory evaluation practice. The following sections summarize the chapters contained in this book.

Issues, Strategies, and Methods

In an important overview chapter, Jim Freedman points out both the simplicities and the complexities of participatory evaluation. He demonstrates the simplicities and common sense of participatory evaluation by making brief references to experience in the management and implementation of sewage and water projects in Ecuador, a marketing cooperative project for fishers in Brazil, and water and health projects in Kenya. However, when viewed in the context of a radical critique of development expertise, participatory evaluation takes on the political and other complexities of development processes.

Scott Clark and John Cove then examine the critical issue of ethics in participatory evaluation. Based on their training and experiences in social anthropology, and drawing on the many decades of struggles by anthropologists that led to the development of codes of ethics in anthropology, they offer stimulating perspectives on the question of ethics in participatory evaluation. They conclude that the evaluator has ethical responsibilities to three parties: project beneficiaries, the funding organization, and the evaluator's discipline.

In relation to the fairly recent shift that has occurred among the major donor agencies in the field of development cooperation from activity-based to results-based management systems, Edward Jackson examines the compatibility of participatory evaluation with results-based management. He makes the case that participatory evaluation can serve the interests of results-oriented development interventions, and vice versa. He cites several specific tools that are emerging in development practice that can enhance the interaction between participatory evaluation and results-based management.

Sulley Gariba analyzes an attempt to use a participatory impact assessment process to foster village-level capacity building in poverty alleviation programs. Based on the experience of evaluating an integrated rural development project in northern Ghana, the analysis concentrates on the process by which an evaluation exercise has been used as an integral part of the development intervention activity, while satisfying the primary objective of assessing impacts. It also reviews the use of tools created by local professionals and community members to assess impacts of development interventions on a continuous basis.

Case Studies

In a pioneering initiative, Kamla Bhasin documents a workshop discussion in India among seven grassroots rural development workers on how to evaluate the process of participatory development that is intended to help the poor collectively analyze the socioeconomic, political, and cultural structures that keep them poor and prevent them from getting organized to challenge these structures.

Marie-Thérèse Feuerstein reviews a participatory evaluation process and its impact on the community in a health project in Patna in the poor, heavily populated state of Bihar in India. She focuses on the role of, and techniques used by, the community health and development team that facilitated this evaluation process.

Yusuf Kassam presents a case study of the combined use of qualitative participatory methodology and quantitative survey methods in evaluating the training impacts of a large, bilateral rural development project involving the landless poor in Bangladesh. He argues that, although the necessity and importance of statistical and quantitative evaluation are not to be denied, qualitative participatory evaluation has an important role to play in producing a body of unique and illuminative data on qualitative development impacts.

Sheila Robinson and Philip Cox describe an alternative evaluation methodology, which they call "process evaluation," and how it was used in a large-scale health development project in Nepal. They provide details of the evaluation methodology and its underlying concepts and discuss lessons learned in the use of this methodology for those involved in international development.

Through a case study of a complex development project involving research and training centers in Southeast Asia and partner Canadian universities and colleges, Gary Anderson and Deborah Gilsig address the question of forms, purposes, and levels of participation by different stakeholders in the aid chain in an evaluation process. This case study illustrates some of the methods and issues of "fourth-generation" evaluation involving interaction by different stakeholders.

Bonnie Mullinix and Marren Akatsa-Bukachi share their experience in Kenya of developing an NGO training program to provide field-workers with the skills and experience to facilitate participatory evaluation with women's groups. This training initiative grew out of the authors' concern that assessments of program impacts are dominated by the needs and voices of donor agencies and project implementers. They believe that the marginalization of program beneficiaries results in the loss of crucial information in development interventions.

Andrew Livingstone summarizes the approaches, methods, and matrices used by a team of Ghanaian and Canadian development specialists in an internal participatory monitoring and evaluation of a water and sanitation project in Ghana. The emphasis of this project was on creating and supporting community water boards as local decision-making structures.

Patricia Ellis analyzes the participatory methodology that was used by community members to evaluate a pilot project for the integration of women in rural development in a small community in Rose Hall in the eastern Caribbean island of St. Vincent. This project, initiated by the Women and Development Unit (WAND) of the University of the West Indies, was itself a participatory, bottom-up development project.

Elizabeth Whitmore recounts a case of conducting a participatory evaluation involving a dairy-goat farmers' cooperative in a small, poor village in Mexico. In light of her experience as a contracted evaluator in this project, she reflects on a number of issues and dilemmas inherent in participatory approaches to evaluation, such as the tension between process and product,

the role of the outside consultant, conflicting interests among different stakeholders, the effectiveness of short-term site visits, and gender issues.

Continuity, Commitment, and Hope

It probably takes half a century for an idea to make a truly significant impact
on the world. The past twenty years have seen participatory evaluation play a
role of increasing importance in international development. Given current
trends in the world at large, in development cooperation, and in this field of
evaluation practice itself, there are strong indications that participatory evaluation may play an even more significant role in the next thirty years. For this to
happen, the involvement of a new generation of young practitioners, scholars,
and policymakers is necessary. The continuity and commitment demonstrated
in past work on participatory evaluation must be carried forward.

References

Beaulieu, R., and V. Manoukian. 1994. "Participatory Development: A Brief Review of
CIDA's Experience and Potential." Policy Branch, Canadian International Develop-
ment Agency, Hull.
Bhasin, K. 1992. "Alternative and Sustainable Development." *Convergence* 25 (2): 26–36.
———. 1994. "Let Us Look Again at Development, Education and Women." *Convergence*
27 (4): 5–14.
Casley, D., and K. Kumar. 1987. *Project Monitoring and Evaluation in Agriculture and Rural
Development*. Baltimore: Johns Hopkins University Press.
Chambers, R. 1995. "Paradigm Shifts and the Practice of Participatory Research and
Development." Pp. 30–42 in *Power and Participatory Development: Theory and Practice*,
edited by N. Nelson and S. Wright. London: Intermediate Technology Publications.
Chaudhary, A., S. Dhar, and R. Tandon. 1989. "Report of International Forum on
Participatory Evaluation." International Council for Adult Education and Society
for Participatory Research in Asia, New Delhi.
Cousins, J. B. 1996. "Consequences of Researcher Involvement in Participatory Evalu-
ation." *Studies in Educational Evaluation* 22 (1): 3–27.
Cousins, J. B., and L. M. Earl. 1992. "The Case for Participatory Evaluation." *Educational
Evaluation and Policy Analysis* 14 (14): 397–418.
Davis-Case, D. 1990. "Community Forestry: Participatory Assessment, Monitoring and
Evaluation." Food and Agriculture Organization.
Ellis, P. 1997. "Gender-Sensitive Participatory Impact Assessment: A Caribbean
Perspective." Special issue of *Knowledge and Policy: The International Journal of
Knowledge Transfer and Utilization* 10 (1/2), edited by Harry Cummings, William
Found, and Terry Smutylo. International Development Research Centre, Ottawa.
Fals-Borda, D., and M. A. Rahman, eds. 1991. *Action and Knowledge: Breaking the Monopoly
with Participatory Action-Research*. New York: Apex Press.
Fernandes, W., and R. Tandon, eds. 1981. *Participatory Research and Evaluation—Experi-
ments in Research as a Process of Liberation*. New Delhi: Indian Social Institute.

Fetterman, D. M. 1996. Empowerment Evaluation: An Introduction to Theory and Practice. Pp. 3–46 in *Empowerment Evaluation: Knowledge and Tools for Self-Assessment and Accountability*, edited by D. M. Fetterman, S. J. Kaftarian, and A. Wandersman. Thousand Oaks, Calif.: Sage.

Feuerstein, M.-T. 1978. "Evaluation in Education—An Appropriate Technology for a Rural Health Programme." *Community Development Journal* 13: 101–5.

———. 1986. *Partners in Evaluation: Evaluating Development and Community Programmes with Participants*. London: Macmillan.

———. 1988. "Finding the Methods to Fit the People: Training for Participatory Evaluation." *Community Development Journal* 23 (1): 16–25.

Foucault, M. 1973. *The Order of Things: An Archaeology of the Human Sciences*. New York: Vintage Books.

———. 1977. *The Archaeology of Knowledge*. London: Tavistock.

Gariba, S., and E. T. Jackson. 1993. "Building Capacity in Monitoring and Evaluation in Africa: The Potential of North-South Partnerships—A Case Study from Ghana." Presented to the annual conference of the Canadian Association for the Study of International Development, Carleton University, Ottawa.

Gariba, S., Y. Kassam, and L. Thibault. 1994. "Report of the Study of Partnership Institutional Strengthening." Prepared by E.T. Jackson and Associates Ltd. and GAS Development Associates, Ltd. Partnership Africa Canada, Ottawa.

Gosling, L. 1993. "Assessment, Monitoring and Review Toolkits." Save the Children Fund, London.

Guba, E. G., and Y. S. Lincoln. 1995. *Fourth Generation Evaluation*, 2d ed. Newberry Park, Calif.: Sage.

Hall, B., A. Etherington, and T. Jackson. 1979. "Evaluation, Participation and Community Health Care: Critique and Lessons." Presented to the American Public Health Association Meeting, New York.

Isham, J., D. Narayan, and L. Pritchett. 1996. "Does Participation Improve Performance? Establishing Causality with Subjective Data." *World Bank Economic Review* 9 (2): 175–200.

Johnson, S. 1994. "Participatory Research: A Selected Annotated Bibliography." International Development Research Centre and Norman Paterson School of International Affairs, Carleton University, Ottawa.

Kumar, K., ed. 1993. *Rapid Appraisal Methods*. Washington, D.C.: World Bank.

Lyotard, J.-F. 1984. *The Postmodern Condition: A Report on Knowledge*. Minneapolis: University of Minnesota Press.

Maguire, P. 1987. *Doing Participatory Research: A Feminist Approach*. Amherst, Mass.: Center for International Education.

———. 1993. "Challenges, Contradictions, and Celebrations: Attempting Participatory Research as a Doctoral Student." Pp. 157–76 in *Voices of Change: Participatory Research in the United States and Canada*, edited by P. Park, M. Brydon-Miller, B. Hall, and T. Jackson. Westport, Conn./Toronto: Bergin and Garvey/OISE Press.

Marsden, D., and P. Oakley, eds. 1990. *Evaluating Social Development Projects*. Development Guidelines No. 5. Oxford: Oxfam UK.

Marsden, D., P. Oakley, and B. Pratt. 1994. *Measuring the Process: Guidelines for Evaluating Social Development*. Oxford: Oxfam UK.

Mathie, A. 1995. "Evaluation in a Result-Oriented Agency Environment: The Case of CUSO." Presented to the International Evaluation Conference, Vancouver.

McPherson, S. 1995. "Participatory Monitoring and Evaluation: PRA Bibliography." *PRA/PLA Notes*. International Institute for Environment and Development, London.

Mebrahtu, E., ed. 1997. "Participatory Monitoring and Evaluation: An Introductory Pak. " Institute of Development Studies, University of Sussex, Brighton.

Mosse, D. 1994. "Authority, Gender and Knowledge: Theoretical Reflections on the Practice of Participatory Rural Appraisal." *Development and Change* 25: 497–526.

Narayan, D. 1993. "Participatory Evaluation: Tools for Managing Change in Water and Sanitation." World Bank Technical Paper No. 27. World Bank, Washington, D.C.

———. 1995. "The Contribution of People's Participation: Evidence from 121 Rural Water Supply Projects." Environmentally Sustainable Development Occasional Paper Series No. 1. World Bank, Washington, D.C.

Narayan, D., and L. Srinivasan. 1995. "Participatory Development Tool Kit: Training Manuals for Agencies and Communities." World Bank, Washington, D.C.

Narayan-Parker, D. 1991. "Participatory Evaluation: Tools for Managing Change in Water/Sanitation." PROWESS/UNDP/IBRD/UNICEF/WHO, New York.

Rebiens, C. 1995. "Participatory Evaluation of Development Interventions: The Concept and Its Practice." Working Paper No. 4, Department of Intercultural Communication and Management, Copenhagen Business School, Denmark.

Rietbergen-McCracken, J., ed. 1996. *Participation in Practice: The Experience of the World Bank and Other Stakeholders.* Washington, D.C.: World Bank.

Salmen, L. A. 1987. *Listen to the People: Participant-Observer Evaluation of Development Projects.* Oxford: Oxford University Press.

Selener, D. 1997. *Participatory Action Research and Social Change.* Ithaca, N.Y.: Cornell Participatory Action Research Network, Cornell University.

Senge, P. 1990. *The Fifth Discipline: The Art and Practice of Organizational Learning.* New York: Doubleday.

Shiva, V. 1993. *Monocultures of the Mind.* London: Zed Books.

Smith, D. 1995. *First Person Plural: A Community Development Approach to Social Change.* Montreal: Black Rose Books.

Smith, S. E., D. G. Willms, with N. A. Johnson, eds. 1997. *Nurtured by Knowledge: Learning to Do Participatory Action-Research.* Ottawa/New York: International Development Research Centre/Apex Press.

Tandon, R. 1990. "Partnership in Social Development Evaluation: Thematic Paper." Pp. 96–101 in *Evaluating Social Development Projects,* edited by D. Marsden and P. Oakely. Oxford: Oxfam UK.

United Nations Development Programme. 1997. *Who Are the Question-makers? A Participatory Evaluation Handbook.* New York: UNDP, Office of Evaluation and Strategic Planning.

Valdez, J., and M. Bamberger, eds. 1994. *Monitoring and Evaluating Social Programs in Developing Countries.* Washington, D.C.: World Bank.

Vio Grossi, F. 1995. "La sociedad ecologica que nace con nosotros." *El Canelo* 64 (June): 30–33.

Waring, M. 1990. *If Women Counted: A New Feminist Economics.* San Francisco: HarperCollins.

World Bank. 1996. *The World Bank Participation Sourcebook.* Washington, D.C.: Sustainable Development Department, World Bank.

Part I

Issues, Strategies, and Methods

1

Simplicities and Complexities of Participatory Evaluation

Jim Freedman

For two years, between 1982 and 1984, Lawrence Salmen experimented with evaluations on sewage and water projects supported by the World Bank in the urban areas of La Paz, Bolivia, and in Guayaquil, Ecuador. During that time he came to what was then a controversial conclusion. He found that the real nemesis of foreign aid was a lack of decent information, in other words, the absence of communication between beneficiaries and project managers. What projects needed most were better ways for managers to know about beneficiaries, and the best way for managers to know about them, he argued even more controversially, was to train beneficiaries as researchers to render what beneficiaries already knew into semiofficial form. He referred to this idea, or method, as "participatory observation," and although this phrase doubtless struck anthropologists as a tired piece of verbiage, his proposal gave a fresh twist to how donors might come to know about projects.

The method, if it can be called that, fulfilled most of Salmen's vaunted claims: it was cheap, it required minimal expertise, it often quickly uncovered problems that plagued projects, and it came up with interesting solutions. It worked well enough that the World Bank decided to use it in other locations. One of them, in 1984, was a project to establish a marketing cooperative for fishermen in Brazil's northeast state of Rio Grande do Norte, where the dilemma was this: fishermen beneficiaries refused to join the cooperative, and the local manager had no idea what the problem might be. Salmen's "experimental" evaluation began by identifying a local fisherman with some university training who would live in two fishing communities for several weeks, listen to the fishermen and fish with them, listen to other actors in the fishing industry in various parts of the region, and make a report.

It seems that the prominent fish buyers, unbeknownst to the project manager, were waging a propaganda campaign against the cooperative and had actually succeeded in convincing most of the fishermen that their own price for fish was higher than the price given by the marketing cooperative. In truth, the reverse was true. But there was another factor. Many of the fishermen had longtime relations of kin or friendship among these influential fish buyers, and when they had to decide whether to believe them or the cooperative's agents, naturally they chose to believe the fish buyers. The only fishermen who decided unequivocally to join the cooperative were those who for one reason or another did not get on well with the fish-buyer middlemen, and the result was that the cooperative had too few members to operate effectively.

No one had bothered to listen to the fishermen during the four years of the cooperative project. In fact, when the cooperative failed to attract the requisite number of members, it never occurred to the cooperative management to initiate a discussion among fishermen. What was needed, obviously, was better communication, which meant, in this case, a campaign to inform fishermen of the short- and long-term benefits of cooperative membership. This was done. Then a new cooperative director was found who built a better rapport with the members and clarified the cooperative's policy of redistributing profits, and not long afterward, the marketing cooperative was attracting more members than it could handle.

In hindsight, Salmen's experimental evaluations seem far from controversial; if anything, they seem banal in their utter simplicity. But this is the point. The principal insights in what are now known as participatory evaluations border perilously on the obvious. They confront the conventions of scientific inquiry and the pretensions to accountability, which for so long encumbered the way donors and administrators learned how projects work, with painfully simple alternatives. Salmen's approach obviated the onerous task of identifying indicators in advance, recognizing that evaluators can rarely know the main issues before project effects make themselves known. The complexities of measuring impact became a secondary concern. The primary concern was instead to provide a mechanism by which useful information could flow from the beneficiaries to project managers, to bother less with describing a project and more with making it work.

A similar experiment was under way in Kenya at the same time under the inspiration of the nongovernmental organization PROWESS, another of the early advocates, like Salmen, of treating evaluations as devices for generating project-useful information (Narayan-Parker 1988). People living along Kenya's southern coastal area suffered from diarrhea and other water-related diseases, and the obvious solution was to make clean water available. This was straightforward enough, since a clean water aquifer lay twenty feet below ground level, easily accessible with hand pumps, but two programs to install hand pumps had already failed. The hand pumps had worked fine for a while, but since the villagers knew nothing of pump mechanics, the pumps eventually fell into disrepair. The broken pumps remained derelict and rusting while the people returned to the unsanitary practice of getting water from hand-dug wells.

A new idea emerged in 1983, sponsored by the African Medical Research Foundation (AMREF) with support from the PROWESS group then associated with the United Nations Development Programme. It was to ask villagers to form associations among themselves with the objective of looking at their needs and how to solve them. The associations started off as evaluators, asking why the hand pumps had failed and what communities could do differently. As evaluators, they learned that they needed spare parts, they needed the money to pay for them, they needed trained technicians, and they needed some way of generating the resources for providing these inputs. Up to this point, their evaluation exercise looked pretty much like any other evaluation, moving from problem to inquiry to recommendations. Conventional evaluations, however, would have stopped once the recommendations were made, but here, the recommendations marked the midpoint, not the end point, of the exercise.

The evaluator groups went on to make contact with AMREF's partner, the Kenya Water and Health Organization (KWAHO), which contracted two sociologists to help them meet the conditions the evaluator groups had identified as lacking. Pump caretakers were trained, and groups were established to generate resources to pay for the pump caretakers and for the parts they needed. Rules were written down for running these new water committees, for choosing leaders, and for holding meetings. The innovation in this evaluation exercise occurred when the evaluator groups, water users themselves, arrived at a common understanding—a body of knowledge known to everyone—of what stood between them and cleaner water. The reason is this: There is a qualitative difference—subtle but dramatic—between separate pieces of information that some people know and a common body of knowledge that everyone knows. In pieces, knowledge is static, a congery of separate inconclusive mysteries, but knowledge shared fully among a concerned group of people turns readily into a plan of action.

Buying locks for the pumps seemed an unnecessary expenditure until everyone realized that there was regular pump damage, and then water users were happy to make an extra contribution. Collective problem identification mobilized, at the same time, resources for the solution. The matter of contributions remained a problem, however, and a thorny one, particularly regarding what to do with members who could not pay. But once the matter was discussed in an open meeting and everyone appreciated firsthand the financial difficulties of the few nonpaying members, the group agreed to allow indigent members to pay in kind instead of in cash. Another problem was solved. The women played active roles in the water committees as treasurers and as mechanics, and this made a few of the men nervous until the majority of men realized the benefits of sharing responsibility with women; the majority of the water committees made money and opened bank accounts under the women's direction, and no one could argue with that.

Toward a Project-Sensitive Epistemology

The difference between conventional and participatory evaluations has in part to do with training beneficiaries as researchers who, with some guidance, undertake an evaluation themselves. There are then two other differences, essential ones, that to some extent evolve out of granting beneficiaries the authority for creating project knowledge and that have far-reaching implications. The first of these is that participatory evaluations gather information that is first and foremost useful for making projects work; participatory evaluations are not concerned, in the first instance, with monitoring performance or expenditures. The second is that the end point of evaluations is a bank account and not the recommendation to open one; the information that evaluations produce is stagnant unless it provides a basis for common understandings that lead to social action.

The rationale for participatory evaluations is that they address those issues that will make projects work for their constituencies in such a way that the constituencies are moved to act on what they know. This seems on first glance innocently straightforward, and although it may be straightforward, it is anything but innocent. The roots of this rationale lie in a radical critique of development expertise, in particular, how and with whose input development understandings are recognized as expertise. Knowledge for and about development has, for the past fifty years, been so shrouded in economic ideology and burdened with the accoutrements of proof imposed by auditors and academics that it was nearly unthinkable that it could come from poor people or that it could be created or used by them.

To a large extent, this was because development and knowledge about development were theaters of the cold war. Gunnar Myrdal opened his great work *Asian Drama* with a cautionary chapter entitled "The Beam in Our Eyes," warning social scientists that they were so overly burdened with political convictions that they were unlikely to solve a problem as politically loaded as poverty (Myrdal 1968). Poverty and its relief were pawns, he said, in the cold war game of power, and social scientists failed to see beyond the ideological tangle of their times, hence the "beam" in their eyes. Development and knowledge about development became pawns in the cold war game, hobbled with so much ideological baggage that those thinkers who really made a difference in the allocation of funds rarely imagined development as more than a contest between the ideology of marketplace individualism and its challengers.

Economists, hawking marketplace solutions to poverty, rose to prominence in these times, though their message was intellectually threadbare. Their message relied heavily on the dubious notion that poor farmers were too poor and knew too little about economic growth to participate in the development process and had to be led out of poverty by the more powerful investors or the more prudent savers. It was unthinkable that a poor woman could pretend to tell experts what was best for her children or her neighbors or her village or would have any idea about how levels of health or income stagnate or decline, much less improve. Poor people did not qualify as actors in the process of growth *because they were poor*, for only those with resources qualified as actors in the marketplace, and among these, only those who could spend and produce in just the right way qualified. Sociologists, progressive economists, and anthropologists all objected loudly. They said that big investors either did not act in the poor people's interests or made it impossible for them to act for themselves, and the result was increasing poverty or increasing inequality or both. But the economists claimed to know better (Freedman 1994).

While economists challenged poor people's knowledge because this knowledge was not relevant to economic growth, bureaucrats challenged it because there was no guarantee that poor people, unassisted, would be forthcoming with accurate information. Gathering good information needed the trappings of science, the appearance of objectivity, random sampling, and numbers for credibility; and credibility was the all-important ingredient in being accountable. It mattered little that scientific designs were inaccessible to beneficiaries; they were not, after all, the ultimate end users of projects. Taxpayers from donor countries were credible, for they, in the end, were paying for the political or economic advantage that development ventures promised.

And the consequence was a body of knowledge about "development" locales that was many times removed from the sites themselves, not to mention the people whom it most intimately concerned; this remove was, furthermore, sanctioned by the academy. Utility, or project problem solving, was not a priority in knowing about projects. The beneficiaries were rarely the end users of what was known, and, more poignantly, since those in the know were rarely those who took action, there was a righteous divide between knowing and doing. The principal reason to officially know about development was for the exchequer to check, or for posterity's sake.

Development knowledge, like the curious oxymoron "military intelligence," became a non sequitur and languished for years bereft of sensible propositions, burdened with ideological agendas and the trappings of scientific method. It was only around the fringes of standard disciplines that alternative criteria for creating knowledge about development emerged. It fell to the rare economists, activists, and progressive philosophers to create a new epistemology that sanctioned such commonsense notions as "local knowledge," "quick and dirty approaches," and "participatory research." In the last decade, a number of writers and practitioners have begun to argue for alternative development epistemologies.

Three, in particular, have had a conspicuous impact on how we now think differently about acquiring and accumulating information for development purposes. Robert Chambers is unquestionably one of these three. For purely practical and pecuniary reasons (it was quicker and cheaper), he proposed to solicit the involvement of poor people in gathering data for project designs, an idea that was enshrined in the phrase rapid rural appraisal (RRA). The idea caught on quickly in spite of the suspicions of bureaucrats and social scientists. But then he carried the idea to its logical conclusion, which was to bestow on poor people the authority for generating data themselves, replacing the predecessor concept of RRA with a newer one, participatory rural appraisal, or PRA. There is nothing ideological about either of these approaches and little that is particularly profound, but they both contain well-tested instruments for engaging beneficiaries in collective research exercises (Chambers 1994a, 1994b, 1994c).

Orlando Fals-Borda represents another of these three. He differs from Chambers in that his ideas are distinctly ideological. Fals-Borda draws on

Paulo Freire's *Pedagogy of the Oppressed*, which views self-knowledge or "conscientization" as a necessary step toward social transformation. Participatory action research (PAR), or participatory research as it is variously called, advocates participatory evaluations because they are political acts capable of rallying the disenfranchised to take actions against exploitation (Fals-Borda and Rahman 1991). However political the theory, and however strenuously Chambers might object to the parallels between PRA and PAR, the practice of PAR does not differ significantly from Chambers's PRA, for they both rely on the premise that there is an undeniable connection between people knowing about a problem and their willingness to take action to solve it.

A third spokesperson for a new, project-sensitive epistemology is Norman Uphoff, whose position comes less from political convictions than from a profound philosophical disquiet about the conventions of standard social science. He uses the efficacy of participatory evaluation as evidence in his case against a social science that indulges in overly mechanistic models and pretensions to precision judgments. The notorious dichotomies that typically frame social science research—objectivity versus subjectivity, altruism versus individualism, knowledge versus action—are false dichotomies and force social thinkers to make unnecessary choices. These rigidities in social science have blinded its disciplines to the real complexity of human society. Uphoff's work, *Learning from Gal Oya* (1992), has strung a theoretical thread between practicing participatory evaluations and propositions for an alternative, more reflective and socially responsible social science.

All three, but especially Uphoff, call attention to the significant role that participatory evaluations play in rearticulating the missions and methods of social science. Although participatory evaluations may be, for Chambers and others, a practical alternative to the standard performance reviews, they really do challenge the way that donor agencies acquire information, as well as the way the grander institutions think about social change. Participatory evaluations are innovations for development practitioners, but the experiments that they inspire regarding how best to know about other people have broad implications. At one level, they are commonsense, even simple methodologies for project management. At another level, however, the rationales that justify them pose complex challenges to the way in which change agents come to know what they are doing.

The Art of Doing Participatory Research

The art of evaluating in the participatory mode entails treading a fine line between adopting procedures for systematically asking and recording the right kind of data and adapting these procedures to the capacities of non-scholarly participants. Conventional evaluations can be needlessly elaborate because evaluators go to great lengths to surround their study with the appearances of rigor in order to withstand the challenge of managers and ministers' offices. They may incorporate elaborate statistical tests, select respondents randomly to guarantee objectivity, and sample control respondents under before and after conditions. Most of this is unnecessary. The art is finding research exercises that participants like to do and that will make them proud of their work, while keeping the technology appropriate. This means using numbers for effect but not for proof, using commonsense methods for assuring fair representations of all beneficiaries, abandoning the strict sense of objectivity, and generally recognizing that compassion works as well as distance in assuring accurate information.

It also means choosing indicators that make sense to participants and their understanding of the project. More to the point, it means avoiding indicators whose principal justification is that they are "standard" indicators or that they ask whether a project met or did not meet its objectives. This seems awkward at first, because benefactors and beneficiaries alike presume that there are certain things that an evaluation is absolutely required to ask. This is not true. The end users of participatory evaluations are beneficiaries, and their questions are the ones to ask.

When water committee members in east Indonesia, villagers in the Wanita Air dan Sanitasi (Water and Sanitation) Project, undertook an evaluation with the help of PROWESS, they puzzled at first over what to ask. Planners would want to know about water-use patterns, hygiene, and maintenance of pumps. The villagers had different questions. The PROWESS facilitators, recognizing that the questions of beneficiaries and planners would be different, encouraged the water committee members to come up with their own indicators. The information they wanted about their sanitation project was whether the women had turned a greater profit selling vegetables since the pumps had been installed. It was a good question because, for the village, one value of more accessible water was having more water to spread on vegetable gardens. So the question was asked and the answers were carefully counted, and it turned out that the proportion of women growing produce for sale and making more cash had increased by nearly 50 percent in the course of the project. It was an interesting conclusion (Narayan-Parker 1989).

Incidentally, the pumps also provided water in a more hygienic way and fewer people were sick, but for the people, this mattered little, even though better hygiene was an original goal of the project. A conventional evaluation would have measured child mortality or diarrhea rates before and after the project, comparing control groups who had no pump installations to groups with pump installations. But this would have been of questionable value. Managers of projects need to have information they can use, information that directly concerns project users. It is hard to use data on diarrhea rates. For most people, changes in diarrhea have little to do with pump installations, or if they do, it is nearly impossible to prove, since so many factors influence health and disease. A control group might well have had less diarrhea than those using project pumps, since there are many causes for diarrhea besides dirty water. But the question of vegetables was easy. Projects need more reliable, local, and concrete justification, and, more importantly, the people themselves need evidence that their work has its rewards. Vegetables, in this case, work better than health.

This is why participatory evaluations ask people to make their own research designs. These designs may not control for extraneous variables; they may have no control groups, no before and after. The question for them is not whether the planners' goals of the project have been met and whether whatever progress has been made toward achieving these goals can be causally linked to the project. Their concern is whether the project has addressed their interests, and they do not worry whether pumps can be linked without question to the things that have happened because of them. The link between vegetables and pumps is too obvious a link to test or control for the link itself. What counts for the people is the immediate and obvious consequence, the things they can feel and consume, not abstract indicators whose proof is, at best, questionable.

Adapting research to a nonscholarly environment continues throughout the research cycle, from research design to data recording and analysis, and especially to presenting the information. Conventional evaluators submit their invoices when the final draft of the report is written, for the job is done when the report is accepted and it disappears into agency files. At this stage, however, the participatory researchers' work has just entered its most critical stage, for they have done nothing if the information they have assembled is not made public. They want others to know what they have discovered, and it is this—dramatizing, disseminating, and mobilizing—that gives these pieces of information their power to mobilize for change.

Reporting the findings of participatory evaluations has an explicit purpose. It is to complete a circuit that takes a group from a process of knowing to doing something about what they know. It takes them from collecting information to depicting their findings in pictures and photos, flyers, puppet shows, and plays, and causing others to take notice. When people know what they need and when the circuit is complete, they are more likely to rise to the occasion to get it. If beneficiaries know for sure that a missing ingredient in a project is better self-management, they are likely to try it. If they know that a lack of women's involvement deprives certain families of a greater potential for income, they will do something about it. When fishermen know that a marketing collective gives better prices for fish than middlemen do, they join, and when farmers realize that preserving their trees is crucial for feeding themselves, they plant trees. But first they must know, firsthand, what these crucial facts are.

In participatory research, they may discover a need for better technology or for more financial resources. More often than not, the crucial facts they discover are social ones. They may discover that, as neighbors and villagers, they fail to act effectively on their own behalf and in the process realize how they might change in order to do so. Participatory research in this way marries research and social action.

This is a simple idea. But putting the idea into practice often seems awkward because it combines two normally distinct activities: social research and social action. Unlike conventional research, which focuses on the one task of compiling information, participatory research does two separate things: it gathers information and creates associations, and it does them together. It creates associations that, in doing research, set in motion a process of acting together, a process that ideally culminates in people acting in concert on matters more bonding than collecting and analyzing information. This combination of efforts—data gathering and social action—places research inside the larger objective of creating viable associations. Research is no longer an end in itself. Evaluations do not begin with experts bringing in questionnaires and knowledge of survey research, nor are they over when reports are submitted.

The Gal Oya irrigation scheme meetings of watercourse groups devised an ingenious way of completing this circuit of exercises all in one sitting. In 1979, the Gal Oya irrigation scheme in Sri Lanka undertook to reverse two decades of irrigation mismanagement. The scheme sought to rehabilitate physical structures that had seriously eroded and, at the same time, sought to revive water management associations that in previous years had nearly ceased to function. The restoration of water management associations relied primarily on introducing mechanisms of self-evaluation as part of the functions of watercourse management groups (Uphoff 1988).

The Gal Oya scheme engaged group promoters to guide watercourse groups through their first self-evaluations, and to do this, the promoters assisted groups in making up a list of questions that members were likely to want answered about themselves. These questions included ones about economic and technical performance; about group dynamics; about how well the group interacted with other such groups, the community, and the state; about self-reliance; and about financial records. The membership chose which questions they wanted, and although the promoters made suggestions, the group's decision was final. In one instance, after reviewing the list, the membership recommended including a question on how many members had participated in an annual harvest festival, and although the promoter was skeptical, the members insisted, claiming that members who attended the festival formed stronger groups. The question was added.

At the meeting, as members discussed each of the questions, the idea was for the membership as a whole to come to a decision about how to answer the questions. A question might ask about conflict resolution, whether conflicts over water were resolved (1) easily, (2) not so easily, (3) with difficulty, or (4) not at all. The membership had to agree, eventually, on one of these answers, and this frequently required lengthy discussion. In this way, the evaluation was planned and implemented, and the answers were made public, all in a single meeting. The ingenious part of this technique is the way it engages all members in witnessing the discourse leading to agreement and causes them to reflect, in the process, on how to alter themselves.

It happened that the watercourse management groups had become aware of the dangers of allowing a single leader to continue to serve year after year, even if that leader was a good one, or even if no one else appeared willing to serve.

Together with facilitators and planners, the groups came to understand that at least one part of the problem had to do with how many members in the group actually wanted to serve as leaders. If the group got together and asked whether there were a lot of people willing to lead, or only a few, or perhaps none other than the leader himself, the members would at least become aware of this part of their problem. So they did. The group met and ranked itself on the issue of whether there were enough members willing to lead, and they ended up giving themselves a poor mark because the group as a whole wanted more leaders. No one felt embarrassed, because the ranking they gave in the end was less important than the discussion itself, and as it turned out, certain young men and women who had previously been overlooked did become known as potential leaders. It was a gentle way to democratize leadership assignments.

Like the science of psychiatry or the art of performance, the art of participatory evaluations lies in someone assembling the intuitions of an audience—in this case, a membership—and giving them shape, bestowing on these once formless intuitions an aura of potency. It is the shaman who, in less mechanistic societies, combined these functions of healing and display—psychiatry and performance—of converting a social illness into a social drama and, with this sleight of the dramatist's hand, resolving critical problems. The ultimate trick, of course, which the psychiatrist and the thespian rarely reveal—much less so the shaman—is to know the right things. A shaman or a sorcerer may appear to "magically" heal a neuropathy by removing an ancestor's tooth embedded in a patient's subcutaneous tissue with the aid of a sucking horn, but we all know that the real shaman's art is to know the social integuments that disturb the sufferer and cause grief. Armed with these key pieces of information, which disturb and move people, the shaman reassembles them in so artful a way as to create a moment of truth for those gathered together, to help the sufferer see the source of misery and to help the consociates take some responsibility for realigning these integuments in the sufferer's favor. This is not to say that beneficiaries are victims—though they may well be—so the analogy stops here. Nor is it to say that participatory evaluators carry anything like the professional credentials of healers or actors, for they are, in the ideal instance, the beneficiaries themselves. But the analogy makes the point that participants in collective research take on the role of shamans; they elicit facts, however arcane or formless or apparently irrelevant, and by organizing them with sharp and meaningful contours, they then create, for themselves and others, a moment of truth.

The Road to Democracy

Ultimately, participatory evaluations aim to promote democracy—no less and no more—the implicit assumption being that the more that disenfranchised people become enfranchised, the more robust their social and economic institutions will be. Furthermore, this spells prosperity. There is a string of associations here, beginning with collective research entailing, among other things, collective knowledge, equitable social institutions, and productive economies, a string of associations that commands attention. One of the few authors to trace these associations and argue strongly for them, largely in this order, is Robert Putnam in his book filled with hard evidence, *Making Democracy Work* (1993). His book speaks directly to the philosophy of participatory evaluations and to the social theory that advocates them.

Putnam's study compares the recent history of northern and southern Italy—the productive provinces around the democratic Milan, on the one hand, with the poor regions of the South, on the other. The question is this: is there something in the social patterns of these respective regions that accounts for their dramatic difference in economic productivity? His evidence is convincing, for politics in the northern provinces bubbles up from myriad soccer associations and police clubs, voting groups, and other voluntary associations, where individuals participate and make their opinions felt. In the north, people act energetically for themselves and for the collective weal. Not so in the south, where the boss rule of patron-client politics subverts democracy and where, discouraged by fatalism, citizens accept the consequent social rigidities by paying corrupt officials and keeping their heads in the hard-rock crevices of an inflexible social life. Why should they vote? Their membership in soccer clubs and village life is little more than a version of paying protection to their political chiefs. It is no surprise that the economy of the north bustles, while the economy of the south flags. There is an important lesson here about development.

The lesson is that economic growth begins with energetic local organizations, locales where individuals can feasibly activate a social network. Where individuals participate in local activities, the gamut of economic possibility grows. Citizens can make their presence felt because there is a safety net to dispel the notorious fatalism of poor people, because they will meet with fair officials from a position of strength, and because in a social environment where there is a civic consciousness, government will provide more and effective services. Where citizens hide from the state and others, the possibility of economic activity narrows, resources are squandered in corrupt extractions, and their efforts are rewarded only if they, in turn, extract the same protection from their fellow citizens. Building local organizations that work democratically and fairly, therefore, seems to be a turnkey for local solvency.

But there is the omnipresent matter of feudalism throughout the postcolonial world. Patterns of ownership and privilege in the villages of poor countries commonly favor a few people and, in doing so, discourage personal initiative among the vast majority of poor who live there. This is an extremely important fact for understanding and dealing with world poverty. Infusions of physical infrastructure, better roads, better irrigation, or productive agricultural inputs will not greatly change these social preconditions of poverty; nor will externally imposed leaner national budgets or better trade balance at the national level. On the contrary, these interventions more commonly reinforce the concentrations of wealth for privileged families. New schools and cleaner water may make the lives of the poor less miserable, but they are unlikely to alter the social circumstances that make unsanitary living conditions endemic. As long as large numbers of individuals and families have little inclination to seek opportunities for personal betterment, they will respond with the kinds of behavior that deepen the roots of poverty. Farmers will cultivate without the motivation to expand production, household heads will continue to seek refuge in the bonds of dependency that suffocate motivation in the first place, and households will continue to rely on large families as the only strategy for increasing household wealth or ensuring survival.

Viable village or neighborhood organizations can change these social environments and provide the majority of persons with the opportunity to participate in a gainful activity. No one knows how to create viable organizations, and barring an unlikely development in social engineering, no one will ever know; however, once such organizations are created, a built-in habit of reflection (participatory evaluation) will reinforce such organizations by promoting equity, and once equity is accepted, accountability is ensured. For all that the mumbling evaluators do about accountability, none of them ever succeeds in increasing it in any measure unless there are equitable groups with decent forms of self-government. Call it whatever—elections or discussion groups, consensual decision making, or participatory evaluation—in spirit they are all the same, for in spirit, they all activate a social conscience and vitiate the invidious social differences that Amartya Sen accurately notes makes all the difference in dismantling poverty.

For all its simplicity, the concept of participatory evaluation contains a complex and wide-reaching promise for social justice. If the art of participatory evaluation is to create a moment of truth, its ultimate role is to reform. By conscripting a community in the simple and sensible act of knowing more about itself, it also engages the members in changing the way they behave politically, for participatory evaluation is a model for democracy and inevitably introduces a democratic routine that everyone can practice. It is indeed a real alternative to conventional evaluations as we know them, for it generates information about projects that is useful and leads to healthy project reform. But the value of participatory evaluation is that it sets in motion a process of social reflection that can lead to social change in ways that traditional concepts of development have failed to do.

References

Chambers, R. 1994a. "Participatory Rural Appraisal (PRA): Analysis of Experience." *World Development* 22 (9): 1253–68.

———. 1994b. "Participatory Rural Appraisal (PRA): Challenges, Potentials and Paradigm." *World Development* 22 (10): 1437–54.

———. 1994c. "The Origins and Practice of Participatory Rural Appraisal." *World Development* 22 (7): 953–69.

Fals-Borda, O., and M. A. Rahman, eds. 1991. *Action and Knowledge: Breaking the Monopoly with Participatory Action Research.* New York: Apex Press.

Freedman, J. 1994. "Participatory Evaluations, Making Projects Work." Dialogue on Development Technical Paper No. TP94/2. Division of International Development, International Centre, University of Calgary.

Myrdal, G. 1968. *Asian Drama: An Inquiry into the Poverty of Nations.* 3 vols. New York: Pantheon.

Narayan-Parker, D. 1988. *Kenya: People, Pumps and Agencies.* New York: PROWESS/ United Nations Development Programme.

———. 1989. *Indonesia: Evaluating Community Management.* New York: PROWESS/United Nations Development Programme.

Putnam, R. 1993. *Making Democracy Work: Civic Traditions in Modern Italy.* Princeton, N.J.: Princeton University Press.

Uphoff, N. 1988. "Participatory Evaluation of Farmer Organizations." *Agricultural Administration and Extension* 30: 43–64.

———. 1992. *Learning from Gal Oya: Possibilities for Participatory Development and Post-Newtonian Social Science.* Ithaca, N.Y.: Cornell University Press.

———— 2 ————

Questions of Ethics in Participatory Evaluation: A View from Anthropology

Scott Clark and John Cove

This chapter addresses ethics in participatory evaluation. Our perspective on the issue derives from our training and experiences as social anthropologists. As anthropologists we come from a discipline for which codes of professional ethics have been written, but in which considerable debate continues. Anthropologists have long struggled with their role in the research process, in large part for two reasons: first, because the quality of their relations with the people with whom they work in the field will determine to a great extent the quality of research results; and second, because their work holds the potential for serious repercussions for the same people. As problems continue to arise for anthropologists and the people with whom they work, the debate goes on. Theorists and practitioners involved in participatory evaluation are bound to face many of the same difficulties. While we are aware that ethical judgments are subjective and cannot be dictated, we believe that a view from anthropology will at least contribute to thinking on the issue.

Contextualizing Ethics in Anthropology

Anthropological debate about the ethics of research is far from new. At the end of World War I, Boas stated his objections about researchers having acted as spies for the U.S. government, and he was censured by the American Anthropological Association for publishing his views in a popular magazine (Lesser 1981, 15–19). In the 1960s, "Project Camelot" raised again the issue of anthropologists being asked to do clandestine research in Latin America and Southeast Asia by U.S. governmental agencies. That topic fueled a major controversy among anthropologists in the United States and Canada over the need for a professional code of ethics (Jorgensen 1971). In the 1980s, similar discussions occurred in Australia and New Zealand. Anthropology in those four countries provides a focus for this section, with particular reference to research on their indigenous peoples.

In commenting on how the New Zealand Association of Social Anthropologists (NZASA) addressed the question of adopting a code of ethics, Goldsmith (1987, 1) notes that the process involved "five years of debate and collective indecision." The Australian literature suggests that the debates there were equally long and sometimes heated. In contrast, the Society of Applied Anthropology in Canada (SAAC) drafted a code seemingly with relative ease in 1983 but never adopted it. The underlying pattern suggests that anthropologists have reached agreement about ethics only with great difficulty. This is in marked contrast to disciplinary consensus that researchers ought to have ethical responsibilities. The difficulties have been in collective efforts to determine the nature of those obligations.

Goldsmith (1987, 3) is insightful here. He argues that the ethics of research is inherently problematic because it is historically and culturally contextualized. The 1960s marked a major change in how anthropologists perceived ethics. Professional codes were one expression; another was the vast quantity of literature on the subject of ethics. In discussing the situation in which anthropological research currently takes place, Geertz (1968, 141) refers to "an altered moral context." It is this notion that will be used to briefly explore the ethical difficulties facing anthropology.

From Nonproblematic to Problematic Ethics

Park (1993) notes that the founders of sociology and, by extension, of social-cultural anthropology, viewed the research enterprise as intrinsically emancipatory. As the distinction between pure and applied research emerged, the former was asserted to have a higher status intellectually and morally because it produced knowledge for its own sake. More generally, both pure and applied anthropology had cultural legitimacy as sciences, science being the exemplar of Western secular rationality (Broad and Wade 1982, 130). The privileged position given to anthropologists was also consistent with their membership in the elite, typically sharing assumptions and interests with other elites, and generally favoring European colonial interests such as the assimilation of indigenous populations. Within elite European intellectual and political discourses, anthropologists could speak not only about indigenous populations but also for them. As Fabian (1971, 230) stated, research ethics involved little more than "conformity with the norms of the society which sponsors the scientific enterprise."

After World War II, there occurred a number of changes in Western societies that made such conformity more difficult. A more pluralistic view of politics began to emerge in Western liberal democracies during the 1940s. This new conception differed from previous ones in key respects (McPherson 1977, 78–79). No moral claims were made about either improving the human condition or reflecting a common good; rather, politics was about competing interests legitimized by different value orientations. Social cleavages were not limited to class, but expanded from the 1960s onward to include gender and ethnicity.

The 1960s involved another political shift: the growth of participatory democracy. For our purposes, its importance lies in an orientation that has been described by Padgett (1986, 172–73) as "post-material values of humanism . . . and social emancipation." In that altered moral context, the cultural "others" who constitute the core of anthropology's subject matter became concerned with defining for themselves what their emancipation might mean, with resultant multiculturalism being one component of a pluralistic society.

If anthropologists began to critically reassess the nature of their research enterprise in the 1950s, and to do so ethically from the 1960s onward, we should not be surprised. Nor is it accidental that women who were anthropologists started to think about those same issues from the vantage point that reflected their previous "otherness." Regardless of gender, anthropologists were forced to confront the history of their discipline and to recognize that it had seldom been emancipatory for its subjects. At the same time, the altered moral climate provided an opportunity to redress that history.

One of the first indications of a change in disciplinary orientation occurred in the early 1950s with the advent of action anthropology (Tax 1952). Its proponents asserted that previous assumptions about differences between applied and pure research were mistaken. Action anthropologists viewed applied research as a basis for developing theory and methods, not merely for using them. Second, they rejected the classic observer-subject dichotomy and defined the latter as clients and active participants in the research process. Third, cultural values were not merely interesting to study but were part of how to define real-life problems and solutions. From the action vantage point, cultural "others" were not outside science with nothing legitimate to say about its assumptions, questions, understandings, and activities. Last, the founder of action anthropology, Sol Tax (1958, 17–19), defined it as "participant interference"— assisting "others" to better understand and change their relations with dominant institutions.

The premises of action anthropology were largely consistent with the altering moral climate. More conventional applied and pure anthropology had to experience the meaning of that new context. Since the 1960s, the discipline's subjects have been increasingly speaking for themselves and about themselves. In so doing, they have confronted themselves as constructed by anthropologists. Not only has the validity of those constructions been challenged, but so has the morality of anthropologists constructing any kind of "otherness."

The reader might well doubt that anthropology has had this degree of significance, yet Australia provides a serious example. The historical absence of treaties in Australia took on symbolic importance for the Aboriginal rights movement in the late 1970s, and the creation and signing of a treaty was seen as appropriate to a formal recognition of those rights. An Aboriginal draft of a possible new treaty identified control over future anthropological research as one item in the creation of a new relationship with Euro-Australians (Wright 1985, 325, 327). From an Aboriginal position, the discipline was seen as inseparable from the history of their interaction with Europeans and the meaning of self-determination. At the same time, anthropological research was deemed to have some use value for achieving Aboriginal political objectives. As one Aborigine stated (English 1985, 258):

> We'll hire our own anthropologist and one on whom we can rely to prepare a report favorable to ourselves. . . . We'll tell you only as much as we think might be necessary to support our claims.

That statement, in one form or another, has been made by indigenous leaders in Canada, the United States, and New Zealand. In essence, an anthropologist doing research in an aboriginal culture is generally required to be an advocate. There is nothing new about advocacy per se. As mentioned, in the past, anthropologists have determined what the interests of indigenous peoples were and have spoken for them. In the altered moral climate, however, that is viewed as paternalistic. What is different about modern advocacy is that such interests are determined by cultural "others," and research is used to assist them to speak for themselves. One anthropologist has referred to advocacy research as "ghostwriting" (Cleave 1992, 81–94).

This new relationship between indigenous peoples and anthropologists has another side. Researchers have had to come to terms with the fact that certain kinds of field studies may not be permitted. Research on purely academic questions and applied research done for parties and interests external to the cultures in question have been rejected. Those doing research for aboriginal clients are required to adopt the basic stance of action anthropology. This is no longer a matter of intellectual or moral choice on the part of the investigator.

This only-as-advocate stance has specific implications for field research, but not all anthropologists have taken that stance. What constrains it is another inescapable reality: virtually anything an anthropologist might wish to say about an indigenous culture can have political importance. Land claims litigation in Canada is illustrative. Both indigenous claimants and the Crown as defendant have used anthropological publications, unpublished papers, and even field notes to support their respective positions. Those uses are independent of the researcher's intent and personal ethical commitments. The courts tend to give more credence to pure research because it is deemed to be disinterested, while ignoring that it may have been framed in terms of theoretical, methodological, and personal interests within academia. The flip side is that advocacy research has been branded by at least one Canadian judge as intrinsically biased and thus readily dismissed (Ridington 1992, 210–12).

For many indigenous organizations, any reliance on anthropologists is problematic. It continues dependency and subordination that cannot be eliminated by either advocacy or aborigines themselves becoming professional researchers. In New Zealand, a number of Maori spokespersons have characterized the discipline as intellectual imperialism and science as a Western cultural institution whose status claims are invalid (Cove 1993). Maori are currently asserting the right to their own science, one derived from traditional values and consistent with contemporary Maori interests. One result is that New Zealand anthropologists, with the exception of a few long-term action anthropologists, have virtually stopped studying Maori (Cleave 1992; Webster 1989).

In the altered moral climate, anthropology has changed and will continue to do so. Changes have involved making political accommodations, interacting with indigenous peoples in radically different ways, exploring new fields of research and abandoning others, considering new theories and methods, and facing difficult ethical questions. However, reminiscent of Firth's definition of anthropology as the "uncomfortable science" (Firth 1981, 198), anthropologists have all too often made relatively comfortable ethical decisions.

Codes of Ethics in Anthropology

The establishment of a code of ethics by a professional association suggests that a relatively high level of consensus has been reached among association members, even if the result is an acceptable lowest common denominator. In anthropology, the process has been complex and sometimes unsuccessful. It has involved recognizing that variability exists among practitioners' interests and situations, which are to some degree mutually exclusive and not restricted to the discipline. The codes themselves are informative, as are debates about adopting such codes.

There are some interesting differences among the three earliest North American anthropological codes. The code of the American Anthropologic Association (AAA) was the only one to recognize that complexities existed in "involvements, misunderstandings, conflicts, and making choices among conflicting values" (AAA 1970, 46). Further, the AAA code asserted that when conflicting interests exist, the first priority is to the peoples studied (AAA 1970, 46). In contrast, the code of the Society for Applied Anthropology (SAA) gave primacy to science and considered only conflicts within communities that might be investigated (SAA 1975, 2). The Canadian Sociology and Anthropology Association (CSAA) code did not acknowledge any sources of potential conflict and made social scientific investigation its first responsibility (CSAA 1978, 3).

The most striking of the above differences is that applied anthropologists in the United States, represented by the SAA, gave priority to science rather than to client-subjects. The most plausible explanation refers to an earlier point about the relative status of applied and pure research. The code drafted, but not adopted, by the Society for Applied Anthropology in Canada (SAAC) in 1983 argues in the preamble that "ethical standards apply to all parties involved in research (clients-hosts-informants and anthropologists)," with primacy given to "interests of participants"—meaning individuals who supply information (SAAC 1994, 38–39). The 1986 Code of the Australian Association for Applied

Anthropology (AAAA) takes a similar position to the AAA code in stressing commitment to "views and interests of subjects studied," with the proviso of not compromising the researcher's "conscience or commitment to truth" (Australian Anthropology Society [AAS] 1989, 35–36).

There are a number of other distinctions between the earlier SAA and the later SAAC and AAAA codes that suggest that changes in the general research situation have taken place. The Canadian and Australian codes view as ethical obligations the establishment of collegial relations with subjects and the encouragement of their full participation in designing and conducting research. The AAAA (AAS 1989, 35) code also makes reference to research done on "unpublished field-work based sources," whereas all the other codes concentrate exclusively on field research.

When the New Zealand Association of Social Anthropologists was considering adoption of a revised form of the AAA code, Goldsmith (1987, 4–5) argued that it was overly complex in identifying six foci of ethical responsibilities. Further, Goldsmith took exception to the 1960s "American worldview" in the NZASA version. From the vantage point of the late 1980s, he proposed the following (Goldsmith 1987, 6):

1. Anthropologists' primary responsibility is to the powerless who may be harmed by anthropological research and publication, not just to prevent harm but also with the view of empowering those people where possible.
2. Anthropologists' next major responsibility is to publicly disseminate the results of their research, with the view to increasing public understanding and, where possible, respect for the subjects of their research.
3. Provided that the first two principles are met . . . anthropologists should also act ethically in dealing with . . . power structures, such as funding agencies and governments.

The first of these principles does away with any and all distinctions about types of anthropological research and asserts that its main if not sole objective is empowerment of those in subordinated positions. In this view, ethics defines the research enterprise rather than being a component of it—a position taken in interdisciplinary cultural studies (Slack and Whitt 1992, 573). Goldsmith's second principle is consistent with this priority and implies that research focusing on purely academic interests and audiences has no place in the discipline. The third principle is essentially residual.

Goldsmith's recommendations are not idiosyncratic. Debates among Australian anthropologists in the 1980s centered on his first two principles. So too do a highly specialized series of debates in Canada around museum representations of Native cultures. By and large, the Australian and Canadian literatures support Goldsmith's position, perhaps with somewhat less concentration on the empowerment of national indigenous populations.

The few dissenting voices in those debates arguably deserve some attention. Their common theme is the legitimacy of anthropological interests and the rejection of the idea that anthropology is ethical only when it supports indigenous political interests (Ames 1992; Harrison 1988; Kolig 1982). For applied or action anthropologists, it is the second component that is most relevant.

A real case is illustrative. The recent controversy in British Columbia over logging Clayaquot Sound has involved a number of parties: various levels of government (provincial, regional, municipal), corporations, environmental organizations, unions, community groups, and aboriginal peoples. Is it ethically appropriate that anthropologists do research only for First Nations involved in the dispute? Should anthropologists refuse to do research for a client having no direct interests in the specific area and the outcome of the dispute? If such research were done, should an anthropologist provide an analysis weighted toward indigenous claims? Are there clients for whom an anthropologist might ethically choose to work who do not demand or require an action or participatory type of research? The next section explores these questions, with specific reference to evaluation research.

Ethics in Participatory Evaluation

We see participatory evaluation as an essential and logical component of the overarching concept of participatory research. It is an example of participatory research, not an alternative. The goal is therefore constant: "to bring about a more just society in which no groups or classes of people suffer from the deprivation of life's essentials, such as food, shelter, clothing, and health, and in which all enjoy basic human freedoms and dignity" (Park 1993, 2).

Moreover, participatory evaluation shares with participatory research the production of the same kinds of knowledge aimed at achieving the stated goal. Park (1993, 4–8) draws on Habermas's critical theory to explain that participatory research necessarily generates the following: (1) instrumental knowledge, aimed at collecting and making sense of "objective facts" through the application of positivist scientific method; (2) interactive knowledge, involving the strengthening, and in some cases the creation, of social bonds among members of a community (which we could define demographically or on the basis of common interests); and (3) critical knowledge, involving research that addresses "questions concerning the life chances we are entitled to as members of a society, as well as . . . the comprehension of the social obstacles standing more immediately in the way of achieving those goals" (Park 1993, 7).

A review of evaluation research undertaken by social scientists in both Northern and Southern regions suggests that there continue to be problems with acquiring even instrumental knowledge. This is ironic, since most social scientists come from a positivist background and would claim the responsible and effective application of scientific method as one of their most valuable skills. This applies equally to anthropologists and others. The importance of instrumental knowledge, as one of three types, and our apparent difficulties in getting it right lead us to believe that it deserves some specific attention in any discussion of participatory evaluation.

Instrumental knowledge is described by Park in the following way:

> It is useful for controlling the physical and social environment in the sense of both passively adapting to it and more actively manipulating it to bring about desired changes. Instrumental knowledge derives its ability to control external events from the structure of its explanatory theories, which are made up of a series of equations essentially expressing causal relationships. (1993, 5)

The difficulties inherent in positivist social science are enumerated and debated constantly in these days of massive global social change and in the realization at long last that our Western sciences are not as effective in knowledge building as we used to claim. The problems can be synthesized to a clear set of three. First, absolute objectivity is not possible, and ignoring this fact may be more dangerous than the actual existence of a scientist's biases. Second, arbitrary distinctions between the researcher and "the other," a particularly acute dilemma for anthropologists, establish a barrier to the transfer of information and the concurrent development of understanding. The barrier is often so solid that scientists are not even able to formulate the right questions, let alone understand the realities that would otherwise inform them. And third, the arbitrary distinction between the researcher and "the other" typically leaves the latter in a vulnerable position that can be acted upon by the researcher or others who claim in some way to own the results of research.

Even though it continues to be problematic, Park correctly points out that instrumental knowledge plays an important role in our understanding of the world. In the context of participatory evaluation, the question therefore becomes: how can we work toward acquiring instrumental knowledge in such a way that it contributes to the broad goals of participatory research, while simultaneously complementing the development of interactive knowledge and critical knowledge?

Although participatory evaluation can be seen as a subset of participatory research, the specifics of actually doing evaluation research are somewhat different, in terms of both immediate objectives and methods. In some ways, evaluation work can be seen as being more utilitarian than other kinds of research. Research is often used to determine the nature of a problem facing a particular group of people, and then to develop ideas about how to address that problem. Evaluation research, in contrast, assumes that there is already something in place to evaluate (for example, a project, a program, a facility, a service*). It therefore tends to be more focused than nonevaluation research in the sense that its immediate objectives refer specifically to the project in question. The objective for any particular evaluation is usually broken down into related subobjectives, most often the measurement of impacts, intended and unintended effects, cost-benefit ratios, efficiency of implementation, and iden-

---

* The thing being evaluated, whether defined as a project, a program, a facility, or a service, is generically referred to as a "project" throughout the rest of this chapter.

tification of reasonable alternatives for achieving the same or better results. But the point remains that evaluation work is often more directed toward one specific project than are other forms of research.

Although differences may exist with varying degrees of subtlety between evaluation research and nonevaluation research, it is important to stress that evaluations can be undertaken in a manner entirely consistent with the same overall objectives and pursuit of knowledge types (instrumental, interactive, and critical) as participatory research. How do we do this, particularly with respect to the acquisition of instrumental knowledge?

Our first premise is that we have at least two and often three sets of commitments: to the people among whom we work, to the organization that hires us to undertake evaluation research, and to our professional disciplines. In cases in which the people affected actually hire the practitioner, the categories of commitment obviously drop to two.

Commitment to "the Other"

The commitment to the people who are directly affected by the project under evaluation extends to the acquisition of instrumental, integrative, and critical knowledge that will culminate in benefits to those people. Benefits include not only substantive knowledge that can be directly applied to the issue at hand but also the building of a capability to do similar work again— with decreased or no involvement by the professional evaluator.

The first step in realizing the commitment is to agree on a mutually understood working relationship with the people whose lives are affected by the project to be evaluated. This is not necessarily an easy task when even the identification of those people can be problematic. In most cases, in both Southern and Northern contexts, the affected people will be an entire community, defined demographically, so that identification is relatively straightforward. However, in terms of a program established for homeless women in the inner city, for example, the community in question must be defined more carefully as individuals sharing certain common characteristics and needs while living among other people who do not share the same characteristics and needs. Cross-cutting a community on the basis of one or more specific criteria can be difficult but sometimes necessary. Identification of the directly affected group helps ensure their inclusion in the research and protects their legitimate input from others who may not have as great an interest in the project being evaluated.

Once the directly affected group has been identified, setting the parameters of the evaluation study can be undertaken jointly with that group. The purpose here is to help ensure that those who are most affected play a significant part in the following: defining the issue for evaluation, identifying the questions to be asked, identifying appropriate information sources, lending their voices to the exercise, and ensuring that the evaluation results are valid and accessible.

It should be stressed that a working relationship between the practitioner and the directly affected community does not imply the exclusion of other groups and individuals not directly affected by the project to be evaluated. Secondary impacts are also important. In terms of the commitment of the evaluator to enhancing interactive knowledge, the involvement of "second-level" groups and individuals is entirely justified because social change will occur most readily when dialogue takes place among all interested parties. To return to an earlier example, the evaluation of a project directly affecting homeless inner-city women might benefit by engaging men and, perhaps, civil authorities in dialogue at some point in the evaluation process.

The evaluator's primary commitment to "the other," however, must remain with those most directly affected by the project. Although this commitment can be manifested in various ways, the most important may be in the evaluator providing an opportunity for the voices of the directly affected individuals to be heard. The idea of "voice" as conceptualized by Smith (1987) is crucial to our tasks as evaluators in the participatory mode. Smith maintains that as researchers we are obliged to provide the mechanism through which the traditional subjects of research convey, first, what the issues are and, second, their own views and experiences concerning those issues. The message is to be conveyed in unadulterated form through the researcher to those awaiting the results of the evaluation. That is to say, the voices of those most directly affected must be presented as originally conveyed. The researcher provides concomitant analysis, but without altering the messages provided by those formerly voiceless individuals.

The provision of an opportunity for subjects' voices to be heard redefines the formerly dichotomous relationship between the researcher-evaluator and "the other." At least at one level of the evaluation process, there is a condition of intersubjectivity, wherein "the other" determines what is to be said and uses the researcher to say it. Evaluation research thus becomes "subjective" to the extent that Western positivist science is not present in the expression of reality through the voice of "the other."

The provision of subjective information by the people directly affected by a project does not deny the value of the information as instrumental knowledge; who better to describe the impacts and effects of a project than those experiencing it? Further, the expression of subjects' voices as part of a group exercise (even if expressed individually) naturally contributes to increases in interactive knowledge and critical knowledge, as defined by Park.

Commitment to the Funding Organization

The involvement of "the other" by the provision of a mechanism for his or her voice to be heard is reminiscent of Tax's action anthropology, whereby the researcher becomes an advocate for "the other." The danger of this approach lies in the likelihood that the organization funding the project under evaluation, as well as the evaluation research, will reject the evaluation results as not credible. This may be a greater problem for evaluators than for other types of researchers, because funders often accept only assessments of their projects based on "hard facts" acquired through the application of scientific method. Where does this leave the researcher who is committed to participatory evaluation?

First, the expression of "voice" by the recipients of the project does not preclude the evaluator contextualizing those messages. There is, after all, a bigger picture of which the subjects may not be aware. Placing the views of the subjects into the larger context thus becomes the job of the evaluator. The message from "the other" then begins to make more sense to the funding organization because it is inserted into the organizational world: What are the technical implications of the message? What are the political implications? What are the implications for other funded projects? What are the implications for modifying the project? What are the implications for further funding? Again, although the voices of the subjects must be clearly represented in a final report, contextualizing their messages helps not only the funding organization but ultimately the subjects. In this way, the evaluator acts as a broker, drawing both the organization and "the other" into the consideration of a single set of messages. While this may not be interactive knowledge as defined by Park, it can nonetheless contribute to breaking down the dichotomous barriers between "organization" and "other."

The evaluator is also obliged to remember that he or she probably entered into a contractual arrangement with the funding organization partly on the understanding that the evaluator would bring to bear on the subject certain professional skills. More likely than not, those skills were assumed to be of the social scientific variety. This is not a bad thing, even though the evaluator may be committed to the voices of the subjects. Again, social scientific skills enable the evaluator to contextualize the messages of "the other"; to take them one step further by giving them meaning in the organizational context.

As well, such skills are necessary in collecting relevant information from other sources. The voices of the subjects of a project should not be the only input to an evaluation study. Factual information gathered from files and from other key informant interviews, for example, is essential to a complete and thorough evaluation. This is the realm of the professional researcher.* By judiciously weighing the evidence from a variety of sources, including the recipients of the project, the evaluator can arrive at reasoned conclusions regarding the project in question. It is hoped that funding organizations will accept this approach, even if part of the evidence derives from "the other."

As a final note on this point, we are of the view that both funders and researchers should be honest from the beginning about the approach to be taken

---

* It should be noted that in the past, even when the recipients of a project were interviewed as part of an evaluation, their message was rarely reported as given; further, primacy was usually accorded to information collected from sources other than the recipients. A responsible evaluator committed to the participatory approach must avoid both these pitfalls.

and the ultimate expectations of one another. If a researcher chooses to commit to breaking down the traditional dichotomies, and if that approach is unacceptable to the funder, then the researcher should not agree to do the evaluation.

Commitment to the Discipline

With respect to our responsibilities to our respective disciplines, a first thought might naturally be to undertake scientifically acceptable research. That thought assumes, of course, that Western positivist science is the only way to proceed. Our position, as suggested earlier in this chapter, is that the positivist approach is only one of a variety of possibilities, and that it can be used in conjunction with other approaches. In our opinion, therefore, the commitment need not be to traditional positivist social science per se.

Instead, we believe that the commitment should be to quality in research. Whether we choose a positivist approach, an approach that projects the voice of "the other," or a combination of approaches, we must ensure accuracy in information collection, analysis, and reporting. We should state our intentions clearly; for example, if we are out to make a point on behalf of an oppressed group, we should say so unequivocally. Further, we should deal with information honestly by not tampering with data, and by reporting on information that might conflict with our objectives. Although these points might seem obvious to professional researchers, they deserve reconsideration. It is, after all, common enough for researchers to be enticed into compromising projects and to then be faced with the dilemma of having to do bad research in order to meet a contractual commitment.

Accuracy and honesty in evaluation research—whatever the approach used—will reflect well on the discipline. The obverse, however, is likely to result in a black mark for the discipline, as well as in difficulties for other researchers who want to enter into contractual arrangements and who must rely on the goodwill of "the other" to do their work. It is our view, again, that any perceived possibility of having to compromise accuracy and honesty in research should be a red flag to the researcher.

The question of ethics is always difficult. We have tried not to sound dictatorial in the discussion above, but rather to present some views based on the struggle by anthropologists in general and on our own experiences in particular. By way of conclusion, we can say that the evaluator has responsibilities in three directions: to the recipients of the project to be evaluated, to the funding organization, and to his or her discipline. None of these should necessarily have primacy over the others. However, if the researcher makes the conscious decision to assign a higher priority to one category, he or she must state that decision clearly and should be aware of the implications of that decision for the other interested parties.

Having said that, we also believe that it is possible to honor responsibilities to all three categories of interested parties. In acting as a broker of information and views between "the other" and the funding organization, the researcher can contribute to meaningful dialogue between the two. Further, if accuracy and honesty characterize the evaluator's work, then his or her discipline and the other interested parties will ultimately benefit.

References

American Anthropologic Association. 1970. "Principles of Professional Responsibility." *American Anthropologic Association Newsletter* 11 (9): 46–48.

Ames, M. 1992. *Cannibal Tours and Glass Boxes: The Anthropology of Museums*. Vancouver: University of British Columbia Press.

Australian Anthropology Society. 1989. "Code of Ethics for Professional Anthropologists in Australia." *AAS Newsletter* 42 (November): 35–39.

Broad, W., and N. Wade. 1982. *Betrayers of the Truth: Fraud and Deceit in the Halls of Science*. New York: Simon and Schuster.

Canadian Sociology and Anthropology Association. 1978. "Code of Ethics." *Canadian Sociology and Anthropology Association Bulletin* 3 (2): 9–12.

Cleave, P. 1992. Mountain-claiming: The Anthropologist as Ghost-writer. In *Other Sites: Social Anthropology and the Politics of Interpretation*, edited by M. Goldsmith and K. Barber. Palmerston North, New Zealand: Massey University Press.

Cove, J. 1993. "Ethnic Relations and the Indigenisation of Science by New Zealand Maaori." Unpublished manuscript.

English, P. 1985. *Land Rights and Birth Rights—The Great Australian Hoax*. Bullshire, Australia: Veritas Publishing Company.

Fabian, J. 1971. "On Professional Ethics and Epistemological Foundations." *Current Anthropology* 12 (7): 222–35.

Firth, R. 1981. "Engagement and Detachment: Reflections on Applying Social Anthropology to Social Affairs." *Human Organization* 40 (3): 190–203.

Geertz, C. 1968. "Thinking as a Moral Act: Ethical Dimensions of Anthropological Fieldwork in the United States." *Antioch Review* 28: 139–59.

Goldsmith, M. 1987. "Power and Ethics in Social Anthropology, or Treating Anthropological Ethics as an Anthropological Problem." Discussion paper presented to the NZASA Conference, Otago University, August.

Harrison, J. 1988. "'The Spirit Sings' and the Future of Anthropology." *Anthropology Today* 4 (6): 6–9.

Jorgensen, J. 1971. "On Ethics and Anthropology." *Current Anthropology* 12 (3): 321–35.

Kolig, E. 1982. "Anthropology: Everyone's Whore?" *AAS Newsletter* 14 (March): 16–19.

Lesser, A. 1981. "Franz Boas." In *Totems and Teachers: Perspectives on the History of Anthropology*, edited by S. Siverman. New York: Columbia University Press.

McPherson, C. B. 1977. *The Life and Times of Liberal Democracy*. Oxford: Oxford University Press.

Padgett, S. 1986. *Political Parties and Elections in West Germany*. London: C. Hurst & Company.

Park, P. 1993. "What Is Participatory Research? A Theoretical and Methodological Perspective." Pp. 1–19 in *Voices of Change: Participatory Research in the United States and Canada*, edited by P. Park, M. Brydon-Miller, B. Hall, and T. Jackson. Toronto: OISE Press.

Ridington, R. 1992. Fieldwork in Courtroom 53: A Witness to *Delgamuuk*. In *Aboriginal Title in British Columbia: Delgamuuk v. the Queen*. Vancouver: Institute for Research on Public Policy.

Slack, J., and L. Whitt. 1992. "Ethics and Cultural Studies." In *Cultural Studies*, edited by L. Grossberg et al. London: Routledge.

Smith, D. E. 1987. *The Everyday World as Problematic: A Feminist Sociology*. Toronto: University of Toronto Press.

Society for Applied Anthropology. 1975. "Statement on Ethical and Professional Responsibilities." *Human Organization* 34: 81–85.

Society for Applied Anthropology in Canada. 1994. "Ethical Guidelines for Applied Anthropologists in Canada." *Proactive* 13 (1): 38–46.

Tax, S. 1952. "Action Anthropology." *America Indigena* 12: 103–9.

———. 1958. "The Fox Project." *Human Organization* 17: 15–23.

Webster, S. 1989. "Maori Studies and the Expert Definition of Maori Culture." *Sites* 18: 35–56.

Wright, J. 1985. *We Call for a Treaty*. Sydney: Collins-Fontana.

———— 3 ————-

Indicators of Change: Results-Based Management and Participatory Evaluation

Edward T. Jackson

Is participatory evaluation compatible with results-based management? This chapter makes the case that participatory evaluation can serve the interests of results-oriented development interventions, and vice versa. Furthermore, there are some specific tools that are emerging in development practice that can enhance the interaction between participatory evaluation and results-based management.

The Shift to Results-Based Management

Recent years have witnessed a shift among the major donor agencies in the field of development cooperation from activity-based management systems toward results-based management systems. In turn, donors are obliging their partner agencies—Southern governments and nongovernmental organizations (NGOs) and private firms in both the North and the South—to adopt results-oriented management practices, as well. This change in approach has been prompted by calls for improved accountability and value for money in foreign-aid spending by deficit-oriented Northern legislatures and electorates, which are making similar demands on other areas of public spending.

While results-based management, or RBM, is only now being applied to development cooperation, its fundamentals are clear. Rather than designing, managing, monitoring, and reporting on inputs and activities of development programs and projects, donor agencies and their fundees and contractees will plan, implement, and assess interventions in terms of the extent to which they achieve their projected results. How these results are achieved is less important than what is, in fact, achieved.

Earlier versions of parts of this chapter were published in 1997 in the special participatory evaluation issue of *Knowledge and Policy: The International Journal of Knowledge Transfer and Utilization,* Vol. 10, No. 1/2, under the sponsorship of the International Development Research Centre, Ottawa.

Categorizing Types of Development Results: A Matrix Approach

Progress is being made in categorizing the types of results that can be generated by development interventions. RBM generally dictates that there are three essential types of results: outputs, outcomes, and long-term impacts.

An *output* is the most immediate, tangible result of an activity. An output could be, for example, the number of persons trained in a course. Outputs can usually be achieved within the period of one month to one year. An *outcome* is a medium-term result that is the logical consequence of the intervention achieving a combination of outputs. For instance, an outcome might be the application of new knowledge and skills by participants following their training course. Outcomes may take one to five years to achieve.

An *impact* is a long-term result that is the logical consequence of the intervention achieving a combination of outcomes and outputs. Carrying our example further, the new knowledge applied by trainees to their work might result in improved quality of life (for example, reduced incidence of disease, improved housing) for the local citizens served by the trainees. The achievement of an impact may require from five to twenty-five years.

The output-outcome-impact "chain" of results is useful in distinguishing among types of development results. However, results can also be defined by the *level* of intervention. Results may be achieved at the *macro*, or policy, level; at the *meso*, or institutional, level; and at the *micro*, or community, household, or individual, level. Successful development interventions are often characterized by mutually reinforcing activities and results "up" and "down" these different levels (see Beaulieu and Manoukian 1994).

Taken together, then, results can be conceived of as a *matrix*, with outputs, outcomes, and impacts across the horizontal axis and macro, meso, and micro levels down the vertical axis. Variations on this type of matrix are being used by the Canadian International Development Agency (CIDA) and its partner NGOs in evaluating, planning, and managing basic human needs, human rights, and poverty-reduction projects. Other development organizations employ variations on this matrix.

At the same time, development agencies are modifying other tools, such as the logical framework analysis, or logframe, from an activity orientation to a results orientation (CIDA 1997). This work continues.

Results-Based Management and Participatory Evaluation: Conflict or Convergence?

While there is growing (though sometimes grudging) recognition that results-based management may, in fact, be a helpful approach for development professionals operating in large bureaucracies, is it compatible with *participatory* forms of development practice? It would appear, perhaps, that the technocratic instruments of RBM represent the antithesis of the approaches used by social-justice activists and engaged scholars advocating participatory interventions.

But think again. When you sit with villagers under a tree, or with barrio residents in a church basement, and discuss their hopes and aspirations for themselves and their children, they usually frame their objectives for the future in terms of *concrete results*. They want better housing, less disease, a cleaner environment, more education, increased income, or greater political decision making. Progress toward these results can be tracked and evaluated, quantitatively and qualitatively. In fact, the ultimate beneficiaries of a development intervention—the poor, the disadvantaged, the disempowered—can, and should, *lead* the effort among stakeholders to define the results to be achieved by a given intervention. And they should be the leaders in reviewing performance on these results, as well.

"Customer-Driven" Development

It may be that the RBM–participatory evaluation combination can provide a vehicle whereby the "customers" of development interventions actually exert substantial influence over the process of defining and evaluating results. Customer-driven product development and service delivery enjoy wide success in both the public and private sectors around the world today. "Ask the customer," exhort prominent management books. While development cooperation is not merely a business or a service, it must, nevertheless, succeed. By using this language, however, practitioners need not abandon their values of social solidarity and the common good.

Building in the Bias: Enabling Participants to Define and Evaluate Results

There is an array of participatory methods that can be used to enable project participants to define and evaluate development cooperation results. The key to all participatory planning and assessment initiatives is ensuring a mechanism for *shared control* by project beneficiaries and other stakeholders. This mechanism might be a study team, research committee, working group, or task force. So powerful are the resources and skills of other stakeholders, though, that a bias must be built into the structure and process to ensure that authentically shared control prevails. This bias must be in favor of the poorest, least literate project participants. Gender differences, class differences, language, medium of communication, meeting times, meeting location, cultural norms and forms, and seasonal rhythms and responsibilities should all be considered in biasing the structure and process in favor of the most marginalized participants.

Once these arrangements have been made, the most appropriate combination of data collection and analysis methods should be selected. As Figure 3.1 shows, one basic decision concerns the mix of qualitative and quantitative methods to be employed. Another decision involves selecting the appropriate combination of qualitative data collection and analysis techniques. Field-based techniques, workshop-based techniques, self-assessment tools, and cultural methods are all possible choices on the methods "menu."

Participatory Tools for Defining and Evaluating Results

A number of tools by which project participants, working with allied professionals, can both define and assess development results of the interventions they are associated with have been developed over the past decade. One group of tools is workshop-based in nature. Workshop-based techniques seek to create a learning atmosphere and a safe environment in which all parties feel free to participate. The workshops usually involve a series of activities designed to build consensus on problem analysis and action to be taken.

One of these tools is *ZOPP*, which was developed by the German technical agency GTZ and its partners in Africa and elsewhere. ZOPP is actually a project planning process that is undertaken through a series of stakeholder workshops. Participants, who include local government officials as well as community representatives from the project area, collectively generate a problem tree that describes relationships among the issues constraining local and regional development. Then, by reversing the problem tree, participants generate an objectives tree, which sets out the actions needed to remove these constraints. The workshops focus on which elements in the objectives tree will be addressed in the project being planned. A project planning matrix or logical framework is then developed by the participants, and the project is sent to each of the stakeholder groups for official approval (World Bank 1996). A variant of the ZOPP approach is *PC/TeamUp*, which places emphasis on team building. PC/TeamUp also uses a special computer software package to assist teams in planning projects. This approach makes use of tree analysis, logical frameworks, SWOT (strengths, weaknesses, opportunities, threats) analysis, bar charts and other scheduling tools, and total-quality management approaches (World Bank 1996).

Another workshop-based technique is *social gender analysis* (SGA). Developed originally by the Coady International Institute of St. Francis Xavier University in Canada, in cooperation with its overseas partners, SGA takes project stakeholders through a series of exercises that analyze the disadvantages faced by various groups in the project area and the resources and strategies required for them to achieve social sustainability. Class, gender, access to and control of resources, benefits from participation, and links between local and national or global levels are all key elements in SGA workshop discussions. The SGA process results in a project strategy that includes clear objectives, an implementation plan, and measures for monitoring and evaluation. SGA is a gender-sensitive tool, but its

Figure 3.1
Possible Methods of Participatory Research and Evaluation

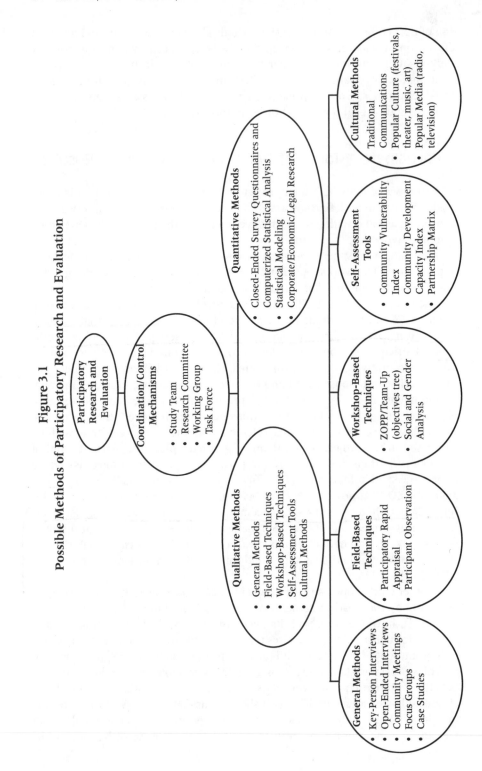

use is not limited to gender concerns. Rather, it is concerned more broadly with social sustainability (see Plewes and Stuart 1991).

Another group of tools involves field-based techniques. Perhaps the best known of these techniques is *participatory rural appraisal* (PRA), which evolved from rapid rural appraisal. Originally developed for rural areas and farming systems by the Institute of Development Studies in Sussex, England, PRA has spread around the world to many other sectors, including projects involving the urban poor. PRA employs group animation techniques and problem analysis exercises to promote sharing of information and joint action among stakeholders. To this end, PRA uses semi-structured interviews, focus groups, wealth ranking, community meetings, needs assessment, mapping, transect walks, and other participant-observer techniques (Chambers 1993, 1994a, 1994b, 1995; Nelson and Wright 1995; Gallardo, Encena, and Bayona 1995; Okali, Sumberg, and Farrington 1994; Scoones and Thompson 1994; Kumar 1993).

Another approach is *participatory research* or *participatory action research* (PR/PAR), representing quite a different tradition. PR/PAR involves both workshops and fieldwork, but with two elements that make it distinct from the other approaches. First, PR/PAR takes a relatively longer time to implement—months, even years, rather than days or weeks. Second, PR/PAR emphasizes issues of *power* more than most other methods, in both its analysis and its action. PR/PAR uses a more oppositional framework vis-à-vis elites than other participatory methods, which tend to try to co-opt elite involvement and acceptance.

Apart from these distinctive features, PR/PAR makes use of a full range of workshop facilitation techniques, field observation methods, and, particularly, group dialogue methods. Projects in this tradition have also employed computerized data analysis, oral history, popular theater and other media, and many other techniques. The insider-outsider dialectic is monitored carefully in PR/PAR, with special efforts made to give voice to the insiders who are on the margins of local communities. The same obstacles faced by other approaches—obstacles related to class, gender, ethnicity, wealth, and power—must be continually addressed by PR/PAR, as well. PR/PAR is often carried out by social movements and frequently has a longer-term goal of broader, structural transformation (see Park et al. 1993; Fals-Borda and Rahman 1991; Manoukian 1996).

Still another cluster of self-assessment tools also uses both workshops and PRA techniques but focuses the analytic work on communities developing their own indices of development for planning and impact assessment. In northern Ghana, for example, a North-South monitoring team on a large rural development project developed a tool entitled the Village Development Capacity Index (VDCI). Funded by the CIDA and the government of Ghana, this index was designed to rank communities in the project area in terms of their performance on poverty indicators and on village development capacity indicators. Poverty indicators, for which data were collected through household interviews, included safety of water sources, literacy rate, food security, and household expenditure patterns. The tool permits other relevant indicators to be added, as appropriate to the project context.

Village development capacity indicators, the data for which were collected through key-person interviews, field observation, and focus groups, included status of village organization, previous experience of the village in managing development interventions, level and types of village cooperation and mutual aid, and the status of infrastructure and assets under village control, both collectively and by individual residents. Stakeholders participated in the process of allocating scores on each of these indicators to the villages under study. Village representatives then reviewed the findings of the VDCI exercise in a workshop, provided feedback, and discussed action to be taken through the overall development project to redress weaknesses identified in the communities. Scores on the VDCI for each village were then tracked by monitoring teams over time in order to assess progress (see Chapter 4).

The same research team then developed a matrix for measuring the extent and nature of partnership between African and Canadian NGOs. A partnership and institution-building matrix was constructed, based on the experience of ten case study partnerships from several subregions in Africa. This matrix included indicators of the compatibility of the two partner-agencies, operational principles, operational mechanisms, commitment, support modes, intervention modes, outcomes, and sustainability of the partnership. Data for these indicators were collected through key-person interviews, document review, field visits, and stakeholder workshops and meetings. Further work on this index has been carried out for additional Canadian-African NGO partnerships (Gariba, Kassam, and Thibault 1995; Kassam, Gariba and Mothenbesoane-Anoh 1996).

Work on both the VDCI and the partnership matrix built on earlier efforts to construct regional and community-based self-assessment tools for use in underdeveloped parts of Canada. In the 1980s, research sponsored by the Economic Council of Canada had resulted in the construction of a development index to measure disparities among subregions. This index was based on more than fifty statistical indicators of economic performance (employment, income), capacity (labor force skills, access to capital), energy (new business start-ups, competitiveness), and policy measures (Lamontagne 1994). Along similar lines, the Canadian Association of Single Industry Towns developed a vulnerability checklist that enables community leaders to assess the extent of economic diversification in the local economy and of existing organizational and material resources on which to build a broader-based and more sustainable economic strategy before a local plant or mine is forced to shut its doors by decision makers far away (Decter 1993).

A more recent generation of this work appeared in aboriginal development organizations in Canada in the early 1990s. Aboriginal leaders and economic consultants, working in a national committee, created a guidebook for aboriginal communities to gather their own data for development planning purposes. The guide helps communities assess the community situation, set development priorities and goals, identify activities to meet those goals, implement development activities, and monitor and evaluate the results. The guide includes advice on selecting indicators to track development progress and worksheets that link strategic goals with specific activities. Most of the indicators suggested by the guide are output indicators, such as community revenue by source and value of loans provided by the local development corporation. Impacts on household incomes and quality of life are not emphasized in the guide but could be easily accommodated. The key here, as with all self-assessment instruments, is that the process calls for the community to choose its key indicators itself (Lamontagne 1994).

Developing Appropriate Results Indicators

Participatory planning and evaluation efforts demand simple, reliable indicators of development results that are agreed to by participants and other stakeholders. In the case of antipoverty, human rights, and basic needs projects, the most crucial results indicators relate to money and power. It is also important that these indicators of results be identified at different levels: macro, meso, and micro. Moreover, *impact* indicators should be emphasized. Although they are the most difficult and complex indicators to achieve, they are, ultimately, the most important tests of whether a development intervention has succeeded.

Micro-Level Impact Indicators

Much work has been done on impact indicators of individual, household, business, and community gains in income by the poor. One finding from this work is that, even at the micro level, there are multiple levels—or sublevels—of impact. In rural development projects, for example, improved grain varieties and expanded irrigation works (inputs) may result in increases in dry-season rice production (output). Such increased production is then sold, generating new income for participating households (impact) (see, for example, van Dusseldorp 1993). In turn, this new income (an impact at another level) is used to purchase rice-milling equipment, start a small kiosk, or construct a new well (impacts), all of which could further influence the quality of life of the household. These potential "onward" impacts must be tracked in the future, as well. Such income gains may also be used by households to pay user fees for village services such as schools, health clinics, or marketing cooperatives, thus boosting infrastructure assets at the community level—and serving as inputs to those services.

Microcredit programs also involve multiple levels of impact. Loans and technical training provided by such programs (inputs) can result in increased owner drawings through improved profitability, expanded sales, and commercial sustainability in participating microbusinesses (enterprise-level impacts). In this way, very small enterprises create employment income for individuals and households (inputs), which generates multiplier effects in the community when households purchase other goods and services and pay taxes or user fees (impacts). The growth of participating microenterprises may also foster the establishment of new businesses by other households to supply the successful enterprises in the program (ACCION/Calmeadow Foundation 1988; Ashe 1992, 1995; Otero and Rhyne 1994). And revenue accruing to each community in which such programs are operated can reinvest taxes and user fees in new infrastructure, services, and training, thereby further building the capacity of the community to develop itself.

Like all development interventions, however, enterprise support programs must assess costs as well as benefits. Fiscal cost-benefit studies seek to assess the return on taxpayer investment. Costs include tax credits and deductions as well as grants associated with the program under study. A percentage of these costs can be allocated to the specific enterprises assessed. Among the benefits calculated for this type of analysis are increased tax revenues from the operations of the enterprises that are attributable to program support and avoided income-support costs (unemployment insurance, welfare). In addition, tax revenues from the firms' suppliers and employees attributable to the support of the program are estimated. Comparing fiscal costs and benefits thus enables evaluators to estimate a payback period for overall public expenditure on the enterprises under study and, if desired, on the program as a whole (Jackson and Lamontagne 1995). Although this approach is obviously more appropriate to Northern contexts, it can be adapted to developing country situations as well.

The work of Moser (1989) and others (Plewes and Stuart 1991) in the field of gender and development has generated useful micro-level impact indicators on power in particular. The gender and development approach is based on an assessment of women's practical and strategic needs, especially as indicated in gender roles in both productive and reproductive work in the household and in managing the community. Practical gender needs relate, for example, to women's access to adequate water supply, health care, and employment. Strategic gender needs relate to the legal and property rights of women, access to credit, equality of wages, freedom from domestic violence, and women's control over their bodies. As the impacts of development interventions yield positive impacts in these areas, women's power increases at all levels: in the household, in the community, in the nation.

Meso-Level Impact Indicators

Increasing the income of the poor also demands impact assessment at the meso, or institutional, level. Institutions promoting poverty alleviation—ministries, NGOs, social movements, and donor agencies—must build their own capacity to assist the poor in achieving gains in income and power. Following Lusthaus, Anderson, and Murphy (1995), all institutional assessments must include analysis of the external environment, organizational motivation, organizational capacity, and organizational performance. With respect to organizational performance, some key impact indicators in antipoverty efforts include financial sustainability of the organization as a whole, self-sufficiency or sustainability of poverty alleviation programs run by the institution, and the percentage of communities assisted by the organization that have moved from being categorized as poor to being categorized as less poor or moderately well-off. Other relevant indicators can include income per capita, unemployment rates, and labor force participation in the area served by the institution, as measured over time.

The relationship between institutional capacity and performance, on the one hand, and community development capacity, on the other, must be assessed in detail. The perceived relevance of the services of the institution to its clients (or "customers") is also a crucial factor deserving careful study. Further, gender-disaggregated data must be collected for all indicators to permit an assessment of the comparative gains made by men and women as a result of the institution's efforts to strengthen itself.

In the field of social development, Oxfam-UK has suggested that indicators of participatory management structures and processes are especially relevant. Such indicators include:

- Evidence of shared decision making among participants and staff;
- Signs of commitment among participants to the group's goals and activities;
- Evidence of shared leadership;
- Signs of solidarity and cohesion;
- Capacity for self-reflection and critical analysis; and
- Capacity to take action in relation to problems identified.

Such indicators may be applied to test the performance of development institutions, NGOs, project management teams, and local-partner organizations (Marsden and Oakley 1990; Marsden, Oakley, and Pratt 1994).

Macro-Level Impact Indicators

All macro-level income gains by the poor can be measured by conventional indicators over time, particularly gross domestic product (GDP) per capita. Other key indicators, some of which are used to calculate the United Nations Development Programme (UNDP) Human Development Index, include share of national income of the lowest 40 percent of households; percentage of the population in absolute poverty; and public expenditures on social programs, health, and education as a percentage of GDP. Additional relevant indicators include daily calorie supply, access to health services, and the prevalence of radios, telephones, and motor vehicles (see UNDP 1994, 1995).

Other indicators can be assessed at the macro level as well. In some cases, new policies and legislation in favor of the poor can be attributed to the demonstration effects of antipoverty projects or to the lobbying of NGOs, government ministries, donor agencies, and social movements on behalf of the poor. Such programs may confer new economic benefits (for example, food prices, credit availability) or civil rights (for example, the general right to organize, women's rights to own land or business assets). These impacts, in turn, will serve as "inputs" that can be transformed, at all levels, into further gains in money and power for the poor. Assessing whether and how such transformation occurs is an important task.

At the national level, research indicates that one year of schooling for girls or young women can reduce the fertility rate by 5 to 10 percent. Reduced fertility boosts economic growth rates on a per capita basis. In addition, increased access to credit for women has been found to do more to reduce poverty and spur investment than does increased credit provision for men (World Bank 1995). At the macro level, educational attainment, fertility rates, and access to credit are all important indicators of gains in power and money by poor women and by women in general.

Useful work had been done on basic indicators of gains (or losses) in human rights in development projects. Norway's Madsen (1991) developed guidelines for project design and evaluation at the micro level that test project performance against international conventions of the Intentional Labor Organization (ILO). The specific rights that Madsen recommends be tested in this way relate to forced removals and resettlements of peoples, land rights, the right to organize, child labor, forced labor, gender discrimination, conditions of employment (including health and safety, as well as worker remuneration), and the rights of participation. The ILO and some Scandinavian aid agencies have included protections for some of these rights in project agreements with Southern government ministries and Northern consulting firms. The World Bank, the Asian Development Bank, and the Organization for Economic Cooperation and Development's Development Assistance Committee published specific guidelines intended to protect project participants against forced resettlement.

Madsen argues, as do most advocates of human rights generally, that project-level—that is, usually micro-level—performance on human rights indicators *must be tested against the standards of international conventions* and, if relevant, national laws. Thus, human rights impact assessment must necessarily be multilevel in nature.

Furthermore, it is likely that, among marginalized peoples whose rights have been systematically denied for centuries, impact assessment practitioners will need to *educate* project participants about their rights while the research is being carried out. There is a moral obligation to do so, as well as a programmatic or professional obligation. Such an educational process can be facilitated greatly by participatory assessment techniques, especially the direct representation of project beneficiaries on assessment teams.

South House Exchange (SHE), a consulting firm specializing in human rights and development, has authored a training curriculum based on case studies of NGO interventions in this field. One case study is about a project involving Guatemalan refugees living in refugee camps in Mexico who are planning their return home. Trainees using the case study are asked to draw up a plan for the refugees' return; the plan must set out the roles of the refugees, a local women's NGO, and foreign partner NGOs. Trainees are also asked to identify "indicators that the plan's elements were working" (SHE 1995, 5). Almost by definition, such indicators must:

- Relate to gains or losses in human rights by the refugees and the local NGO, measured through the application of international standards;
- Disaggregate data by gender;
- Assess the effectiveness of the intervention at the micro (individual) and meso (institutional) levels in the South and at the meso level in the North; and
- Pay special attention to impacts related to NGO capacity-building and North-South partnerships.

Such multilevel, multidimensional impact assessment can be significantly enhanced by participatory methods. The participation of women refugees in a Southern-led project evaluation process would yield especially rich insights and also build additional project commitment and capacity among participants.

Moving the Practice Forward

Clearly, the potential (and the limitations) of the relationship between participatory evaluation and results-based management is only beginning to be understood. It will be through collective action and reflection, globally and locally, that this area of development cooperation practice can be advanced. There will be pitfalls and complexities. But substantive gains can be made, especially if engaged practitioners are able to regularly exchange views, experiences, and techniques at the country, regional, and global levels. Networks, newsletters, monographs, and case studies would contribute much to this learning process.

Participatory evaluation can be compatible with results-based management. Whereas advocates and practitioners of RBM are not necessarily interested in participatory development approaches, advocates and practitioners of participatory evaluation can find productive ways of blending RBM into their work. There is already an array of practical tools and indicators that can be mobilized to this end. The convergence of RBM and participatory development promises to be a rich and creative site of development cooperation practice in the years ahead.

References

ACCION International and the Calmeadow Foundation. 1988. *An Operational Guide for Micro-Enterprise Projects*. Toronto: Authors.

Ashe, J. 1992. "Microlending Programs." Pp. 559–69 in *The Social Investment Almanac*, edited by P. D. Kinder, S. D. Lyndenberg, and A. L. Domini. New York: Holt.

———. 1995. "Strategies for Financing Micro-Enterprises: The Working Capital Model." Working Paper, Centre for the Study of Training, Investment and Economic Restructuring, Carleton University, Ottawa.

Beaulieu, R., and V. Manoukian. 1994. "Participatory Development: A Brief Review of CIDA's Experience and Potential." Policy Branch, Canadian International Development Agency, Hull.

Canadian International Development Agency. 1997. "The Logical Framework: Making It Results-Oriented." Performance Review Branch and the Bilateral Branches, CIDA, Hull.

Chambers, R. 1993. *Challenging the Professions: Frontiers for Rural Development*. London: Intermediate Technology Publications.

———. 1994a. "The Origins and Practice of Participatory Rural Appraisal." *World Development* 22 (7): 953–69.

———. 1994b. "Participatory Rural Appraisal (PIA): Analysis of Experience." *World Development* 22 (9): 1253–68.

———. 1995. "Paradigm Shifts and the Practice of Participatory Research and Development." Pp. 30–42 in *Power and Participatory Development: Theory and Practice*, edited by N. Nelson and S. Wright. London: Intermediate Technology Publications.

Decter, M. B. 1993. "What We Can Do for Ourselves: Diversification and Single Industry Communities." Pp. 136–200 in *Regional Development from the Bottom Up*, edited by M. Lewis and D. McNair. Vancouver: Westcoast Development Group and the Centre for Community Enterprise.

Fals-Borda, O., and M. A. Rahman, eds. 1991. *Action and Knowledge: Breaking the Monopoly with Participatory Action-Research*. New York: Apex Press.

Gallardo, W. G., V. C. Encena, and N. C. Bayona. 1995. "Rapid Rural Appraisal and Participatory Research in the Philippines." *Community Development Journal* 30 (3): 265–75.

Gariba, S., Y. Kassam, and L. Thibault. 1995. "Report of the Study of Partnership Institutional Strengthening." Partnership Africa Canada, Ottawa.

Jackson, E. T., and F. Lamontagne. 1995. "Adding Value: The Economic and Social Impacts of Labor-Sponsored Venture Capital Corporations on their Investee Firms." Canadian Labor Market and Productivity Centre, Ottawa.

Kassam, Y., S. Gariba, and E. Mothenbesoane-Anoh. 1996. "Strengthening Partnerships for Community Health: Report of the Evaluation of the Impact of Partnership for Capacity Building in Canada's International Immunization Program." Canadian Public Health Association, Ottawa.

Kumar, K., ed. 1993. *Rapid Appraisal Methods*. Washington, D.C.: World Bank.

Lamontagne, F. 1994. "Development Indicators and Development Planning: A Case Study." Pp. 208–22 in *Community Economic Development: Perspectives on Research and Policy*, edited by B. Galway and J. Hudson. Toronto: Thompson Educational Publishing.

Lusthaus, C., G. Anderson, and E. Murphy. 1995. *Institutional Assessment: A Framework for Strengthening Organizational Capacity for IDRC's Research Partners.* Ottawa: International Development Research Centre.

Madsen, H. L. 1991. "Towards Human Rights Assessments of Development Projects." Working Paper, Program of Human Rights Studies, Chr. Michelson Institute, Fantoft, Norway.

Manoukian, V. 1996. Guest lecture on participation. Presented to the graduate course on Project Management in Developing Countries, School of Public Administration, Carleton University, Ottawa.

Marsden, D., and P. Oakley, eds. 1990. *Evaluating Social Development Projects.* Development Guidelines No. 5. Oxford: Oxfam UK.

Marsden, D., P. Oakley, and B. Pratt. 1994. *Measuring the Process: Guidelines for Evaluating Social Development.* London: David Bruman Associates.

Moser, C. 1989. "Gender Planning in the Third World: Meeting Practical and Strategic Needs." *World Development* 17 (11): 1799–1825.

Nelson, N., and S. Wright, eds. 1995. *Power and Participatory Development: Theory and Practice.* London: Intermediate Technology Publications.

Okali, C., J. Sumberg, and J. Farrington. 1994. *Farmer Participatory Research: Rhetoric and Reality.* London: Intermediate Technology Publications.

Otero, M., and E. Rhyne, eds. 1994. *The New World of Microenterprise Finance.* West Hartford, Conn.: Kumarian Press.

Park, P., M. Brydon-Miller, B. Hall, and T. Jackson, eds. 1993. *Voices of Change: Participatory Research in the United States and Canada.* Toronto/Westport, Conn.: OISE Press/Bergin and Garvey.

Plewes, B., and R. Stuart. 1991. "Women and Development Revisited: The Case for a Gender and Development Approach." Pp. 107–32 in *Conflicts of Interest: Canada and the Third World,* edited by J. Swift and B. Tomlinson. Toronto: Between the Lines.

Scoones, I., and J. Thompson, eds. 1994. *Beyond Farmer First.* London: Intermediate Technology Publications.

South House Exchange. 1995. "Guatemalan Refugees: Preparing for the Return Home— A Case Study." SHE, Ottawa.

United Nations Development Programme. 1994. *Human Development Report 1994.* New York: Oxford University Press.

———. 1995. *Human Development Report 1995.* New York: Oxford University Press.

van Dusseldorp, D. B. W. M. 1993. *Projects for Rural Development in the Third World: Preparation and Implementation.* Wageningen, Netherlands: Wageningen Agricultural University.

World Bank. 1995. "Toward Gender Equality: The Role of Public Policy." World Bank, Washington, D.C.

———. 1996. *World Bank Sourcebook on Participation.* Washington, D.C.: World Bank.

———— 4 ————

Participatory Impact Assessment as a Tool for Change: Lessons from Poverty Alleviation Projects in Africa

Sulley Gariba

The 1990s have witnessed a deepening fatigue among the development assistance community toward sustained investments in poverty alleviation. This frustration stems from both a lack of concrete results in poverty alleviation projects and the inability of development practitioners to convey the real impacts of their work to the sponsors of such projects. The subject of this chapter, the evaluation of an integrated rural development program funded by the Canadian International Development Agency (CIDA) in northern Ghana, has already paid the ultimate price of the donor fatigue: termination of support.

This kind of "undifferentiated gloom and doom is not justified" (Cornia, van der Hoeven, and Mkanadwire 1992, 2), essentially because, in many countries of Africa, there is scattered but growing evidence of progress at the grassroots and sectoral levels in improving agricultural systems and water conservation, in raising efficiency in education, and in extending key health services, such as child immunization, even though recovery at the aggregate level is not yet apparent.

What remains to be determined is the most effective means of assessing and analyzing the growth and development of human capacity and the "intangible" interventions that coalesce to generate increased capacities for development at the grassroots. This chapter illustrates how partners in development are tackling issues of participatory impact assessment.

Scope of the Chapter

This chapter focuses on the attempt to use a participatory impact assessment process to foster village-level capacity building in poverty alleviation

Some parts of this chapter were first published in *Knowledge and Policy: The International Journal of Knowledge Transfer and Utilization*, Vol. 10, No. 1/2, under the title "Participatory Impact Assessment for Poverty Alleviation: Opportunities for Communities and Development Agencies." Reprinted by permission of Transaction Publishers, New Brunswick, New Jersey.

programs. It concentrates on the process by which an evaluation exercise has been used as an integral part of the development intervention activity, while satisfying the primary objective of assessing impacts.

This chapter describes the background of the program that was being evaluated, describes divergent purposes of the evaluation, and examines the extent to which the participatory methods adopted influenced the program in question. Finally, this chapter analyzes the wider implications of this approach to evaluation, both for the specific project and for the broader network of promoters, implementers, and beneficiaries of a more transparent process of development interventions in general.

Project Background: Bedrock of Competing Interests

The Northern Region Rural Integrated Program (NORRIP) was initiated over a decade ago by the government of Ghana, with funding from CIDA, to promote regional and integrated rural development in Ghana's underdeveloped northern region. Phase I of the program, undertaken in the early to mid-1980s, involved the establishment of a regional development secretariat (known as the NORRIP office) to undertake a variety of regional-level sectoral studies and produce a comprehensive program implementation plan. After some delays, the implementation phase of the program (NORRIP phase II) began in 1988, with the NORRIP office, in conjunction with a Canadian executing agency, charged with the mandate of strengthening the planning and program delivery capacity of line agencies of the government of Ghana and testing innovative means of delivering social and economic services to villages in two project districts, namely, the Yendi and East Mamprusi districts in the northern region.

Between 1988 and 1990, the stakeholders in NORRIP II significantly redesigned and refocused the implementation phase of the program. In particular, it was decided that the lead sectors of the project would be rural water supplies (village-operated hand pumps) and related education and training, together with primary health care services. The approved inception report for this phase determined that the project would install 350 hand pumps in the newly reconstituted districts of East Mamprusi and Yendi, where it was estimated that there were some 250 villages eligible for this improved water supply.

This major redesign brought to the fore the conflicting expectations of development programs that seek to address the problems of poverty in rural areas. Growing frustrations with the pace of "tangible" outputs led the funding agency, CIDA, to emphasize the objectives relating to the installation of facilities—in this case, new water supply facilities. Yet the rationale for the program, and ultimately the long-term objective, related to sustainability and capacity building for the concerned villages and communities to manage their own development, including the newly installed water supply and sanitation facilities. Thus, water supply and related sanitation facilities were merely means for enhancing the capacity of the communities to work toward alleviating their poverty rather than ends in themselves.

In 1989, CIDA engaged the services of an evaluation and monitoring consultant to provide ongoing professional advice on the effectiveness, efficiency, and impacts of NORRIP II, through twice-yearly monitoring missions and more detailed baseline and evaluation studies. The evaluation consultant, a Canadian firm, undertook these activities in partnership with a Ghanaian firm with extensive experience in the northern region of Ghana to actively promote capacity building among local consultants in evaluation and monitoring (the results of this collaboration have been presented; see Gariba and Jackson 1993).

What to Evaluate and How

Two specific problems confronted this evaluation mandate. The first was a question of what specifically to evaluate, arising from the divergent expectations of the different stakeholders; the second was that of which evaluation methodology would ensure satisfactory outcomes for the main stakeholders in the program.

The contending objectives of village-level capacity building for sustained development and the immediate delivery of improved water supply raised crucial questions of what to evaluate. The main promoter of the NORRIP program, CIDA, was interested primarily in the type of evaluation that would convey immediate impacts of the investment in water supply and sanitation, as emphasized in the program redesign. This was a logical defense against the growing pressures to reduce budgets for development projects commonly faced by the aid bureaucracy.

However, it is commonly recognized that the health impacts of water supply and sanitation projects are difficult and expensive to measure on a routine basis. Further, the investments in the project, while supporting water supply and sanitation improvements, also involved fundamental areas of capacity building, at both the village and the development agency levels. Therefore, it would have been extremely limiting for the evaluation exercise to have focused exclusively on the long-term health impacts of improved water supply.

The evaluation activities were therefore designed to foster a combination of the capacity-building objectives and those targeted at measuring the impact of delivery of new water supplies into one objective: assessing the impact of capacity building on access to improved water supply and sanitation services.

The Evaluation Methodology

As the implementation stage of the project started up in early 1989, it became clear that an early baseline study—prior to implementation—was not welcomed by village leadership in the project area; nor would it have been ethical. Villagers and other institutional partners had waited ten years for the delivery of services promised by the project and were unlikely to cooperate with yet another study until some concrete evidence of implementation (boreholes, hand pumps, health services, and the planned village-level capacity building) was forthcoming.

The methodology and implementation of the evaluation study were therefore conditioned by the peculiar circumstances of the NORRIP II program in order that the results would be useful and reflect the needs and expectations of the project stakeholders.

The Evaluator's Dilemma in Selecting a Methodology

In developing countries, the word *evaluation* has often evoked mixed reactions from promoters and implementers of development projects. For the promoters, mainly Western donor agencies, evaluation has been used as the yardstick for "extending" or "terminating" project mandates and funding. For project implementers, evaluation has been, at best, a means for vindicating their approaches to project management and, at worst, the vilification of their chosen techniques. Caught in between these divergent purposes and perceptions of evaluation is the evaluator, who, for the most part, satisfies neither the promoters nor the implementers of development interventions. In this chapter, evaluation is viewed as a systematic way of learning from experience, whereby the partners in the development endeavor draw lessons from their interaction and take corrective actions to improve the effectiveness or efficiency of their ongoing future activities.

Thus, the participatory impact assessment method of evaluation was selected, to emphasize the process of collaborative problem solving through the generation of knowledge and its use. A number of critical elements of this method need to be mentioned before we describe how they were actually implemented.

Evaluation as a Learning Tool. This principle formed the main paradigm of choice. The purpose was not to investigate but to create an opportunity for all the stakeholders, the donors included, to learn from their particular roles in the development intervention exercise.

Evaluation as Part of the Development Process. The evaluation activity is not discrete and separable from the development process itself. The results and corresponding tools become, in effect, tools for change rather than historical reports.

Evaluation as a Partnership and Sharing of Responsibility. This is in sharp contrast to the tendency for evaluators to establish a syndrome of "we" the professionals and "they" the project actors and beneficiaries. In the participatory impact assessment methodology, all the actors have more or less equal weight.

In this context, the evaluator becomes readily transformed from an investigator to a promoter, and from persecutor to participant.

Assessing Capacity and Its Impact on Development

In the baseline study for NORRIP II, the entire data collection exercise was orchestrated around an attempt to study the knowledge, attitudes, and practices (KAP) of rural residents of the survey area related to various socioeconomic phenomena, some of which the NORRIP program was attempting to change by its interventions. For this reason, the purpose, methods, and outcomes of the evaluation study were tailored to facilitate this complex interplay between what villagers already knew and current practice (or lack thereof). The underpinning assumption was that, physical access notwithstanding, the capacity to analyze their situation and understand their environment was a critical indicator of whether or not rural residents could benefit from any poverty alleviation measures made available to them, no matter how minuscule.

In more practical terms, the KAP approach was selected on the assumption that understanding the extent of current knowledge (or lack thereof) would facilitate the design and targeting of "appropriate" information and development interventions. As well, understanding the attitudes, sources of misconception, and myths prevalent in target communities would likely affect strategies for presenting new information and even credible personalities for such delivery. Finally, understanding the current practice would enable change agents to discourage inappropriate behavior (with new evidence of the reality) or reinforce appropriate practices.

Organizing for Change

A further aspect of the participatory impact assessment process is that of a conscious attempt to organize rural residents into groups for the purpose of analyzing their objective reality in the context of the development intervention. Experiences in Latin America, Asia, and elsewhere show that rural populations are seldom able to find solutions to their problems unless they can organize themselves to achieve objectives that they themselves understand and set, drawing on their own resources to do so (Isely and Martin 1977).

Montis (1985, 2–3), in her work on Nicaragua, proposed three interrelated stages of participatory investigation:

1. Inquiry about the socioeconomic characteristics of the study area.
2. Evaluation of the functioning of the project, from the point of view of acquiring the critical knowledge for developing new and superior forms of economic and social organization.
3. Evaluation of the way this critical knowledge is manifesting itself in the development and functioning of the water supply and sanitation system.

These three stages, according to Montis, are predicated on a conscious organization of the participants into consistent groups that have common reference points in relation to the exercise at hand.

In the NORRIP evaluation exercise, the entry point for the village data collection exercise was a series of village-based focus group workshops involving groups consciously organized for that purpose. The main criterion of group information was the preexisting organizational dynamic of decision making in the community. Thus, groups of female youth were set aside from female adults; these, in turn, were separated from male youth and male elders. The specific interests, expertise, and capacities of each group were explored separately, in order to arrive at a complete picture of the village dynamic.

Two other dimensions were used to supplement this village organizational basis of data collection. The first was the extensive use of village informants, one female and one male, to collect pertinent and commonly known factual information about the village, such as community infrastructure and location of facilities. The second was the use of a cross section of the disaggregated groups identified during the focus group workshops to verify information collected from the key informants and other sources. The rationale for this was to establish a quality control mechanism and thereby avoid unnecessary bias that could arise from particular individuals.

Findings: The Macro Environment of Poverty

Since the village is the main focus of analysis of macro-level manifestations of poverty, it is important to understand how these impinge on village-level capacity and what tools are needed to both understand the dynamic and influence change. Using the combination of processes identified above, the baseline study revealed that four main characteristics of poverty stand out distinctly in the study area:

Food insecurity was a critical indicator of worsening poverty in the northern region.

At the time of planning NORRIP, the overwhelming expectation was that the project would assist peasant farmers to reinforce their preexisting subsistence security and increase their productivity in a manner that would not altogether destroy their social and cultural specificity (see Gariba 1989, chap. 4). By anticipating interventions in agricultural production and value-added food processing, potable water supply, education, and the development of rural infrastructure, such as feeder roads, NORRIP proposed to enhance the productive capacity of rural producers, making their surpluses available to a wider domestic market, without altogether destroying them.

- The project did not embark on any of the production enhancement proposals originally contained in its plan of action. The consequence, as evidenced by the baseline study, was a high incidence of food insecurity, with more than 70 percent of the survey area running out of food before the end of the critical lean season.

- The bulk of this survey area received little or no agricultural extension services. In fact, the East Mamprusi district had been virtually ceded to two small nongovernmental organizations (NGOs) providing limited coverage in agricultural extension. Consequently, the chances that peasant producers would receive any sustained support to avoid starvation were increasingly diminishing. No forms of credit or farmer support services could be found in the area that might allow farmers access to needed resources for productivity enhancements.
- The seasonal stock of peasant surpluses then got sucked quickly into the cash economy and urban markets, leaving peasant producers with little or no food when they needed it most—in the lean season.

The level of coverage in basic social amenities was so low that the majority of the residents in the region were constantly at risk of water source contamination and disease exposure.

- The northern region of Ghana still ranked as the lowest in terms of access to potable water, education, and health amenities in the country. Although the NORRIP intervention introduced a marked improvement in water supply, this was limited in two out of thirteen districts, providing a mere 350 point sources of potable water in a region of over one million residents. By contrast, CIDA investments made earlier (in the 1970s and 1980s in the upper regions of Ghana) provided over 2,600 point sources of potable water, for a population less than 70 percent that of the northern region.*
- The little that was provided in terms of coverage and scope now stood the risk of not being sustained, due in part to a disastrous ethnic conflict that wiped out about 40 percent of the villages in which NORRIP had installed water and health facilities. The imminent termination of support to the NORRIP program by both partners at this critical moment did not augur well for sustainability of the remaining investments. The consequence could be a reversion to the "old ways and old sources" of water and attendant practices, thereby deepening the poverty situation.

High rates of illiteracy among women exacerbated the ignorance of residents of this region on the risks associated with inappropriate water utilization and sanitation practices.

- Notwithstanding the few potable water sources offered by NORRIP, the majority of the residents of the survey area still used water from unsafe

---

* The Upper Region Water Supply and Utilization Project, though limited to the water sector and sanitation education, had a sustained and significant coverage. To date, the project is in its third phase, having been initiated in 1974.

sources, largely due to their proximity and to ignorance about the disease implications of unsafe drinking water and sanitation practices.
- The higher incidence of illiteracy among women made the effects of this life-threatening poverty indicator more serious for the rest of the family, as the major decisions on water, sanitation, family care, and the management of health were made primarily by women.

Deepening poverty undermined social-economic harmony and the legitimacy of the formal state or government. This could exacerbate existing ethnic tensions and conflicts over land and production assets.

- The economic mode of production throughout northern Ghana was peasant based, with a predominance of a subsistence ethic. Production was organized mainly by family labor primarily for its own consumption. Under these circumstances, land and labor were the most important factors of production, and their abundance was held sacrosanct. Consequently, the issue of land and the size of families became virtually nonnegotiable, if subsistence security was to be maintained at current population growth rates. Any disequilibrium in the critical balance between the productivity of land and the size of families, clans, or tribes resulted in serious conflicts of untold proportions (see Schejtmann 1984).
- Under the peasant-based mode of production, political office was based primarily on the clan and tribe, with the chief retaining overwhelming authority, which was often shared by various clan leaders (elders) and a variety of traditional opinion leaders, including women. Here, the secular authority of the central state, regional, and district administrations had not yet gained wide acceptance or creditability (Ray 1984; see also Skalnick 1983).
- The only means by which this formal authority (the government) gained any measure of acceptance was through the investments it made in poverty alleviation, production, and development. Where this was lacking, as in northern Ghana, traditional societies held steadfastly to their traditional state, and when conflicts over resources emerged, these state forms held the authority.
- At the root of the recent northern region ethnic conflicts was the issue of land and production rights, as a result of rapidly diminishing arable land. The trigger for the conflict, the issue of autonomy of various chieftaincies, related essentially to which chief had authority over which land. The consequences were the disastrous "peasant wars" in the northern region, which claimed over 4,000 lives (Wolf 1969).

Tools for Change: The Village Development Capacity Index

If monitors and evaluators are to be seen as partners in the development effort (not mere critics of it), the question that comes to mind is what value does evaluation add to the development process?

At the start of the monitoring and evaluation process, two outputs were expected. The first was that a process of longitudinal evaluation, including a detailed baseline study, would allow the evaluation consultants to contribute consistently to the process of program formulation in response to emerging issues during periodic monitoring missions and diagnostic studies. The expectation was met largely by frequent missions, also involving intense dialogue and stakeholder consultations. The second expectation was that a new methodology would evolve that would permit the evaluation or assessment of impacts in a qualitative as well as quantitative manner.

As CIDA and the government of Ghana contemplate new forms of intervention to alleviate poverty and increase community governance capacity, it is timely to propose tools, coming out of the extensive experiences of the NOR-RIP monitoring and evaluation process. One of the objectives of the baseline study was to attempt to prepare a methodology by which village development could be monitored and evaluated. This section outlines a framework for the use of the Village Development Capacity Index (VDCI) as a means of both planning and assessing village development on a continuous basis.

The central idea of the VDCI is that each village, as a community, has a unique combination of social, political, economic, and cultural characteristics that determine its status and prospects for development. Understanding and documenting these characteristics at the start of a project (intervention) can allow development agents and agencies to

1. Recognize the strengths (capabilities) as well as the weaknesses (needs) at the start of the project;
2. Plan appropriate and desirable interventions in any particular community;
3. Monitor the effects that planned interventions are having on the weaknesses identified, while tracking the status of the existing strengths (capabilities) identified in the community;
4. Evaluate the extent to which planned interventions have had impacts on development, and how existing capabilities have changed over a specified period of time; and
5. Isolate which new factors or variables have emerged in the course of the planned intervention that were not considered at the start of the project.

Building Indicators

Ideally, the planning of a project should begin with a set of objective conditions that require change. This can be the result of a study of the conditions of poverty, outlining salient characteristics of that phenomenon that can be changed through precise interventions. The developmental conditions in a given community can be recorded in two forms:

1. The status of community infrastructure and socioeconomic services; and
2. The status of community and village development capacity—including prevailing values, customs, traditions, and socioeconomic as well as political systems at the village level.

In the case of the NORRIP program, although the planning phase did a thorough assessment of the existing physical infrastructure and the associated development constraints, there was no coherent database of existing conditions as defined in (2) above. For this reason, the baseline study* designed a specific instrument to collect socioeconomic status data in a qualitative and quantitative manner. The first step in the process of collecting data was the village profile. This involved the determination of indicators that would depict the current status of village development and capacity.

These indicators were determined by the evaluation consultant, in consultation with NORRIP. The following indicators then served as discussion guides in male and female focus group workshops in all thirty villages surveyed.

1. **Status of village organizations:** includes the number and variety of village-initiated groups and women's groups and the decision-making ability of these groups.
2. **Previous development experience of the village** in planning and sustaining development projects, with particular emphasis on projects initiated by the villagers themselves, women's projects, and the ability of the village to raise funds in support of projects receiving external support.
3. **The status of agriculture and control of resources** in the village, focusing on range of crops produced, production techniques and technology, control of food within households, control of natural produce such as fruits, women's access to land, and opportunities for women to increase their role and benefits from agriculture.
4. **The level and range of village cooperation,** including different forms of organizing labor for production, communal work, and social obligations; the types of traditional savings and credit; and access to formal loans.
5. **The range of economic assets and income-generating activities** in the village, with emphasis on which of the gender groups engage in more income-generating activities in the wet and dry seasons. Also in this section, emphasis is put on the ability of the village to sustain its

---

* Ironically, the baseline study came at the end of the project, making it impossible for NORRIP to benefit from these results.

labor force throughout the dry season, without resorting to seasonal migration to augment family subsistence.

6. **Status of village leadership:** an analysis of the political dynamics in decision making, focusing on whether the village is fractured by conflict, ruled by strong leadership, or operating on a system of consensus and collective leadership.

7. **The leadership's perception of the major constraints to village development**, and the level of understanding of the causes of these constraints, as well as the solutions they would propose to overcome these.

8. **The village's knowledge of NORRIP**, its expectations from NORRIP, and whether or not it benefits from other donors, government agencies, NGOs, and extension services.

Supplementing these qualitative indicators were other forms of rudimentary data constituting poverty indicators extracted from the quantitative survey of over 400 rural households in the two target districts.

Poverty Indicators

Based on the analysis of the macro environment, certain indicators were extrapolated that impact heavily on the ability of rural residents to overcome their current situation of deprivation. In the specific context of the NORRIP project, these included:

1. **Risk of contamination:** the risk factor determined by the village water sources in wet and dry seasons, prevailing sanitation practices and availability of sanitation facilities such as latrines, and exposure to diseases such as malaria, diarrhea, and guinea worm. If the village has potable water, this risk will be low; if it obtains water from unsafe sources all year-round, it will record a high risk.

2. **Knowledge of diseases (diarrhea)**, including knowledge on how the disease can be contracted and prevailing practices to treat and/or prevent it.

3. **Knowledge of guinea worm**, including knowledge on how the disease can be contracted and prevailing practices to treat and/or prevent the infection.

4. **Literacy (extent of ignorance)**
   • general rates of formal literacy
   • knowledge of causes of illness (mainly waterborne)
   • knowledge of disease prevention or avoidance practices
   • knowledge of treatment methods
   • knowledge of benefits of child immunization

5. **Risk of hunger/food security**, involving an examination of when stored grain is finished from the granaries, and the extent to which food produced is adequate to feed the population year-round.

6. **Level of expenditure**, a crude estimate of disposable income.

Constructing the VDCI

Upon completing both the quantitative and qualitative surveys, the VDCI can be constructed by using Figure 4.1.

Allocating Scores to the VDCI

The exercise of scoring needs to be participatory, involving the major stakeholders, including the village leadership. The following guidelines might be useful to incorporate in the planning process for scoring VDCI.

Beneficiary Workshop. The beneficiaries on whom the data were collected should be given an opportunity to review and discuss the data on their status, with respect to poverty and their village development capacity. This will assist the evaluators to correct any wrong information and to update any new information that may have been missed during the survey period. It will also serve as a forum for feedback to the beneficiaries of the survey.

Stakeholder Forum for Scoring. Once the feedback with beneficiaries has occurred, they are asked to select their representatives for an exercise in scoring. Village representatives, the implementing agencies, the donor, and other allied agencies with knowledge about development in the area are then invited to a workshop on scoring the indicators.

Prior to this workshop, all participants must be provided with adequate information on the data collected on each village, both the qualitative and the quantitative data.*

At the workshop, dialogue and consensus building should characterize the scoring process. Where participants have reason to score high or low on any indicator, adequate reasons must be presented. If these reasons constitute new information that was missed during the survey, that particular section of the village profile data needs to be reviewed and updated accordingly, to correspond with the agreed score.

Using the Score Range. The score range suggested is on the scale of 1 to 5: 1 signifies low, 2 fair, 3 average, 4 high, and 5 very high. This allows the flexibility of dialogue and consensus in the process of development and capacity building.

Uses of the VDCI

Monitoring and Evaluation of Indicators. After an index is established for each village, specific indicators can be tracked over time. Thus, for instance, if access to safe drinking water (physical presence and proximity) in Village 1 was high (i.e., 5) and the knowledge, attitudes, and practices on disease pre-

---

* In the case of the baseline study, a detailed report was produced on each village, covering the village profile and a set of quantitative data from the household survey.

Figure 4.1: Village Development Capacity Index

Elements/Indicators	Score/Index by Village				
Poverty Indicators (From Household Survey)	V1	V2	V3	V4	V5
Safety of water sources year-round (if low score 1...if high score 5)					
Knowledge of diarrhea diseases (if low score 1...if high score 5)					
Knowledge of guinea worm (if low score 1....if high score 5)					
Literacy (extent of ignorance) (if low score 1...if high score 5)					
Food security (if low score 1...if high score 5)					
Level of expenditure (if low score 1...if high score 5)					
(You may add any number of poverty indicators for which you have collected data)					
Subtotal (Poverty Indicators)					
Village Development Capacity Indicators	V1	V2	V3	V4	V5
Status of village organizations (if weak and few score 1...if strong and varied score 5)					
Previous development experience of the village (if poor score 1...if strong score 5)					
The status of agriculture and control of resources (if few score 1...if diverse with gender-balanced control score 5)					
The level and range of village cooperation (if weak and uncooperative score 1...if strong and cooperative score 5)					
The range of economics assets and income-generating activities (if weak and few score 1...if high and varied score 5)					
Status of village leadership (if weak and conflict-prone score 1...if strong and consensual score 5)					
The leadership's perception of the major constraints to village development (if uncertain score 1...if clear and perceptive score 5)					
Villager's knowledge of their development partners (if not known and not understood score 1...if known and compatible score 5)					
Total Score/Index (By Village)					

vention were very low (say 1) due to poor literacy (say 2) in a survey carried out in 1992, these particular indicators can be monitored periodically when the project (interventions) is being implemented.

Tools for Analysis and Planning of Interventions. A major application of the VDCI is as a tool for analysis and planning of development interventions. The experience of NORRIP and other integrated rural development programs shows that, while basic services, such as water, are paramount needs in rural northern Ghana, not all villages require the same types of intervention. Further, the specific permutation of development interventions can assure proper targeting needs:

- A detailed analysis of village vulnerabilities
- A correct appraisal of village capacity and development capabilities

By using the VDCI, such indicators can be clearly spelled out and researched, with the full involvement and cooperation of the beneficiaries.

The VDCI Worksheet

This study cannot usefully be concluded without providing a practical tool for development practitioners seeking to effect change in developing societies. The VDCI worksheet will assist development workers and villagers to analyze their situations objectively and to plan appropriate interventions.

The VDCI worksheets[*] are forms that can be used by partner agencies, extension workers, and monitoring and evaluation practitioners to

1. Outline poverty alleviation and village development goals;
2. Relate these goals to various development indicators;
3. Evaluate their present development strategies and intervention activities against these goals; and
4. Arrive at their own assessment of the level of development capacity attained and what is required to upgrade this performance to higher forms of village development and empowerment.

In this worksheet, each of the elements of poverty alleviation and village development capacity building identified during the baseline study is regarded as a strategic goal;[**] each goal then has a set of goal indicators. The development agents (donors, executing agencies, extension workers, and villagers themselves) and the partners are then required to complete the last two columns on the right-hand side of each worksheet by

---

[*] These worksheets were adapted from *Using Development Indicators for Aboriginal Development, A Guidebook,* by the Development Indicator Project Steering Committee, Department of Indian Affairs and Northern Development (DIAND), Canada, September 1991.

[**] Development agencies and village leaders are encouraged to select from this menu any set of strategic goals consistent with their chemistry, or add others that are not described here.

Figure 4.2:
Village Development Capacity Index Worksheet

Strategic Goals on Poverty Alleviation	Goal Indicators	Activities/ Interventions	Enhancement Strategies
Eliminate the risk of disease contamination	provide a variety of potable water points year-round		
	water sources are close enough to villagers, women		
	the technology of water delivery is simple and reliable		
Improve knowledge, attitudes, and practices related to diarrheal and other waterborne diseases	most villagers know that diarrhea, guinea worm, and malaria are caused by drinking infected water or unsafe sanitation		
	most villagers know how to prevent waterborne diseases		
	villagers' water utilization practices are safer		
Improve literacy for development	overall literacy rates are improved		
	women are specifically targeted in literacy activities		
	functional literacy is emphasized		
Eliminate the risk of hunger	productivity is improved through soil and water conservation		
	storage of food is improved through reduction of post-harvest losses		
	food processing is enhanced through use of appropriate and affordable technology		
Improve incomes	sources of rural incomes are diversified		
	women are specifically assisted to increase their income		
	opportunities to market goods and services are increased year-round		

Strategic Goals on Village Development Capacity	Goal Indicators	Activities/ Interventions	Enhancement Strategies
Strengthen village-based development organizations	level of functional village organizations		
Reinforce positive development experiences of the village	extent to which village self-learning is enhanced		
Improve agricultural productivity and foster equitable distribution of benefits	extent to which environmental factors inhibiting agriculture are addressed		
	level, type, and appropriateness of agriculture and agro-processing technology		
	extent to which the burden and benefits of agriculture are shared in a gender-balanced manner		
Reinforce village cooperation	extent to which cooperative labor systems are reinforced		
	extent to which exploitation of child and female labor is reduced		
Improve the range of productivity of value-added investments in village	range of value-added production enterprises		
	extent of gender balance in investments		
	extent of savings		
Work with village leadership and acceptable structures	extent to which existing structures are reinforced and improved		
Train leadership on development	extent to which analytical tools for development are shared		
Foster an understanding and negotiation with a variety of development partners	tendency toward mutual trust		
	extent of transparency and openness		
	sensitivity to partner's socioeconomic and cultural context		
	extent of endurance and long-term commitment		

1. Summarizing the activities currently in place to foster the attainment of that goal indicator; and
2. Suggesting strategies to improve the attainment of higher forms of that indicator.

Some Cautions and Further Work

Using the participatory impact assessment method for baseline study raises an important question that is often unanswered: in what ways can the parameters of data collection for the baseline be simplified to provide a consistent mechanism for tracking performance over time? Most KAP studies tend to be rather complex and diffuse, detailing current reality at the time of data collection to the point where use of the data over time as a baseline for assessing impacts in the future becomes problematic (see Isely and Martin 1977, 315).

Further, it is important to emphasize that poverty indicators cannot easily be aggregated, as the phenomenon tends to affect some households more than others (see Roe, Schneider, and Pyatt 1992, 103–15). A group organizational approach works better, hence the validity of the participatory impact assessment model. In village discussions on the willingness and ability to pay for improved water supply, a consensus by the village on what, collectively, it is able to pay for water is, in effect, the median of what the average household will be able to afford. This has further implications for the establishment of indicators to assess the extent to which communities have made good their commitment to pay for improved water supplies. Under conventional evaluation, the onus is on the evaluator to determine such an indicator, and the responsibility falls on project management to explain outcomes. Under participatory impact assessment, the community, in collaboration with the other stakeholders, determines indicators for assessing impact.

This chapter depicts the use of tools fabricated by local professionals and community members to assess impacts of development interventions on a continuous basis. By focusing on capacity-building indicators on the one hand, while tracking poverty indicators on the other, the model presents a hybrid between nebulous analysis and too discrete counting. It also offers opportunities for both donors and developing country partners to record, analyze, and document the real changes that are occurring as a result of investments in poverty alleviation.

Finally, there is an intrinsic strategic value in the alliances between evaluators and project stakeholders to devise methods that can contribute positively to change rather than render retribution for how badly projects are managed. The prevailing perception among donors and development workers that portrays evaluators as "policemen" needs to be discarded and replaced by a partnership for progress. Valuable information about the project gathered through the participatory assessment of impacts needs to be fed into the development process in a dynamic and constructive manner. The collectors and analyzers of the information, being themselves stakeholders, build their capacity to internalize the implications of that information and hone in on the strategies to generate change. This is the essence of participatory impact assessment.

References

Cornia, G., R. van der Hoeven, and T. Mkandawire, eds. 1992. *Africa's Recovery in the 1990s: From Stagnation and Adjustment to Human Development*. New York: St. Martin's Press, UNICEF.

Gariba, S. 1989. "Peasantry and the State in Northern Ghana: The Political Economy of Agrarian Stagnation and Rural Development in the Northern Region of Ghana." Doctoral diss., Carleton University, Ottawa, Canada.

Gariba, S., and T. Jackson. 1993. "Enhancing North-South Partnerships in Evaluation." Paper presented at the conference of the Canadian Association for the Study of International Development, Ottawa, June.

Isely, B., and F. Martin. 1977. "The Village Health Committee: Starting Point for Rural Development." *WHO Chronicle* 31: 307–15.

Montis, M. de. 1985. "Participatory Research in Nicaragua." Translated by M. A. Rahman. Rural Employment Policies Branch, International Labor Organization, Geneva.

Ray, D. 1984. "The State Traditional Authority and Development in Ghana." Paper presented at the 14th annual conference of the Canadian Association of African Studies, Antigonish, Nova Scotia, May.

Schejtmann, A. 1984. "The Peasant Economy: Internal Logic, Articulation, and Persistence." Pp. 274–98 in *The Political Economy of Development and Underdevelopment*, 3d ed., edited by C. Wilbur. New York: Random House.

Skalnick, P. 1983. "Questioning the Concept of the State in Indigenous Africa." *Social Dynamics* 9 (2): 11–28.

Wolf, E. 1969 *Peasant Wars of the 20th Century*. New York: Harper and Row.

My gratitude goes to my Canadian partner, Dr. Ted Jackson, and all the staff and associates of E.T. Jackson and Associates for the high level of collaboration in producing this chapter. Special thanks go to Ms. Huguette Rutera, who worked with me in Ghana to collect and analyze the data and is now dedicating herself to similar work in Rwanda, against all odds. Thanks are also due to IDRC for sponsoring my participation in the conference and to my wife and business partner, Neo, for intensely scrutinizing the manuscript.

Part II

Case Studies

—————— 5 ——————

Are We on the Right Track?
Report of a Workshop on
Participatory Evaluation

Kamla Bhasin

In January 1983 seven of us who had been involved with rural development for several years spent three days in Secunderabad, India, discussing how to evaluate the process of participatory development. Our meetings were held in the office of the Rural Development Advisory Service, and five of us also stayed there. Getting to know one another during and outside the meeting was as rewarding an experience as the discussions themselves. At the end of the three days, all of us felt satisfied with the consensus and mutual understanding we had managed to arrive at and the friendships we had built. This chapter is an attempt to share our discussions with those who were not with us but who are as interested in these issues as we were and continue to be.

What follows is a more or less verbatim reproduction of our discussions, albeit arranged a little more systematically. We are sharing our discussions with you in the hope that this document will lead to further discussion and greater clarity about the evaluation of development activities.

Background

Different development approaches and strategies require different kinds of evaluation methods and techniques. If development projects are top-down, started by people from outside the community (governmental or nongovernmental organizations or agencies) to provide services such as health and education and to bring about certain changes in production methods and techniques, then the local people are merely recipients, targets, or objects of development. People for whom development is supposedly intended have little or no say in the con-

The workshop participants were Abha Bhaiya, Aruna Roy, Datta Savale, Kamla Bhasin, M. Kurian, M. V. Shastri, and Vikas Bhai.

An earlier version of this chapter was first published by Freedom from Hunger Campaign/Action for Development Program of the Food and Agriculture Office in New Delhi, India.

tent and direction of such efforts. With hindsight it can be said that top-down, centralized development projects seldom help the really poor and needy because the real causes of poverty are left unquestioned and unchallenged. The evaluation of such projects is also, quite logically, top-down, geared and done by the decision makers without any participation of the local people. Those from whom information and opinions are gathered are not even informed about the evaluation outcome. In fact, often even the project holders have no say. For them, more often than not, evaluation is like an inspection being carried out by outsiders at the insistence of funding agencies, and they feel threatened by it. The main purpose of such an evaluation is clearly one of financial accountability, and emphasis is on physical targets. Because this model of development does not insist on starting a process of consciousness-raising, increasing awareness, and mobilization, little attention is paid to the assessment of intangibles such as people's participation, the decision-making process, level of awareness, and practice of democracy.

Development, however, can also be understood as a means of helping the poor to collectively analyze the socioeconomic, political, and cultural structures that keep them poor and get organized to challenge these structures. In such a development model, the oppressed people are seen as subjects, not merely objects of their own development. The program is a partnership between the local masses and outsiders. Its strength is concomitant with that of the people's organizations (POs) that emerge, their democratic functioning, and the actions they take to tilt the balance of power and resources in favor of the exploited masses. The evaluation of such efforts for development and organization has a different purpose and demands other methods, techniques, and indicators.

We who met in Secunderabad were interested only in the evaluation of the second type of development efforts. All of us felt that although a large number of action groups (AGs) are now concentrating on the mobilization and organization of the poor, there is little clarity on how these efforts should be assessed. The purpose of our talks was to achieve some common understanding on the basis of the experience and ideas we all had on evaluation.

Some Important Considerations

We agreed that the evaluation of people-centered and people-oriented efforts at consciousness-raising, mobilization, organization, and action should consider several key points.

Evaluation Is Reflection on Action

Evaluation, as we see it, is collective reflection on the actions taken by individuals within a group and by the group itself, and on the methods of functioning of a group. Its purpose is improvement both in the understanding and analysis of reality and issues and in future action. Thus seen, it is an important method of group education and learning.

Built-in and Ongoing Evaluation

For a group interested in improving not only the socioeconomic position of the poor but also the methods of functioning and the understanding of everyone involved in the work, evaluation has to be built-in and ongoing. Reflection based on concrete information has to be closely linked to action. In addition to ongoing evaluation, at the end of one or two years, there can be an overall, time-bound evaluation that is a cumulative assessment of what has taken place over a decade.

The experience of the Comprehensive Rural Operations Service Society (CROSS) shared by M. Kurian illustrated very well the method and importance of ongoing evaluation and its culmination into an annual exercise. The village *sanghams* (small, face-to-face groups of rural poor) initiated by CROSS assess their activities and the performance of the functionaries every month. In addition, they assess every major action undertaken by them. Evaluation sessions are also organized every three months at the cluster and area level. Apart from these evaluations by the local people, CROSS staff meets once a month to take stock of its activities and methods of functioning. Annual self-evaluation is done in January of every year.

Emphasis on Self-Evaluation

The emphasis of a people-centered and people-oriented program or organization has to be on self-evaluation in which the people and the organizers not only participate but also decide about its parameters, form, and methods. The final judges of a program's effectiveness must be the people themselves.

Evaluation of Tangibles, Intangibles, and Processes

If the objectives of development are both tangibles (such as improved economic status, improved health) and intangibles (such as increased awareness, people's participation, and democratic decision making), then obviously evaluation must also focus on both these aspects. There are techniques available for assessing tangibles, but we need to develop methods and indicators as far as intangibles and processes are concerned.

The process a group goes through to reach decisions and act is as important as the outcome of the action. We have to understand how people move toward the achievement of their objectives. It is necessary to understand how the processes within POs and AGs are related to general processes in society and how they affect each other. Their context has to be understood.

Just as there is a close relationship between action and reflection, theory and practice, there is also one between tangible objectives, such as increased access to land or higher wages, and intangible ones, such as improved level of awareness and strength of POs. Ideally, the achievement of one should lead to improvement of the other.

POs might be fighting for economic benefits, but unlike the usual development projects, POs emphasize the processes and use each struggle to educate and strengthen themselves. After achieving some small victories, POs cannot sit quietly and smugly, but need to constantly ask how much space has been created by a campaign and how that space should be used for future action. For them, the process of structural change should be an ongoing one that does not stop at any particular point. This is different from target-bound projects, considered terminated on completion of a certain number of wells, the installation of pump sets, the production of biogas, and so forth.

False Dichotomy between Consciousness-Raising and Economic Development

When the entire emphasis of development programs is on material development, quantitative analysis is primary. But when the emphasis of development efforts is on the growth of people and their organization, qualitative analysis assumes more importance. Because material development and the development of people's consciousness and their organization do (and must) go together, quantitative and qualitative analysis cannot be exclusive of each other. Some groups take an extreme position and reject all quantitative data and measurement of material development. They talk only of intangibles like consciousness-raising or increasing the level of awareness. We felt a need to have a good synthesis of evaluating tangibles and intangibles, quantitative and qualitative results. If one is working with the really poor, their material conditions have to be improved fast (mainly, of course, through their own efforts). The poor are not going to be interested in consciousness-raising for its own sake. All consciousness-raising must lead to an improvement in their material conditions, and vice versa. In fact, this dichotomy between organizational work and programs for economic development is false and misleading. Groups primarily doing organizational work also improve the economic status of the poor at least as much, if not more, as the so-called projects for income generation do. Organizations such as Bhoomi Sena, Shramik Sangathana, and CROSS have achieved tremendous economic benefits for the poor through their struggles to recover alienated lands, provide higher wages and employment opportunities, lower interest rates, fight corruption, reduce the power of middlemen, and so forth. The economic position of the poor can be improved by removing insecurity and exploitation, and if these two tasks go on simultaneously, it is ideal.

The attempts to organize the poor also improve their receiving mechanism and bargaining power and thereby enable them to make increased use of government schemes, bank loans, and the like. To recapitulate, economic development and people's organizations and action are—and should be—dialectically related. Every struggle by the oppressed should create more space for their economic development, and their improved economic status should in turn strengthen their organization.

Need to Look at Three Kinds of Processes

We need to evaluate processes in three areas or realities, and also to look at the interplay among these three:

1. The AG's reality and the processes within it.
2. The community within which the AG is working and the processes within the community.
3. The larger socioeconomic and political reality in which both AGs and oppressed communities are situated.

It is important to analyze and understand why some people form an AG, why they want to relate to a certain oppressed community, what their perception of the larger reality and structures is, what conception of change they have, and what their goals and aspirations are. Is there any homogeneity between the aspirations and understanding of the AGs and those of the community within which they work? How realistic are the objectives set by them in the context of opposition forces?

Interplay of Aspirations and Reality

It is also important to look at the objectives and aspirations of AGs and POs in the context of the forces of reality. We have to see the dynamics between both. The reality exists and operates independently of aspirations of AGs and POs that intervene to change it according to their own understanding. So we must understand the totality of the forces of society and see what the intervention has succeeded in achieving.

Not only is there need to assess the extent to which the objectives and aspirations have been achieved, but they, themselves, have to be constantly reviewed and readjusted according to changing reality and changes in AGs' and POs' understanding. We need methods and tools to assess the AGs' and POs' goals in the context of their aspirations and hypothesis, and of the larger reality.

It is only when action is taken after a systematic analysis of the overall situation and reality that it becomes meaningful and effective. For example, if one does community theater without understanding the context, and if it is not related to any action, it provides, at best, some entertainment. People's theater can inspire and lead to action only if it is done with a perception of reality, and of the needs and aspirations of the masses. When divorced from POs and from action, theater, nonformal education, or consciousness-raising efforts are uninspiring and uninnovative and lead to no change in the oppressive situation and structures.

The Role of Outsiders in Self-Evaluation

Emphasis on self-evaluation does not mean that we took the extreme position that local people and AGs can assess their work themselves. We recognized that every perception has its limitations. Just as outsiders' perception might be limited because of their lack of knowledge and acquaintance with local realities, local people's perception might be limited because of their particularity. The interaction of perceptions and views (both of insiders and of outsiders) can therefore be very beneficial.

The presence of an experienced and sensitive outsider can encourage the group to formulate and articulate its thoughts more systematically and objectively. A sensitive outsider can enrich the discussions by bringing in other experiences, perceptions, perspectives, and dimensions. There can be areas that local people either forget to look at or do not want to look at. It is the outsiders' role to bring these forgotten elements or reality into discussion, however unpleasant this might be. Local people and AGs have to be helped to realize that unpleasant facts cannot be wished away. An outsider plays an important role by asking the right kind of questions and providing useful insights for dealing with dilemmas and uncertainties.

Outsiders can play this role effectively only if they are actually insiders in more than one way. They have to be known and acceptable to the people who are assessing themselves, should identify with the group's objectives, and should be involved in the same kinds of struggles and processes, although in another area or at a different level. Insofar as they are involved and have a commitment to the same goals, they are not "objective" evaluators. Has not the myth of evaluation being objective been exploded?

For helping in assessing various aspects of work, we might need different kinds of outsiders, for example, someone acquainted with health issues when it is about a community health program.

It must be remembered that an insensitive outsider can ruin all efforts at a genuine self-evaluation; instead of leading to a common understanding she or he can further divide the people and generally harm the organization and action.

In order to be effective, an outsider has to be thoroughly prepared by gathering whatever information is available about the organizations and the local and natural realities within which they are operating and that they want to change through their interaction.

It was pointed out that AGs can also help each other in their self-evaluation. The same is possible between communities and groups. Experienced members of one group can help others in their self-evaluation. Such interaction strengthens the links between different groups and thus increases their joint strength.

Self-Evaluation Is Possible Only If the AG Is Ready for It

It was stated that all AGs do not recognize the need for an honest self-evaluation. Some of them consider it a waste of time. They want to get along with action and see reflection as separate from it. For them, reflection is unnecessary theorizing that delays action. Of course, when taken to an extreme kind of "hair-splitting," reflection can indeed delay action; in fact, at times, it becomes its substitute. But reflection is absolutely necessary (in right measures), especially to avoid the other extremes of activism.

Some AGs might recognize the need for self-evaluation but might not be ready for it, because it analyzes all aspects of work and relationships, and this can be a very painful process, especially in the beginning. It requires a certain self-confidence, the ability to look at oneself critically and to listen to criticism without getting defensive or aggressive.

It is only when at least some members of the AG recognize the need for a self-evaluation that its process can be started. As the latter goes on, other members might also recognize its usefulness and importance and join it.

Self-Evaluation: An Illustration

Aruna Roy shared with us the experience of her group, the Social Work and Resource Centre (SWRC), with a self-evaluation process. Her case study shows how, through it, changes took place in their understanding and analysis of the reality around them, and their own role vis-à-vis this reality.

SWRC started work in 1972. Initially it was primarily a group of professionals trying to provide technical and managerial solutions to the problem of poverty and injustice. At that time SWRC did not work exclusively with the poor, nor did it have their organization as its objective. In the course of the first three to four years, some questions cropped up in some of the workers' minds about the larger reality, the community within which the AG should work, the adequacy of technical solutions, the role of professionals, and so forth. This questioning by individuals within the AG led to some creative tension and changes in the work, but for another two years there was neither a collective questioning nor a clearly expressed need for evaluation. In 1978, eight to ten members started to concretize the issues, and a debate began within the group on the need for self-questioning. This small group started meeting informally to formulate the questions that were in their minds. They reflected on all issues bothering them and on the relationship of this questioning to their understanding, their work, and local reality. They also identified problems in the following areas of their work and group functioning:

- Communication within the AG itself and between its members and local people;
- Different kinds of inequalities and differences in status within the AG;
- Concentration of decision making in a few hands, and the need to create structures that would ensure broader participation and reduce the exercise of informal power; and
- Place of economic development and its relationship with politics, social change, and so forth.

The group, small at the beginning, gradually expanded to reach eighteen to twenty members. They once sat almost every day for about six weeks during which their own work was more or less suspended. This activity was not seen very favorably by some other AG members, but they did not object to it. Watching cautiously, they even joined some of the sessions, but distrustingly. The ball that had been set rolling moved on. Later a group of forty had two four-day sessions with eight outsiders well known to them and who, it was felt, would be able to help them deal with certain dilemmas faced and questions they had regarding the nature and direction of their work, the role of an institution like theirs, development programs versus organization, and the like.

There was a tremendous heterogeneity among the members in terms of their social and educational backgrounds, understanding and articulation of issues, and commitment to change. The pace of discussions was therefore slow, and everyone did not participate equally.

The kinds of questions raised and answers attempted are given here in Aruna's own words: "We demanded openness and ability to discuss even personal commitments and aspirations. We broke the barriers between our professional and personal lives. We realized that our objectives had been too general. We narrowed them down. We decided we should work mainly with the poor. We formulated a decision-making process which was participatory. We wanted a forum in which every worker could effectively take part. We decided we should evaluate ourselves (our attitudes, behavior, understanding) once a year—how honest are we, how democratic, how open, how caste-minded? What is our understanding of issues? We discussed questions like what is more important for a worker—a Ph.D. or a capacity to communicate with people and elicit people's participation? But this process of personal evaluation when related to salary structures was not very successful. Subjective factors played too important a role and did not allow for the personal evaluation to become operational in relation to judgments by peers on one another's salaries. This power was vested by the group in its director, accepting its own failure.

"Also at the village level we had talks with people who had participated in our programs. We met them at one of the five field centers once a month on the new moon day and reviewed the various programs. Meetings were sometimes held with special-interest or program groups like crafts group, health group, and so on.

"We concluded that there was a role for an institution like ours. We discussed its role in development, 'agitation,' in trying to bring about structural changes. We also discussed whether it was possible for a development group like this to shift gear and go into organizational activity. Some felt it could be done, others that it could not, and should not."

The long talks obviously led to several changes in their work, in the decision-making process, and in interpersonal relationships. These changes led to the need for more discussion and clarity. In the end, a dialectical relationship seems to have been established between action and reflection, theory and practice.

Perceived Advantages of Self-Evaluation

According to Aruna, these self-evaluation sessions were extremely useful. At the end of it all, most participants realized that this kind of communication and openness is necessary for improving a group's effectiveness and impact.

Self-evaluation can help everyone to think and learn collectively, to articulate better. If carried on sensitively, it can make every participant more honest, sensitive, analytical, and open to change. It changes everybody's awareness and consciousness, as well as people's attitudes, and helps them to cope better with conflicts.

Self-evaluation can improve a group's inner functioning by creating better relationships between the different AG members. Open discussion on certain issues removes unnecessary misunderstandings. By talking frankly, even about sensitive issues, people begin to see and appreciate others' viewpoints.

Self-evaluation helps in evolving a common perspective, a shared commitment to action, and thus transforms a loose group of individuals into a cohesive and effective AG. As the analysis of the group improves, it understands better the larger realities and the interaction of its work with them. By making members critically conscious of their actions, it improves both a group's inner functioning and the work it does with people. According to Aruna, "an attempt to resolve our own dilemmas and conflicts led to greater clarity."

Such a process alters the relationships within the group and the relationship of the AG with the people. Because the AG becomes a cohesive group and develops a certain focus, AG members do not say different things about their work, and this improves the AG's image vis-à-vis the people. The misunderstanding or confusion that people might have about the AG's role, real motivation, and so on is reduced when it develops an open dialogue with local people and also involves them in the assessment of the work initiated.

Systematic self-evaluation requires that AGs develop methods of gathering and documenting information and of conducting free interaction and discussions and keeping records of these. AGs also have to look for indicators of consciousness and articulation. Because of all these conscious efforts at evaluation, the AGs' work improves.

In addition to improvement in the above-mentioned areas, which are mainly intangible, experience shows that self-evaluation improves the achievement of tangible results. This happens because action becomes much more relevant, conscious, and focused. As part of their self-evaluation, SWRC also did qualitative analysis and found that the former had led to better tangible results. (This was also Kurian's experience in CROSS.)

Some Examples of Bad External Evaluations

We also heard examples of some bad external evaluations conducted by social scientists and rural development and management experts, using the latest cost-benefit and social cost-benefit analysis. In order to get a good analysis of their work, CROSS got an evaluation done by a well-known organization. At the end of the elaborate questioning, data collecting, and processing, what CROSS got was merely a description of its work without any analysis. The evaluation failed to provide any guidelines for future action, which was the main purpose of having it done, and ended up giving CROSS a very good chit and a substantial bill. Similarly, some management people had gone to SWRC to conduct social cost-benefit analysis, and its outcome was not helpful either, at least not to the AG and local people.

The sharing of these experiences made us realize that there are no ready-made "scientific" tools available for the evaluation of efforts to raise people's consciousness and mobilize them. Established academic institutions cannot, for obvious reasons, be expected to provide the necessary help in this matter. AGs and mass organizations, together with some sensitive academics, will have to evolve methods and tools for assessing their work.

6

Participatory Evaluation: Primary Health Care in Patna, India

Marie-Thérèse Feuerstein

Acommunity health and development team working in the poor, heavily populated Indian state of Bihar has found new direction and a new level of commitment from the community as a result of incorporating participatory evaluation into its expanding program.

On the banks of the Ganges River at Patna, northeastern India, stands the Kurji Holy Family Hospital. It is a 275-bed teaching hospital serving Patna, the capital of Bihar, the second most populous state of India. For more than thirty years, the hospital has run a community health program with the aim of reaching out to the poorest in the surrounding area. An estimated two-thirds of the population of Bihar are living below the poverty line. Twenty percent of the state's population in 1988 comprised tribal people and Harijans or "untouchables," who now refer to themselves as Dalits.

The poverty in Bihar has little to do with the quality of the land. Bihar is made up of fertile plains, and the southern plateau of the state provides 40 percent of India's minerals. The lack of development has more to do with the meager industrial development and the neglect of the state's infrastructure. Farmers have to manage without roads and power supplies, let alone the benefits of modern agricultural technology.

The unequal distribution of land is another serious barrier to progress. Most of the cultivated areas produce zero or low growth due to poor irrigation and lack of modern inputs and extension services. Wealthy landlords continue to own huge tracts of land but offer little support to those who work on their estates. The remaining cultivable land is divided into plots that are often too small to be efficient. Most of the tribal and Dalit families are landless. They are forced to hire themselves out, mainly as farm laborers, on a daily basis.

Community Health

The Kurji Holy Family Hospital decided to start using a room in the hospital as a community health department in 1959. The aim was to familiarize staff

This chapter was first published in *Contact* 32 (August 1993).

with the conditions of the poor living in periurban areas of Patna. By 1968, the department had its own Urban Health Centre in a separate building on the hospital grounds.

A year later, a request from a priest working in a particularly poor, rural area twenty-one kilometers from the hospital heralded the start of an outreach program. He requested weekly clinics for the people of Maner, an area extending westward along the Ganges. The work in Maner flourished, and in 1978, the Maner Community Health Centre was built by the Catholic Medical Missionaries.

Since then, the program has increasingly emphasized social development. A number of community workers are employed in what is now a multidisciplinary team.

The Evaluation Process

Deciding to Evaluate

Prior to the participatory evaluation, there had been several earlier efforts in studying the progress of the program. One was undertaken in 1976 by a hospital management team, and another by the Voluntary Health Association of India (VHAI) in the early 1980s. VHAI recommended better definition of target areas, more preventive and promotive health services, such as for tuberculosis and leprosy, and a greater emphasis on maternal and child health (MCH) care. At that time, men—as the workers and income earners—received considerably more attention from the health services than did their wives and children.

A few years later, two members of the community health department staff attended a seminar on social analysis and began to feel that the program needed to focus even more intensively on the poorest people in the communities. The participatory approach interested these two individuals. It was an approach that made reaching the poorest a priority, and it involved health workers and the community in making their own evaluation and their own recommendations for adjustments to the program.

However, to most of the members of the health staff team, the idea that they were to evaluate the program for themselves seemed ambitious. They had very little baseline data, and some of the community health workers (CHWs) and community development workers (CDWs) were unable to read or write.

Finally, the team invited Marie-Thérèse Feuerstein, a facilitator in participatory evaluation, to come and visit them to explain the process. The visit was made possible through funding from the program's partner, Misereor, Germany.

In Patna, the facilitator described to the health team how each of them—whatever their background—would be able to participate in an evaluation of their program. They soon became convinced that they would like to adopt such an approach and, together, set dates for her return.

Defining the Objectives of the Evaluation and Choosing Evaluation Methods

Six months later, in October 1988, the evaluation facilitator returned to Patna to join the twenty staff members working on the community health and development team. Half of them were based at the Kurji Urban Health Centre and the other half at the Maner Community Health Centre. The intention was to evaluate the progress of the past four years (1984–1988).

The first event was a six-day training workshop to plan and prepare for the evaluation. The first task was to define the objectives of the evaluation. All were agreed that the main objective of the program as a whole was to help people meet more of their basic needs. The problem then was how to measure progress toward this objective.

The facilitator asked the team to think about the life conditions that were influencing the health and social development of families in the communities they aimed to serve. From a primary focus of looking at family needs, participants then "scaled up" to look at community needs. They drew up a list of factors affecting health development, including education, food, housing, and so on.

When discussion moved specifically to health needs, each requirement that was mentioned was drawn on the blackboard, forming a primary health care circle around a family group. The team discussed the links between achieving the components in the primary health care circle and achieving other basic needs.

The list of conditions affecting people's health and lives provided indicators, or markers, for measuring progress in different areas. For example, an increase in the percentage of people living in good-quality homes would constitute progress in living conditions.

In order to measure changes in the indicators of progress, the team realized that there were key questions that needed to be answered in order to establish whether components of the program were successful. For example, how extensive was their health program, and had it improved the health of school-children? Questions were decided upon for the four main activity areas of the program: health activities, social support activities, program organization and management, and training.

Next, the team worked out how to collect the information. They decided on nine main evaluation methods:

- Analysis of records and documentation
- Survey of MCH from a sample of women aged fifteen to forty-nine
- Mid-upper-arm circumference measurement of children aged one to four
- Flash cards, weight-by-height chart, and puppetry for schoolchildren
- Village meetings and focus group discussions
- Special staff meetings
- Group questionnaire on community health to nursing and midwifery students
- Observations
- Visits to key informants

The team also had to delegate responsibilities; decide the sequence in which evaluation preparation, implementation, and analysis would take place; and make plans about how to present and use the evaluation results. In all, it took the team two and a half days of the six-day workshop to complete the detailed plan.

Preparing and Pretesting the Evaluation Methods or "Tools"

Another two days of the workshop were devoted to training and designing and developing the evaluation tools. The health center staff, including CHWs and CDWs, and students were trained in interview techniques. Everyone also had to learn how to organize focus group discussions and to understand how to develop the "tools," such as the model for the survey forms.

To obtain the additional MCH information needed, a three-page questionnaire was prepared for the survey. The questionnaire was then pretested on a random sample of mothers attending the community health department's Urban Health Centre at the hospital site in Kurji.

It was decided that focus group discussions should be held with those involved in milk cooperatives, for example, to find out what had been achieved. The focus group discussions involved a team member acting as facilitator to steer a discussion. He or she prepared several key questions in advance, and the discussion provoked by the questions would identify factors that had contributed to or impeded success.

Preparation of a number of evaluation tools was necessary for the evaluation of the primary school program. For example, in order to check for physical development, Save the Children Fund weight-for-height charts were made more durable by sticking red, green, and yellow insulating tape onto the different bands. Strips of X-ray film had to be cut and strategically colored to measure the mid-upper-arm circumference of the children. In order to evaluate the health education program in the schools, team members produced sets of hand-drawn and painted flash cards. These cards were used to test how much the children understood about the links between health and hygiene as a result of the health education they had received. Staff also made puppets that they used to entertain the children and communicate specific health information after a particular evaluation session had been completed.

Collecting New Information Using the Evaluation Tools and Selecting Existing Information (Data) to Evaluate the Program

As mentioned earlier, the four components of the program were health activities, social support activities, organization and management, and training. Each member of the evaluation team took responsibility for collecting the data in one of these four areas of activity. The questions relating to the different components had already been discussed and agreed upon during the evaluation workshop.

Health Activities

Maternal and Child Health. Many of the activities of the Urban Health Centre at Kurji and the Maner Community Health Centre in the rural area catered to mothers and small children. There was, therefore, a considerable amount of information (data) available. For example, analysis of some of the program records indicated that few women were receiving antenatal care. At the evaluation planning workshop, all were agreed that the most important questions in the evaluation would relate to achievements and shortcomings in MCH.

The team decided to use a survey as a major evaluation tool. This was not initially a unanimous decision. Some team members, and even the facilitator herself, would not necessarily have chosen to undertake a survey as the major evaluation tool. The facilitator felt that the process could be too time-consuming within the overall evaluation, and that more active participation of villagers with poor literacy skills might be achieved by focus group discussions. However, other team members felt that a survey would not only raise awareness in the villages but also help team members themselves to strengthen their own survey and evaluation skills.

The survey sample included a total of 441 women aged fifteen to forty-nine. They were interviewed in the health centers, in the villages, and at work in surrounding fields. Over half the women were aged twenty-two to thirty, and approximately three-quarters of them were living in the target area for program activities.

The interviewers reported that they were well received by most of the village women. Although some women were reluctant at first to answer questions because there were no free handouts, most offered their time willingly. Some women even said that they liked being asked questions. They said that it gave them an opportunity to think about aspects of their lives that they had not considered before. For example, they were particularly interested in talking about the dowry system and about their own experiences of marriage and pregnancy.

The interviewers reported that carrying out the survey had helped them get to know the women better. "I was surprised that village women were prepared to answer questions," said one member of the team. "Even our male interviewers found that the women were cooperative and very willing to discuss openly."

School Health. Of the twenty-nine schools involved in the program's health activities, three were selected for evaluation—two in urban areas and one in a rural area. The sets of hand-drawn flash cards were used by the evaluation team to assess the children's knowledge of three common health problems, namely, diarrhea, scabies, and eye infections.

The team also decided to build new skills into the school health evaluation "package." They therefore introduced aspects of the child-to-child approach as part of the evaluation. In the child-to-child method, older children spread health messages to younger children, peers, families, and communities.

Teachers helped to identify students who would work with the evaluation team and become key actors in the evaluation. These older children weighed and measured the younger pupils, using the weight-for-height chart.

The final part of the school health evaluation provided an opportunity for the children to improve their health knowledge. Members of the team used their handmade puppets to present a story. The puppet characters were based on those the children had seen in the flash cards. In telling the story, the puppets answered the questions the children had been asked during the evaluation. In this way, the children enjoyed themselves and had the opportunity to learn all the right answers to the questions they had been asked while being shown the flash cards.

Social Support Activities

A second area of program activity was the social development program that had started years earlier. The activities included assistance to local people in taking advantage of government welfare schemes, support for cooperatives, lobbying work with bonded laborers, and encouragement for youth drama and women's activities.

During the evaluation planning, the team had decided to use focus group discussions to evaluate these activities. This decision was made partly because focus group discussions allowed further participation of those who could not read and write and partly because there were no baseline income data on which to base a survey.

Government Welfare Schemes. Focus group discussions with villagers during the evaluation revealed that, in the words of some villagers: "Government tries to give people good quality—but they end up getting bad quality."

The main problem appeared to be that even when people did manage to receive food or livestock through the schemes, they were sometimes of poor quality or inappropriate to the family's needs. For example, the grain given in return for work on roads, construction of schools, and social forestry was often substandard. The goats supplied on loan were often sick or producing very little milk. Families were not always trained to handle the animals or items they received, for example, a horse and cart. Some families felt that they had actually become poorer, as they now had the added burden of loan repayment. This perception was particularly true in cases where their animals had died.

Another problem was that obtaining a loan was made difficult by the corruption among local officials and local bank clerks. Families were often asked for bribes of 10 percent or more of the loan, and the bank officials receiving the advance would take their own share before releasing the money.

Milk Cooperatives. One of the three milk cooperatives established through the program produced considerable benefits for the fifty-two members involved. Focus group discussion revealed that average family income of the members had risen well above the average. Motivation and literacy had increased through having to keep accounts and write business letters. Having the status of a registered body also made it easier for the members of the milk cooperative community to apply for government schemes. As a result, they planned to start poultry farming, a fair-price shop, and a preschool for young children. However, two other milk cooperatives failed. They ran into financial and management problems because too few people had adequate business skills.

Bonded Laborers. During the focus group discussion, it emerged that 600 bonded laborers had organized a rally about their situation to present their case to state-level officials. The program had started to support the activities of these men because of the extreme deprivation of life as a bonded laborer.

Youth Drama. Evaluation of the youth activities of the program was hampered because the youth group had not yet been re-formed. Unfortunately, a misappropriation of funds had occurred, leading to a loss of public support and eventually to the group being disbanded.

Women's Activities. With funds from a government scheme, the program had helped twenty-five Dalit women to attend a three-month training for self-employment. The evaluation revealed, through focus group discussions, that although some women had initially succeeded in self-employment schemes, such as making and selling fans, they had later run into difficulties in buying raw materials.

Program Organization and Management

The process of evaluating the program's organization and management was comprised mainly of drawing together existing information (data) that would be needed for the overall evaluation analysis. For example, it was necessary to prepare information about target areas, details of program costs, and arrangements for program monitoring and networking.

Program Training

Although the program had trained a diverse range of personnel, including *dais* or traditional midwives, community health workers, and government workers such as kindergarten teachers, the evaluation focused on the community training of student nurses and midwives and of the novices—young women who had been received into the house of Medical Mission Sisters but who had not yet taken their vows.

A number of different evaluation tools were used, including both individual and group interviews and focus group discussions. The students and novices participated actively, particularly in the group interviews about their training for community health. They answered key questions while a facilitator arranged their answers in table form on the blackboard.

Analyzing the Data Collected, Reaching Conclusions, and Producing Recommendations

With the questionnaires of the MCH survey completed, the long and arduous task of pulling together and analyzing the results began. Working in rotation, a team of ten in the urban health center and of six in the rural community health center each took more than two days to count the results and to present them in the form of tables. One member of each team drew empty "dummy" tables on the blackboard to receive the data and totals. Both teams used pocket calculators to work out percentages, averages, and ratios, as necessary.

The team at the rural health center in Maner had eight deliveries to attend to while the data analysis was taking place. Fortunately, all births were normal, and despite the interruptions and the long working hours, the team completed the tasks of analyzing data, reaching conclusions, and making recommendations.

By the time all the results were tabulated, most team members considered the survey to have been worthwhile. In fact, those staff members who had been most against it at the start were among those who quoted the survey findings most frequently.

Maternal and Child Health Care

Some of the survey findings were surprising and, in some cases, even shocking. For example, among 217 women interviewed in the rural area, more than 85 percent had received no antenatal care. A similar proportion had never used family planning (see Table 6.1).

Results such as these caused anxiety. "If this is the situation in the villages where we have been working, the situation must be much worse in other villages," said one concerned team member. The school health evaluation provided some small-scale but useful data for the evaluation. For example, it was clear that some children were seriously underweight. The evaluation also showed that the children's knowledge of the causes of common health problems was poor. For example, half of the children in the rural schools did not connect flies and contaminated food with diarrhea.

Although pleased with the achievements of the school health evaluation, the team working in the two schools in the urban area were concerned by the absence of girls in the classrooms. Girls growing up in urban areas are often expected to care for younger children and livestock or to become "rag pickers," collecting waste paper, plastic, or tins to sell by the kilo. It was therefore decided that some out-of-school activities should be planned to reach the children who do not attend school.

Milk Cooperatives

The conclusion of the evaluation of the government welfare schemes was that although the activities were helping to link people with the government schemes, more attention needed to be given to preventing bribery and illegal bank practices and to understanding how those families living in extreme

Table 6.1: Some Surprises from the MCH Survey, Patna 1988

	Urban	Rural
441 female respondents aged fifteen to forty-nine	n = 224	n = 217
• Never used any family planning method	83.9%	86.6%
• Never received any antenatal care	37.0%	86.6%
140 children, aged one to four		
Mid-upper-arm circumference		
• In red section	20%	19%
• In yellow section	20%	34%
Socioeconomic factors		
• Average number of household members	6.9	7.1
• Average number of rooms in house	1.9	2.1
• Family members owning warm clothes	37%	50%
• % of thirty-six urban and forty-two rural families who could not repay loans	66.7%	73.0%
Main problems (164 urban families and 174 rural families)		
• Lack of money	80.4%	72.4%
• Lack of employment	64.0%	48.0%
• Alcoholism	18.9%	2.2%
• Housing	45.7%	14.1%

Source: MCH Survey, Urban and Maner Health Centres, Table MCH/U2–9 and 11, and Tables MCH/M2–9 and 11.

poverty might be better able to benefit from the schemes.

One conclusion of the evaluation of the work with milk cooperatives was that more training in bookkeeping, writing business letters, and leadership should be made available so that a larger network of people could be drawn upon to develop milk and other cooperatives.

Bonded Laborers

The focus group discussion with bonded laborers revealed that, as a result of new awareness, the landlords were more willing to release workers. However, this did not mean that these men could necessarily find jobs and homes. What was needed was more support for these men on their release. Otherwise, some were forced to return to the very landlords from whom they had been set free.

Youth and Women: A Future Priority

Even though the youth drama and the women's activities programs had faced problems, both were considered to be very important areas for the continuing and future success of the overall program.

Program Organization and Management

As part of the process of analysis and recommendation, discussion of program organization and management revealed the need to incorporate additional monitoring and evaluation procedures into future program activities. Program recordkeeping would have to be partly redesigned, and monthly monitoring meetings would be held.

Staff also recognized that there was a need to redefine appropriate target areas. For example, the Maner Community Health Centre was especially active in fifteen villages, with a population of between 1,000 and 3,000 in each. The large size of this population compromised the program's ability to follow up all the social support activities. Management and organization of the health activities, however, appeared to be working well.

During the evaluation, analysis of program costs and expenditures also took place, and the team decided that greater contact with other health and development programs in India would be useful.

The "Social Cement" of the Program

Although several criticisms of the community training were voiced, such as rapid student turnover, most felt that it was the presence of the students and novices in the villages during training that contributed "social cement" for the entire community health program. Although the majority of the general nurses would not subsequently be working outside a hospital setting, it was felt that their community training would enable them to give better and more realistic patient care in hospitals. At the community level, villagers in the program did not generally know who were staff and who were students.

The commitment and affection shown toward the villagers by the novices, who spent several months actually living with Dalit families, were singled out for special mention. During their community training, the novices took their turns in fetching water, carrying out household tasks, and harvesting rice.

Both teams produced a list of recommendations. The urban group produced fifteen recommendations and the rural group eighteen. They were short and practical and emerged directly from analysis and discussion of the evaluation findings. However, each set of recommendations took a considerable length of time to secure because it was essential to achieve a consensus. Without full agreement, the group commitment needed for implementing the recommendations would be weak.

Even before the evaluation process was over, members of the team were exhibiting a new enthusiasm toward their program. "This experience has helped us see that our work is bearing fruit," one member of the evaluation team said. They also felt that the participatory evaluation approach had stimulated interest in the community itself and created a new closeness between the program staff and those it was trying to reach. "I feel that I now know the village women in a deeper way," said another team member during one of the closing sessions. At the conclusion of the evaluation, the team's hope was that the new closeness and understanding would strengthen the continuing program.

Preparing the Report in Forms Suitable for Sharing with Various Groups

Each section of the report was prepared by different individuals or groups from within the evaluation team. Most members of the team had done nothing like that before. The facilitator assisted by carrying out some basic editing, but she made every effort to keep as many of the original expressions and styles as possible.

In retrospect, the evaluation team felt that it would have been better to have allowed more time for them to produce charts, posters, and other visual aids to accompany their own part of the report. However, the full sixty-eight-page document was eventually typed, stenciled, and bound in attractive, locally produced covers that had been prepared in advance.

Sharing the Findings of the Report

Community members were invited to come and hear about the findings of the evaluation. The interviewers in the urban area had specifically invited the women respondents to hear about the results. The response was overwhelming. More than 100 women arrived at the meeting room, some followed by protective fathers-in-law who sat on a mat at the back of the hall.

The meeting was extremely lively and lasted three hours. Thanks to extensive preparation by members of the team, activities included awareness-raising games and songs, role play, and picture graphics—all of which included messages from the survey findings. In this way, the statistical results of the survey were turned into pictures and actions.

For example, one member of the team had prepared "flannelgraph stories." From flannel material, she had cut out shapes of women in saris and stuck them on the board. In one story, three women were in red saris and seven women in green, showing that only 30 percent of village women were receiving antenatal care.

Some of the students had also composed an "Antenatal Song," which was sung loudly and with great enthusiasm by the women and members of the evaluation team. The lyrics of the song encouraged women to think about their needs during pregnancy, and especially about the need to seek antenatal care.

The evaluation team presented a mimed role play about the difficulties of a village woman during pregnancy and childbirth. This was the first time that a drama had been presented in this form. Many of the women discussed at length what they had seen in the role play. Others remained silent, knowing that they were not allowed to speak in the presence of fathers-in-law who had accompanied them to this unaccustomed outing.

A final three-day workshop brought together the evaluation teams from the urban and the rural centers plus senior hospital officials and invited guests. The purpose was to share and analyze all the results of the evaluation and to decide which recommendations should be for short-term, and which for long-term, action. It was also an opportunity to make a general plan of the program's work for the coming year and to decide on a schedule for the next evaluation.

Putting the Recommendations into Practice in the Ongoing Program

Follow-Up

This section is based on a report from Sister Grace Pullumakal, who wrote to CMC in 1993 with reports from the Urban and Maner Community Health Centres.

In January this year, hospital administrator Sister Grace Pullumakal reported that the hopes of those involved in the participatory evaluation were being realized. Today, the community health program is flourishing. "More and more people are fighting for their rights. They are now very aware of the need for education and immunization, for example," she says.

Sister Grace says that a clear sign of the new community orientation at the urban clinic is the fact that it has been renamed. "We now call it the Community Health Centre Kurji instead of the Urban Health Centre."

Focus on Women

The changes go far deeper than the change of name. In both Kurji and Maner, the greater recognition of the need for participation has created a new focus on women's development. It is now recognized that without specific efforts to support women, little progress can be made in increasing community participation. Maner has opened three women's literacy centers, and at Kurji, health education sessions are included in regular sewing classes.

A priority at both of the health centers is the immunization program. Tremendous strides have been made since the evaluation in 1988. That year, the survey revealed that in the Maner catchment area, only 17 percent of the children aged six months to five years were fully immunized. The follow-up report, written in 1993, showed that two-thirds (66 percent) of the children under five years old were fully immunized.

It has proved much more difficult to increase attendance at antenatal and postnatal clinics. Instead, the health staff at both Kurji and Maner make a special effort to give attention to the mothers when they come to the clinics with their children. In Maner, there is an additional scheme in which two or three people in each village are asked to keep an eye on pregnant and lactating women and to report any cases that might need follow-up by health staff.

The school health programs in both areas continue to be very successful. In Kurji, the aim is now to extend the child-to-child approach to all schools in the catchment area. The program has found that the interest and cooperation of the school principal are very important to their efforts.

The youth drama program is back in full force. Last year, there were 150 performances in Maner, many of which helped people to understand their situation better and to seek solutions. In Kurji, the theater's message has concentrated on the need for education. Drama performances and meetings in one area led people of four villages to get together to build a straw room for a school. Afterwards, they hired a teacher and are now collectively paying his salary.

Schools for "Rag Pickers"

The continuing social support activities include organizing discussion groups about government welfare schemes and support for a milk cooperative, as well as new projects in community participation for safe water and nonformal education for women and children. In Kurji, there are now five nonformal schools for dropouts and for the "rag pickers" who otherwise miss school because they have to do their work in the mornings. Parents value these nonformal schools not only because of the education their children receive but because it helps keep the children from becoming involved in drinking, drug taking, and other addictive habits.

The program is associating more with other voluntary groups. The centers have worked with UNICEF on their immunization programs, and with several women's organizations.

Much has also been achieved in the area of training. For example, at the Kurji Community Health Centre, there is now a better-planned program for the nurses and midwives during their time spent in the community. The students become actively involved in surveys, case studies, and street dramas, and also in the village meetings where the important plans and decisions are made.

Lalti's Story

Finally, an individual example of personal success since the participatory evaluation in 1988 is the experience of a Dalit woman called Lalti. She had been a very enthusiastic participant during the evaluation that took place in her home village of Binteoli. She was identified at that time by members of the evaluation team as a possible future leader for women in her own community.

With her follow-up report, Sister Grace told us that ever since Lalti took part in the evaluation and feedback session, she has been very active in stimulating community initiatives in her own village. Her involvement in the community health program has helped her grow in self-confidence and ability. Lalti now has regular employment as a *dai* in private practice. Sister Grace says that Lalti's employment takes her enthusiasm for community participation and development beyond the limits of her own village. Sister Grace concludes: "With her home-visiting, Lalti now reaches out to many."

$$7$$

Combining Participatory and Survey Methodologies in Evaluation: The Case of a Rural Development Project in Bangladesh

Yusuf Kassam

Most development projects in developing countries funded by development assistance agencies, especially those large-scale projects implemented by the governments of the recipient countries, involve external and internal evaluations that are predominantly quantitative in nature involving a lot of statistics. The evaluation of the *developmental impacts* of these projects is also portrayed in numbers and statistical configurations. Very little attention is paid to the qualitative empowering impacts of development processes that require the use of a participatory evaluation methodology.

Several reasons can be cited to account for the neglect of undertaking participatory evaluation and obtaining qualitative data:

- The institutional demands to justify the significant investment of large sums of money and to lubricate the chain of accountability make it imperative to obtain the so-called hard data on project performance.
- Participatory evaluation in terms of its value and methodological validity is either not well understood or not fully recognized by the donors.
- The bureaucrats in the funding agencies and other stakeholders working under considerable pressure and stress do not have enough time or patience to plow through the long and detailed texts generated by participatory evaluation methods. They tend to prefer "at-a-glance" information presented through statistical tables.
- In many quarters, development work is still perceived predominantly as a technical and mechanistic exercise rather than as a complex and dynamic *process* of transformation.

This chapter was first published in *Knowledge and Policy: The International Journal of Knowledge Transfer and Utilization*, Vol. 10, No. 1/2, under the title "The Combined Use of the Participatory Dialogue Method and Survey Methodology to Evaluate Development Projects: A Case Study of a Rural Development Project in Bangladesh." Reprinted by permission of Transaction Publishers, New Brunswick, New Jersey.

- The constraints of evaluation budgets inhibit the use of participatory evaluation, which is time-consuming and therefore more costly.
- Many consultants hired to carry out evaluations are either not well versed in or do not recognize the legitimacy and value of participatory evaluation approaches and techniques, according to their norms of what constitutes a "scientific, objective, and empirical" inquiry. It is argued that participatory evaluation produces knowledge that is "subjective, soft, and impressionistic."

While the necessity and importance of statistical and quantitative evaluation—especially of large-scale projects involving a large number of beneficiaries—are not denied, qualitative participatory evaluation has a complementary role to play in producing a body of unique and illuminative data that cannot be produced by the conventional research methodology. Participatory evaluation produces insights and perceptions that, at the very least, represent value added. Knowledge produced by participatory evaluation transcends the statistical silhouette of reality and presents a project's "flesh and blood," as it were, thereby giving a more intimate feel of the "pulse" of a project.

The combined use of survey and participatory evaluation methodologies produces macro- and microknowledge of reality, each informing and enriching the other. It enables one to see, so to speak, both the canopy of a forest as well as the individual trees, plants, and creatures underneath that canopy. What is often and sadly not realized by the project stakeholders is that their evaluation needs and objectives are better served and enriched by undertaking an evaluation that combines both traditional and participatory methodologies.

This case study is an example of an internal evaluation of the training component of a massive, long-term, and multimillion-dollar rural development project in Bangladesh conducted by the author and his Bangladeshi counterpart (Kassam and Kamal 1992) that combined both the traditional survey and participatory evaluation methods. The evaluation was greatly facilitated by the project's Canadian resource team based in Dhaka, as well as by the Bangladesh Rural Development Board, the project's implementing agency.

The Project

The project, named RD-12, is a rural development project for the assetless rural poor (the *bittaheen*), funded by the government of Bangladesh and the Canadian International Development Agency (CIDA) and implemented by the Bangladesh Rural Development Board (BRDB), a governmental agency. It started in 1988 as a five-year project—a continuation and expansion, with some modifications, of a previous phase of the project called RD-2 and funded by CIDA as well. The project was extended to June 1997.

The purpose of the project is, first, to assist assetless rural men and women by providing them with skills, training, and credit necessary for income generation. In addition, the project is intended to strengthen the capacity of BRDB to plan, implement, and sustain development among the rural poor.

The project promotes the creation of organizational structures of and for the rural poor designed to foster local leadership and reduce exploitation, enabling participation of the rural poor in local affairs and markets and thus helping to ensure an adequate supply of inputs and services to them. At the same time, the project contributes to institution building within the government of Bangladesh by continuing to improve awareness of the needs and constraints of the rural poor, the institutional requirements for addressing these needs, and the ability of the BRDB and key government ministries to meet these requirements.

E.T. Jackson and Associates Ltd., an Ottawa-based management consulting firm, has served as the Canadian Executing Agency (CEA) for the project. The firm supports the delivery of credit, training, and organizational services by the BRDB. CIDA provides $53 million toward this bilateral project, including $13 million for a revolving loan fund, and the government of Bangladesh contributes $3 million.

By the end of the initial five-year period ending in June 1994, RD-12 had mobilized 16,366 village-based Bittaheen Cooperative Societies in seventeen districts (six greater districts) of the project area. An estimated 500,000 members of the new *bittaheen* societies benefit directly. Almost 3 million household members benefit indirectly. Three-quarters of the society members have borrowed funds to start income-generating activities or microenterprises, and the average loan recovery rate has been about 94 percent. Between 1990 and 1994, RD-12 delivered two million person-days of training to the project participants across Bangladesh. BRDB staff received over 70,000 person-days of training during the same period. The large numbers of people trained in RD-12 make this project the largest human resource development project that CIDA has supported.

Through the management of the project by Jackson and Associates as the CEA, gender equity and social development strategy have remained important priorities for the project right from the inception mission. The firm contracted Bangladeshi and Canadian specialists to provide training for BRDB in gender and social analysis (GSA) and has promoted employment equity at all levels of the project.

Over 70 percent of RD-12's borrowers are now women. More than two-thirds of about 11,500 loan societies organized by the project staff are women's societies. The repayment rate for the women's societies outpaces that of the men's groups. Women members also mobilize higher average savings than their male counterparts. Furthermore, 47 percent of the 2,500 field staff of the BRDB are women, a percentage that has set a new standard for employment equity in the government of Bangladesh.

The firm's commissioned study that assessed progress on GSA found that RD-12 has achieved much in terms of promoting the integration of women in the development process but still could do more to facilitate attitudinal change on gender issues among men at all levels of the project.

Project Evaluation Methodology

The methodology used to carry out the evaluation of the training component of RD-12 consisted of documentary review, survey methods, and participatory evaluation methods. The survey methodology included an interview questionnaire that contained both closed- and open-ended questions, and this instrument was used with a sample of 2,104 beneficiaries and 126 field functionaries. The survey was conducted by a team of twenty Bangladeshi researchers with an equal gender balance. In addition, case studies of four men's and four women's cooperative societies were prepared, focusing on their development, achievements or failures, and problems encountered.

Under participatory evaluation, dialogues were conducted with a random sample of ten beneficiaries (members of cooperative societies), five women and five men. The dialogue method was used in order to gain a deeper and qualitative understanding of the dynamics of social and economic transformation among the beneficiaries, including the psychosocial and other developmental impacts on the beneficiaries of the project.

The Use of the Dialogue Method and Its Conceptual Context

In addition to the purpose of illuminating the qualitative developmental changes that occurred among the beneficiaries, the dialogues were intended to complement, supplement, and enrich the quantified data obtained through the interview questionnaire, case studies, and file review. In this way, the dialogues provided "flesh and blood" to the quantified findings on the impacts of training and the overall project performance that could not possibly be obtained by conventional research instruments. Furthermore, arising out of the priority placed on the gender dimension of the project, the dialogues were also intended to give a voice to the women beneficiaries.

The dialogues were conducted by two Bangladeshi researchers (one woman and one man), who were given a special orientation on how to conduct the dialogues. Using open-ended and nonleading questions, the dialogues were taped and transcribed verbatim. In conducting the dialogues, what was crucial was not only to record the participants' own thoughts and feelings but to do so in their own words and idiom and in their own style of expression. In transcribing the dialogues, they were not tampered with in any other way except for minimal editing for linguistic errors. After a dialogue was taped, it was played back to the participant.

The dialogue method is part of qualitative and participatory research and evaluation methodologies (see Kassam and Mustafa 1982) based on the work of, among others, Paulo Freire (1970b), Orlando Fals-Borda (1977), Budd Hall (1975), W. Filstead (1970), Kathleen Rockhill (1976), M. Parlett and D. Hamilton (1972), Michael Pilsworth and Ralph Ruddock (1975), R. Chambers (1978), Peter Oakley (1986), M. Patton (1987), H. Richards (1985), and C. Weiss (1972).

The investigation of psychosocial and qualitative changes in people's lives can best be illuminated by adopting an *anthropocentric* approach, which involves the *interpretation of reality exclusively in terms of human values and experience* (Kassam 1979). The dialogue method helps to portray the uniqueness of individual perceptions of and experiences in a development process. Whereas the information obtained through the use of conventional evaluation instruments such as questionnaires, interview schedules, or checklists superimposes the description of empirical social reality on to a predetermined framework of that reality, genuine dialogue eliminates most of the preconceived and preconstructed elements of the traditional evaluation process. Epistemologically, therefore, the dialogue provides a more accurate and authentic reflection of social reality. The dialogue makes it possible for social reality to be described on a "clean slate," as it were, and fills in the silhouette produced by the use of quantitative survey methodology. The dialogue helps to capture and portray the dynamics of the social and economic transformation among the beneficiaries of a development project.

The dialogue method is used not to quantify, verify, or predict the personal and qualitative social impact of a development program but rather to "illuminate" it (see Parlett and Hamilton 1972). While the dialogue method makes it possible to get a more accurate glimpse of the total human context with all its complexities and social interactions, the very *process* of dialogue serves a number of other important purposes. Through dialogue, the people participate actively in the evaluation process, whereas the conventional methods and instruments treat people as those who are "researched upon" and as mere sources of information. Through dialogue, the participants of a development process are treated as central subjects and actors of that process and are given the opportunity, to use Freire's words, to "name the world." The dialogue very often serves as a liberating experience for the participants.

An Example of a Dialogue

The following dialogue was conducted with Ms. Mosammat Jainab Bibi, the manager of Shahapur Bittaheen Women's Cooperative Society in the district of Jamalpur.

Ms. Bibi joined the society in 1984 and is now the manager. She has studied up to Class III and has one son and two daughters. Her son attends Class X and one daughter is married. She is involved in paddy-husking and poultry-rearing activities. She received training on members' education, cow rearing, and poultry. She is also attending the manager's training regularly.

"I joined the society in 1984. Mr. Tara, the local upazila official, had distributed fifteen wheat feeding cards among fifteen vulnerable female villagers. One day he told us to mobilize another fifteen women to form a society. We did it and he helped us to form a BRDB society. We deposited Tk. 1 per week as savings. We were not united then. We did not know each other. When the other fifteen women joined us we held a weekly meeting. We continued it and Mr. Tara would also attend. We generated a little fund and Mr. Tara and we deposited it at BRDB office. With our consent he formed a BRDB society for us. We deposited Tk. 1 or 2 as savings in 1984. We did everything by ourselves like raising savings, depositing them at the bank, issuing verity vouchers, taking receipts from bank, etc. We registered our society on 30.3.85. It is nearly seven or eight years that we have been running our society.

"Look, we are poor. We had no dignity in the local area. We worked in others' houses. At that time they helped us know the path of life. They invited us to receive training from BRDB so we could run the society smoothly. Our husbands were very cruel to us then. They threatened us in many ways. They challenged us saying what sort of law the government had established that all the women should have to hold meetings neglecting all their household work. Not only that—the rich also taunted us and ostracized us.

"We requested the BRDB to help us with credit support so that we could husk paddy. My husband works all day. We thought if we could husk paddy by taking a loan we could deposit Tk. 1 or 2 as savings besides repaying the loan. Considering our request, they provided each of us with Tk. 500 as credit support. We bought 2 maunds of paddy each and husked it. We repaid the loan installments and deposited Tk. 1 or 2 as savings from the profits we earned by paddy husking. We had no poultry so we bought some through the profit.

"We take a loan every year and husk paddy which provides us with some profit. We spend a little of that for the education of our children. Previously the Railway School was completely reluctant to admit our children. The directors of BRDB asked us once: 'How many are you?' We answered we were forty-six. They replied that means at least forty-six children and advised us to go and admit our children in the Railway School and gave us hope that they would help us. When we went there, the teachers were in panic. We asked them: 'Why do you not want to admit our children—because we are poor? Since we have no clean clothes? Why do you admit rich children?' Then the teachers agreed to admit our children.

"They told us to pay Tk. 10 for each boy or girl as an admission fee. We had protested earlier but realized very soon that we had to pay Tk. 10 because it was compulsory for everyone. They gave us seven days to collect the money. We collected the money and admitted our children in the school. That's how we overcame that problem.

"One of our members lost her husband. They were poor though they had a rich neighbor. The whole day had passed but she could not perform the funeral ceremony due to lack of money. She requested the rich neighbors to help her but they did not respond. Having no alternative, she came to us. We called all forty-six members and held a meeting. We took a decision to contribute according to our ability, whether it was Tk. 5 or 10. We raised Tk. 200 and purchased cloth for Tk. 110 and spent the rest for soap and other things.

Ten of us read the Holy Quran and buried the dead body after the Jumma prayer. That was another problem we had overcome.

"The rich persons took the matter negatively. They were in fear that their prestige would suffer by our united movement. They expressed their bitter opinions: 'These women worked in our houses earlier. What is happening to them? Why are they educating themselves? We would like to help them to bury the dead man, but those women do the job without taking any help! Our prestige will sink!' They held a meeting afterward.

"One man had a shop on a pucca [paved] road where members dry their paddy. The elites wanted to stop us drying paddy on the road but our members ignored them. They said the government is the owner of this road and if government puts any objection then we will not dry our paddy on the road. A son of a member went to that shop to buy molasses. But the shopkeeper did not want to sell to him. He asked the grocer: 'Why do you not sell to me? I have money!' The grocer stopped him and punched him on the chest. The boy returned home crying. His mother informed the society about the incident and sought justice. We went to Mr. Ibrahim, our Union Member, and appealed for justice. He advised as to go to the shop. We went there along with other poor villagers. The grocer taunted us and said: 'How dare these women not keep purdah! Why are they holding a meeting in my shop? I am a Mondal [his family name]! Why have these shameless beggars come here?' We replied that our son had been assaulted by you and we want justice. The Upazila Member came and called the grocer. He reproached him severely and asked him to beg pardon. At last the grocer gave us Tk. 300 for medicine for the injured boy and another Tk. 200, totally Tk. 500 as penalty.

"Through the Society I have received skill development and membership education training. I have conducted weekly meetings of the members. I have received poultry and cow rearing training and I cultivate fish and vegetables. I have learned how to rear poultry and how to keep the poultry shed. Shock sick birds should be kept separately. Dead birds should be buried in a hole. Rani khet is a disease of poultry birds. I have told all these thing to the members in our weekly meetings. I have recommended they rear poultry and to sell their eggs to generate savings. Fowls can be sold for Tk.100. Cloth can be purchased from it. Thus we have been trained. The symptoms of Rani khet are lime-like stools and drowsiness of the birds with a high temperature.

"We cultivate fish collectively. We have no pond but we requested one old man to provide us with his pond for fish culture. 'We will cultivate fingerlings or young fish in your pond. We will sell the fish after two to three months regularly and the rest will be yours,' we said. We took the pond under this condition and we earned Tk. 880 in two months. We have been cultivating fish for five to six years and earn Tk. 500–600 each two to three months. We maintain the pond and take care of it, catch the fish, and sell them. We do not get the help of any men. We have utilized our training fully.

"We also rear cows. Presently there are two or three cows which provide two or three sheer of milk daily. We know from our training that straw mixed up with urea and potash is a good feed for cows. We provide it to them and the milk quantity has increased four to five times.

"There are no conflicts in our society. Unity prevails among us. Before we were in misery. Now we are working unitedly and our distress is disappearing.

"Previously we worked as maid servants grinding spices. Our hands swelled. We would be the poorest if BRDB had not supported us with loans. These loans saved us from going to others' houses for work. We have taken loans six times from RD-12. We have taken loans twice earlier, both for Tk. 5,000 and have bought cows with these loans. I sold my first cow since it became sick. I bought a cow again and reared it according to the training I received. We need more education. We make mistakes due to insufficient education. Training helps us to increase our income. We could earn more if we were provided with more training. For example, they advised us to apply lime after drying the pond—1 sheer of lime in 1 decimal area of a pond. Urea also should be applied.

"We hold weekly meetings in addition to monthly meetings. We do everything collectively such as fish culture and vegetable cultivation. We gain profit by selling bran. Everyone has planted a palm tree in their homesteads. Other members suggested we do that. The age of the society and the palm tree is the same and all of those trees are bearing fruit. The society improved us a lot. We had no house and no tin roof. We had a roof made of straw. I have taken a Tk. 500 loan from the savings deposit and bought a betel leaf shop for my husband. He is earning Tk. 20–25 daily from that shop. I have saved the money and built this house. At the initial stage we deposited Tk. 1 and later Tk. 2. We worked and have developed our status. Now we deposit Tk. 5 and are trying to increase it.

"The society is our future. My son is studying at school. Savings deposits help us in time of need. All forty-six members pay attention to each others' problem. If ten members sign the resolution book, we can get the money. But we rarely do it. We are depositing the money for our future.

"Presently I am involved in paddy husking and poultry rearing. I am educating my children. I have given my two daughters into marriage with the help of the society without which it would have been difficult for me. In earlier days we starved day after day. Now we can save Tk. 1,000 to 1,500 after all household expenditures. Husband and wife together are running our family. When my husband ran our family alone, we were in severe trouble. We could not even buy a pen for our children. It stopped them from going to school. Now I husk paddy, sell the rice and bran and pay the educational expenses for our children. I have raised savings by selling chicken eggs. I gave my two daughters into marriage with this extra income. My son is a student of Class X. I deposited money by selling rice bran. I could not buy cloth in the early days. Now I can buy *suti sharee* [cotton sari]. When my husband earned for family, we could not even eat. According to the advice of BRDB I have started working, rearing poultry birds and purchasing cloth by selling them.

"Thank God our condition has improved. Now we need more loans and training which will be more useful. I read up to Class III. Training of BRDB enriched us. I have one son and two daughters. I have stopped having more children. Family planning training taught us this. One boy and one girl are enough. We teach the members to have only one or two children through the society.

"Now my life is good enough. I had no house before—now I own a house and I husk paddy. I could not speak in those earlier days. I was afraid of the sir [authorities]. People taunted me. They called me shameless. My relations from my husband's side also taunted me. But I encouraged myself with the thought: 'What would it be like if we the poor worked together?' I have observed improvement. I have received loans. I have undertaken activities with this loan assistance. It has improved our condition. The people who taunted us earlier now pay us proper respect. Now we do not go to the rich people for help. The Society has provided us with a house. Rich people can see it. They thought they would take loans for house building. But the chance comes to us. It is an intolerable matter to the elites that the resourceless people are now becoming resourceful.

"Now we can take meals three times a day. We can purchase clothes and educate our children. Due to dowry we could not give our daughters into marriage. Now we have taken a decision that we will not take dowry and will arrange dowryless marriages.

"We know about nutrition—that vegetables, pulses, and eggs provide calcium which keeps our health good. We drink tubewell water although we had no tubewell in previous days. Diarrhea will appear if we do not drink tubewell water. We have come to know these things through training. Every member accepts family planning methods. No one has more than two or three children. In case of any problem, first we try to solve it by ourselves. We do not go to other person if the problem is solved by us. If it is not, then we seek others' help. In case of any disease of our livestock or poultry, we go to the veterinary doctors. Our Organizer Madam and others help us.

"Training has taught us how to speak. We hope to receive training on sewing. Members are interested to work on block printing; paddy husking is not so suitable. We can print clothes if we have a printing factory, something our members saw at BRAC [Bangladesh Rural Advancement Committee, a large national NGO].

"Now we are not afraid of rich and powerful persons. In previous days they had taunted us. But now they don't have the temerity to taunt us. If we want justice from the Upazila Member, he gives top priority on our case even it is the case of one of our members. They are afraid of us because we move collectively and unitedly.

"At the primary stage my husband was unwilling to allow me to attend the meeting of the society. Now he realizes that besides the husband, the wife can also help run the family. So he has become enthusiastic. He is of the opinion that the women should work collectively. It is good we are improving. We also make them understand that we are poor. BRDB is providing as with advice. Let us see what comes of it.

"We will need no loans after two to four years. We needed work since we were poor but now we are going to overcome poverty. Now we know that capital can be formed by rearing poultry. We help each other. We help other members to marry their daughter. We give gifts also. If a member cannot give her installment for two to four weeks due to any ailment, we collectively help her to pay the installment. We help each other in illness by raising funds at Tk. 1 or 2 per person.

"We made and provided saline when one of us was attacked with diarrhea. Most of the members have bought one or two decimals of land. I have bought five decimals of land. For this I sold the calf which I bought by loan and added my savings. Everyone has two to four hens. Altogether we have 500 hens presently. I took Tk. 100 from profits from paddy trading and bought three hens. Today I have fifteen hens and many fowl.

"I have formed another three societies in the neighboring areas. They are running well.

"We have been awarded the national prize. It is a shield of silver. The society is good. Savings and shares are satisfactory. Prime Minister Khaleda Zia gave us a prize last December as we are the number one society in Jamalpur. Besides that we got a cassette recorder from Jamalpur administration.

"The name of this society is Shahapur MBSS. We hope we will win more prizes in the future."

A Brief Analysis of the Dialogue as a Source of Qualitative Data

A brief analysis of the dialogue quoted above is presented here to illustrate the significance of the information contained in the dialogue as a source of qualitative data.

The dialogue revealed how one beneficiary and her cooperative society, on whose behalf she spoke, benefited and were empowered by their participation in the project. The dialogue describes how the society members tackled the different problems and issues that faced them, such as how they confronted the school authorities to admit their children, how they asserted their right to dry their paddy on a paved road, how they sought justice from the grocer who assaulted the son of one of the society members, and how they used their entrepreneurial skills in negotiating the use of a pond from a community member for starting their fish culture project. The dialogue also describes how they used their acquired knowledge on health, nutrition, and family planning in their daily living; their awareness of their basic human rights; their unity, solidarity, and self-reliance; their collective and group decision-making actions in dealing with other social problems and events; the management of their income-generating activities; the loans they took; the savings they made; the ways in which they used the income that they derived; the kinds of further investments they made from their incomes; their increased awareness of the importance of the education of their children; and how they have overcome their fear of the "authorities."

These examples of how the society members managed their lives, their families, and their communities, as demonstrated by both the substance and the tone of the dialogue, showed a powerful and profound impact on the social and economic development of the members of the cooperative society.

At the level of social development, the changes in their self-perceptions and other psychosocial changes resulted in their social empowerment. At a broad level, this empowerment included their sense of feeling liberated from their former conditions of marginalization and oppression, their acquisition of more control over their lives and destiny, and their capacity to resist exploitation and injustice by the rich and powerful. Other elements of their empowerment relate to the achievement of self-confidence, self-assertiveness, moral courage, group solidarity, collective and democratic decision making through the society, and higher aspirations for themselves and their children.

In terms of economic development, their economic empowerment included such elements as the acquisition of income-generating skills, the ways in which they manage their income-generating projects, the reinvestment of the money earned from their projects, the accumulation of their savings and shares, and the development of entrepreneurial skills.

All these elements of the beneficiaries' social and economic empowerment constitute many of the necessary conditions for achieving the sustainability of developmental impacts.

The findings on the social and economic impacts of the project obtained through the dialogue corroborated the findings from the survey questionnaire. In addition, they enriched and provided more intimate qualitative details and insights that interfaced with the bare-bones statistics and their analysis. Such an in-depth, qualitative, and more comprehensive body of knowledge on the development process could not be elicited from the survey questionnaire. More importantly, the developmental impacts were described and viewed from the beneficiaries' own perceptions, perspectives, and frames of reference, and in their own words, idiom, and style—not those of the researcher. The beneficiaries' own perceptions and perspectives represent an important and more authoritative evaluation feedback to the project's stakeholders.

Lessons Learned

In using the qualitative and participatory dialogue method in combination with the survey methodology in carrying out the evaluation of the developmental impacts of this program, some major lessons have been learned concerning approaches, methods, and presentation of findings that affect how evaluation is perceived, carried out, used, and valued. These lessons include the following:

1. The combined use of survey and participatory evaluation methodology certainly enriches the evaluation findings of a development project, par-

ticularly its qualitative social impacts, and makes the reading of the evaluation report more interesting and stimulating, as was intimated by the project's stakeholders.

2. One of the strengths of this evaluation study was that it treated and presented the verbatim transcriptions of the dialogues as an *integral* part of the *main* findings of the study. They served as a key body of self-contained information, standing on their own rather than being tucked away in the shadow of appendices. The content of the dialogues is at least as substantive, valid, and authoritative as the quantified and statistical data. In addition, some relevant excerpts and quotations from the different dialogues were incorporated, along with the quantified data, into the body of a key chapter called "Impacts of Training."

3. The qualitative findings obtained through the dialogues were instrumental in making BRDB officials understand and recognize the importance and significance of the qualitative social impact of the project on the beneficiaries. Before the study was conducted, BRDB tended to be almost exclusively preoccupied with the credit performance and economic impact of the project, as indicated by the number of income-generating activities initiated, level of loan disbursements, loan recovery rate, frequency of loans taken, increase in income, and so forth. Only peripheral attention was paid to those project interventions that were intended to promote social development of the beneficiaries.

    As part of the follow-up of this evaluation study, the author was then able to build a more convincing case (based on the profound social impacts as revealed by the dialogues) that, while economic development is certainly one of the critical goals of the project, a development process needs to be viewed more holistically. The argument for this case was made along the following lines: For the credit component of the project to succeed, training for social development is equally as important as the training for economic development. It was recognized that credit was the backbone of the project. However, access to and productive utilization of credit should be seen as a means to an end, namely, economic and social development that culminates in empowerment. If economic development is to become sustainable, it cannot occur without social development, and sustainable social development cannot occur without economic development. The dynamics of a sustainable development process require that economic and social development be perceived in an interactive manner and not be dichotomized as an either-or situation. Failure or reluctance to recognize the complementariness of economic and social development will, in the long run, undermine the success of the credit program. The mutual reinforcement of economic and social development will create the necessary conditions and environment that will enhance the prospects of achieving *sustainable* economic and social development.

4. The use of the dialogue method, like any other participatory evaluation method, has its own limitations and constraints. The researchers have to

devote much more time in conducting the dialogues than in administering interview questionnaires. Consequently, it is more costly to conduct an evaluation that uses such methods. However, in the case of this evaluation study, since only ten beneficiaries were involved in the dialogues out of a total sample of 2,104 beneficiaries, the extra cost was negligible.

5. The researchers assigned to conduct dialogues need special orientation in the development philosophy underlying the dialogue approach and training in the skills of using the dialogue method effectively, and they also need to be quite sensitive and sophisticated in establishing a rapport with the participants.

6. The other limitation with using the dialogue method is the representativeness of the participants with whom the dialogue is conducted, since the participants selected have to be articulate. This factor tends to delimit the use of random sampling in favor of a more selective sampling of those participants who are more self-confident, more assertive, and willing to describe their experiences and express their views without any inhibitions.

7. The dialogue method also imposes a constraint on the size of the sample chosen, which again has implications for its representativeness. Because the use of the dialogue method is time-consuming and produces long texts, the sample needs to be much smaller than a sample selected for a survey questionnaire.

8. It would have been value added if the project could have found a mechanism to share the dialogues with the other beneficiaries of the project. In this way, the sharing of self-evaluated development experiences with other beneficiaries can become an educational process through which the beneficiaries can get an opportunity to discuss and reflect on developmental changes and impacts. Such a process would give them the opportunity to get some idea of their own potential for development, and promote a feeling of solidarity. The text of the dialogues could also be used to serve as highly motivating and relevant literacy follow-up reading materials in the same project.

References

Chambers, R. 1978. *Rural Poverty-Oriented Monitoring and Evaluation.* Brighton: Institute of Development Studies, University of Sussex.

Fals-Borda, O. 1977. "For Praxis: The Problem of How to Investigate Reality in Order to Transform It." Paper presented at Symposium on Action Research and Scientific Analysis, Cartagena.

Filstead, W. J. 1970. *Qualitative Methodology.* Chicago: Markham.

Freire, P. 1970a. *Cultural Action for Freedom.* Middlesex: Penguin Books.

———. 1970b. *Pedagogy of the Oppressed.* New York: Herder and Herder.

Hall, B. 1975. "Participatory Research: An Approach for Change." *Convergence* 8 (2): 24–32.

Kassam, Y. 1979. *The Voices of New Literates from Tanzania*. Dar es Salaam: Tanzania Publishing House.

Kassam, Y., and M. Kamal. 1992. "Report of the Evaluation Study of the Training Component of RD–12." Ottawa: E.T. Jackson and Associates Ltd.

Kassam, Y., and K. Mustafa, eds. 1982. *Participatory Research: An Emerging Alternative Methodology in Social Science Research*. Toronto: International Council for Adult Education.

Oakley, P. 1986. "Evaluating Social Development." *Journal of Social Development in Africa* (1).

Parlett, M., and D. Hamilton. 1972. *Evaluation as Illumination: A New Approach to the Study of Innovatory Programmes*. Edinburgh: Centre for Research in the Education Sciences, University of Edinburgh.

Patton, M.Q. 1987. *How to Use Qualitative Methods in Evaluation*. London: Sage.

Pilsworth, M., and R. Ruddock. 1975. "Some Criticisms of Survey Research Methods in Adult Education." *Convergence* 7 (2): 33–43.

Richards, H. 1985. *The Evaluation of Cultural Action*. Basingstoke: Macmillan.

Rockhill, K. 1976. "The Uses of Qualitative Research in Adult Education to 'Enlighten, Enoble, and Enable.'" Paper presented at the International Conference on Adult Education and Development, International Council for Adult Education, Dar es Salaam.

Weiss, C. 1972. *Evaluation Research*. Englewood Cliffs, N.J.: Prentice-Hall.

8

Process Evaluation: The Nepal Health Development Project

Sheila A. Robinson and Philip Cox

This case study discusses an alternative evaluation methodology known as process evaluation and its application to the Nepal Health Development Project (HDP). It describes the HDP, provide details of the evaluation methodology and underlying concepts, and recount the various stages of implementation. The latter part of the chapter summarizes major findings and discusses lessons learned and benefits and costs of the methodology.

Brief Project History

The HDP is a participatory health development project of the University of Calgary's Division of International Development, the Institute of Medicine (IOM) at Tribhuvan University in Nepal, and the Ministry of Health. The first seven-year phase of the project ended in March 1995, and a second phase is under way. Project funding provided by the Canadian International Development Agency (CIDA) for the first phase was Cdn. $4.6 million.

Three evaluations of the HDP were conducted, all of them at the initiative of the HDP partnership. The 1989 and 1991 evaluations used a combination of conventional and participatory methodologies. The HDP subsequently developed the process evaluation methodology for tracking human resource development (capacity-building) initiatives and their outcomes. This methodology was implemented in the final year of the first phase of the project.

The Nepal Health Development Project

Project Setting

Nepal is a country of 20 million people, bordered on the north by Tibet and on the west, south, and east by India. It comprises three distinct topographical zones: the Himalayas in the north, the foothills in the center, and the Gangetic plains, or Terai, along the southern margin.

To a large extent, Nepal was isolated from the rest of the world until 1954, when the traditionalist monarchy was forced by internal and external pressures to initiate a multiparty democracy. This pluralist system was quickly replaced by a one-party, palace-controlled government that lasted three decades. However, the process of opening the country to outside influences continued. In 1991, after a brief popular uprising, there was a return to a multiparty parliamentary system. There has been a continuing commitment since then to pursue broad-based development goals through democratization and decentralization.

Administratively, the country is divided into seventy-five districts. Each district has been divided into municipalities and clusters of villages called Village Development Committees (VDCs). Altogether, there are thirty-six municipalities and 3,995 VDCs.

The Ministry of Health is responsible for providing curative and preventative services through a network of hospitals and remote rural health posts. Primary objectives of the government's national health policy are to upgrade the health status of the majority in rural areas by extending basic primary health services to the village level, and to provide accessible and effective referral services.

Project Description

The HDP developed in response to what the project partners perceived as a gap between the Ministry of Health's stated intentions to raise the level of health in rural areas and its actual performance. Specifically, the gaps were perceived to exist on three levels:

- Between the ministry's stated programs and the ability of regional and district-level managers to implement these programs;
- Between the expectations of the regional and district managers and the performance of extension workers in the field; and
- Between actions of the extension workers throughout the district and the services required by community members.

Thus, the stated purpose of the HDP was:

To strengthen the capacity of the government's health-related institutions and rural communities in Surkhet District to meet health needs through community-based participatory development, management strategies, and the training of generalist physicians.

At the peak of the project, there were twenty-seven full-time and eight part-time staff in VDCs, Surkhet District, and in Kathmandu. Four equivalent staff positions were held by Canadians acting as counterparts to Nepalis in the following roles: project coordination, community health and development, district management, physician training, and documentation and research. The Canadian coordinator and documentation and research officer worked part-time from the project's Calgary office.

Three Streams of Project Activity

The evaluators used the process evaluation methodology to focus on the capacity-building experience resulting from the three streams of project activity: community development, district health strengthening, and generalist physician training.

Community Development Stream

HDP was active in five VDCs in Surkhet District. These VDCs, with a combined population of 35,000, are remote agricultural communities located in the foothills. Project community development staff and local facilitators were trained in participatory research and participatory appraisal techniques, which they utilized in their work with village groups.* These processes were designed and utilized to empower villagers, independently and as a group, to address community issues.

In all the communities, villagers have organized themselves at the ward level according to interest, such as women's health or forestry groups. These neighborhood groups meet monthly to address local issues. From time to time, representatives meet to share, exchange, and plan at the village (VDC) level. Initiatives arising from this community development process include irrigation and clean water schemes, forest conservation, vented stove construction, women's literacy, microenterprise development, and savings and credit schemes.

As the project "worked itself out" of a VDC, it assisted ward groups to relate to one another across VDCs so as to form a local "people's" organization. These self-help nongovernmental organizations (NGOs) are able to establish cooperatives, access external funds, and organize collaborative village development schemes. They can also better advocate for community interests with government agencies such as the Ministry of Health.

---

* Participatory appraisal has its roots in participatory action research (PAR) and rapid rural appraisal (RRA). It features an interdisciplinary group assessment process in a style that uses multiple techniques for data acquisition and analysis. It is people oriented and locale specific. It pursues an increasingly accurate understanding through rapid rounds of field interaction. Participatory appraisal, in particular, places the "subjects" of research in the center of the design and implementation of the research process. It taps local knowledge and combines it with modern scientific expertise. And it provides those in positions to make changes with useful information as a guide to action.

District Health Strengthening Stream

The second stream of activity addresses the delivery of health programs at the district level. The focal point of this stream of activities is the Ministry of Health's district public health office, which manages preventative, promotional, and curative health services through a network of health posts, sub-health posts, and a twenty-bed district hospital.

The project's aim is to strengthen the ministry's capacity to operate in a decentralizing bureaucracy. HDP staff assisted ministry staff to develop information-gathering systems and methods for planning and managing district health activities, and to improve the functioning of the outlying health posts, the district hospital, and the referral system that links the two. Activities within Surkhet District included needs assessment of staff, in-service training, and the development of community-managed health post drug schemes. In addition, project staff collaborated in the training of female health post auxiliaries, traditional birth attendants, and community volunteers. At the national level, the project contributed to health policy and planning through the development of policy and program alternatives and participation on national task forces related to district health services.

Training of Generalist Physicians

From the IOM's main campus in Kathmandu, the project, along with the newly developed Faculty of General Practice, coordinates a three-year postgraduate general practitioner training program. Most districts outside Kathmandu have poorly equipped hospitals and medical doctors without the requisite skills to perform emergency and obstetric surgery. The objective of the program is to place specially prepared generalist physicians with appropriate clinical and managerial skills into district hospitals. Consistent with the institutional capacity-building goal of the HDP, most of these residents come to the program from within the Ministry of Health and, upon completion, return to a government district hospital.

Focus of the Evaluation

The process evaluation examined the extent and the process by which the HDP achieved its purpose of capacity building. The evaluators were interested in seeing how the capacity-building efforts of the project had assisted in meeting needs and improving performance in the community and the health system in Surkhet.

Purpose of the Process Evaluation

1. To assess the capacity-building process by which the project has achieved its outputs and outcomes;
2. To assist the broad range of stakeholders refine the project's operational effectiveness, and to enhance the capacity of these groups to plan for the future;
3. To create an additional project output, a field-tested evaluation methodology for measuring changes in human resource development/capacity-building projects like the HDP.

Process Evaluation Methodology

The process evaluation methodology has four key elements:

- Use of a conceptual model around which to examine capacity building;
- Reliance on participatory strategies;
- Adoption of participatory appraisal techniques; and
- A qualitative approach to indicator development and field investigation.

No one element is new to the world of evaluation, yet combined, the HDP's recent experience suggests that these elements offer an accessible, action-oriented assessment tool for human resource development projects.

Use of a Conceptual Model

Human resource development or capacity-building projects like the HDP emphasize the *process* of matching beneficiary needs and competencies with financial resources, staffing, equipment, supplies, and time, and then transforming this collection of inputs into plans and activities that build human and organizational potential.

Those responsible for implementing project activities are keen to know how activities generate knowledge, attitudes, and skills, and how the learning in turn influences others who are not directly involved. Further, they want to know whether learning actually changes the way things are done in an organization or community, and whether these changes are sustainable.

Often the environment around the project has much to do with sustainability. Implementers are thus also interested in understanding social, economic, political, administrative, cultural, and other cross-currents that enable or impede capacity building.

A conceptual model addressing these issues is used to link the evaluator to the theory of development underlying the way the project was designed. The model helps keep the evaluation focused on what the project or activity is trying to achieve. In human resource development projects such as the HDP, the conceptual model provides a framework to clearly reflect the intent of capacity-building initiatives. In so doing, it enables the evaluator to assess progress in the *process* of building human or organizational capacity. Using the model to analyze the findings of the evaluation can, in turn, allow project managers to build on their understanding of development and make better decisions.

The "spiral" model of capacity building, developed by the HDP for this evaluation and described later in this chapter, assumes that behind every new latrine, weaving loom, or irrigation canal in a village, for example, there are less visible but equally important changes in individual and group knowledge, skills, and attitudes. Similarly, it assumes that behind every improvement in the design and delivery of health services provided by the local health post or district hospital, there are changes in the way health personnel view their roles, those of their colleagues, and the needs of their consumers. Indeed, the model assumes that even where there are no visible improvements to look behind, there may be important changes taking place in the capacity of people and organizations to improve the quality of life.

Reliance on Participatory Strategies

Participation is a cornerstone of effective process evaluation. The people who most need to know how well or poorly project activities are building capacity are those who carry them out. These are the people in charge of the construction of latrines or irrigation ditches at the village level, the people responsible for health post staff supervision and training at the district level, or the people responsible for the management of the project as a whole.

In designing the process evaluation methodology for the HDP, its originators recognized the wide range of stakeholders within the project. Among the groups and individuals directly related to the HDP, there are two types of stakeholders. There are those people whose lives and work are directly affected by the activities of the HDP. There are also those people implementing or supporting the project who stand to learn from the evaluation results. In order to be an effective guide to these stakeholders, the designers realized that process evaluation had to be *relevant* to each of their varying information needs.

Therefore, to be *participatory* and *relevant*, representatives from stakeholder groups had to be genuine participants in the design, data gathering, analysis, and reporting phases of the exercise. Where this was possible, the stakeholders would have a greater sense of ownership of and accountability for the evaluation. As a result, they would be more likely to respond to the research findings and recommendations.

This evaluation used a core team of four evaluators, three of whom were external to the project. This was an interdisciplinary team. Combined, it gathered expertise in evaluation, community health and medicine, cultural anthro-

Figure 8.1: Composition of the HDP Process Evaluation Team

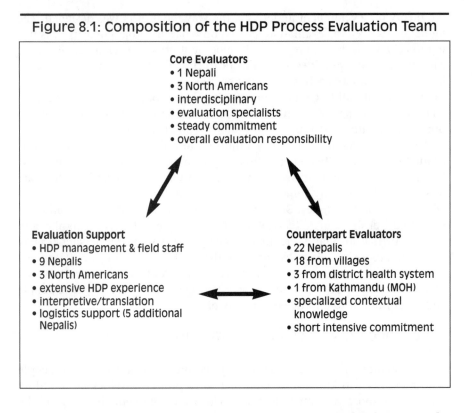

Core Evaluators
- 1 Nepali
- 3 North Americans
- interdisciplinary
- evaluation specialists
- steady commitment
- overall evaluation responsibility

Evaluation Support
- HDP management & field staff
- 9 Nepalis
- 3 North Americans
- extensive HDP experience
- interpretive/translation
- logistics support (5 additional Nepalis)

Counterpart Evaluators
- 22 Nepalis
- 18 from villages
- 3 from district health system
- 1 from Kathmandu (MOH)
- specialized contextual knowledge
- short intensive commitment

pology, health economics, social policy, and community development. The core team was joined by counterpart evaluators from the Surkhet office of the Ministry of Health, the district hospital, and the three VDCs participating in the exercise (six villagers per VDC). This joint team was supported by HDP staff and representatives of the major stakeholder organizations: the IOM, the University of Calgary, and the Central Office of the Ministry of Health. The composition of the process evaluation team is illustrated in Figure 8.1.

Staff supplied insights into the operations of the project. Villagers and Ministry of Health officials provided an understanding about the context of the project. The core evaluators contributed their own disciplinary perspectives. Given their relative distance from the day-to-day project routine, they asked probing questions and brought a broader perspective to the research. They also contributed a technical understanding of evaluation.

Adoption of Participatory Appraisal Techniques

Participatory appraisal provides a toolbox of techniques to help interdisciplinary teams function effectively and efficiently. These techniques—semi-structured interviews, focus groups, social/community mapping, accidental interviews, group treks, and many others—help evaluators talk with and listen to local people and other team members, observe local conditions, and study preexisting information.

While guided on a daily basis by the conceptual model and the parameters of the project/activity's design, the team was free to choose the information-gathering instrument and angle of inquiry that made sense at the time. Sometimes, these choices were made ahead of time in planning sessions; sometimes, they were not.

Team members primarily worked together so that each individual could exchange her or his interpretation of the same observation. Daily debriefing was essential to order and synthesize the information that rapidly accrued. At these sessions, the benefits of interdisciplinary team research became clear. Members contributed their various perceptions, often complementing each other's insights to build a better understanding. Sometimes, when individual perceptions clashed, the team decided whether more information was needed on the same topic, and if so, it planned the agenda and use of appraisal techniques accordingly.

Qualitative Approach

A quantitative approach is necessary but not sufficient to evaluate human and organizational capacity building. For example, quantitative information does not convey changes in attitudes and behaviors, nor does it address the question of sustainability, all of which are intrinsic to the goal of capacity-building projects. While visible outputs—the latrines, literacy students, trained physicians, and so forth—can and should be counted as indicators of progress, such information must be balanced with qualitative information within a qualitative conceptual framework.

The qualitative framework, in this case the conceptual model of capacity building, embraces the full life cycle of a project or activity—from inputs to impacts. The model guides evaluators in identifying key questions and in seeking out, testing, and verifying indicators of capacity building for each stage in the life cycle. The model, key questions, and indicators lend themselves to a qualitative approach to data gathering and indicator development.

The Spiral Model of Capacity Building

The Spiral Concept

The conceptual model for this process evaluation was based on the assumption that new knowledge, skills, and attitudes influence ever larger circles of people within an organization, institution, or community. Understanding the capacity-building process is essential, as it represents the means by which the HDP achieves its purpose—a closer fit between consumer need and health service delivery.

Figure 8.2: Spiral Model of Capacity Building

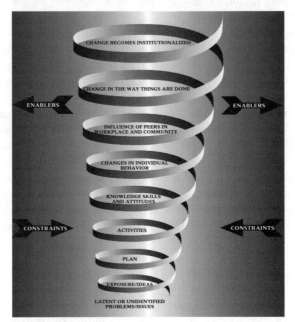

This concept is represented schematically in Figure 8.2. The figure shows a spiral in a box. The spiral is narrow at the bottom and becomes wider as it winds upward. At the bottom of the schematic is the initial exposure to problems and ideas. As the ideas are discussed, they generate enough support to be transformed into a plan of action. Contained in this plan are one or more activities. The activities of a capacity-building process may bring together groups of people who can effect the desired changes with those organizing the activity. Once in contact, existing knowledge, skills, and attitudes are sharpened and new knowledge, skills, and attitudes are acquired.

From this point on, changes in knowledge, skills, and attitudes begin to affect ever-widening circles of people, leading to corresponding changes in individual behavior. Changes in behavior, exhibited by the persons directly involved in the activity, influence changes in their own immediate workplace or community settings. This leads to concrete changes in the way things are done. Others start to notice the changes and, if they like them, support the new ways of doing things. Indeed, this level of support increases to a point where the changes become institutionalized—a part of the way things are usually done. Herein lie the seeds of sustainability.

The designers delineated five "zones" of capacity building to simplify data collection, analysis, and the presentation of the results: mobilization, planning and organization, learning, diffusion, and institutionalization. The zones overlay on the spiral and reflect aspects of the capacity-building process detailed

Figure 8.3: Spiral Model of Capacity-Building Zones

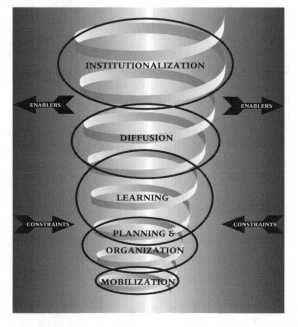

above. As illustrated in Figure 8.3, these zones of capacity building overlap. Learning, for example, takes place throughout a large portion of the capacity-building activity.

As applied to the HDP, there are—within each of the three streams—a multitude of activities. Some activities are large scale, some small; some activities are slow to come to fruition, some are much faster to take hold. It is intended that each activity in some way contributes to the achievement of the purpose of the HDP.

There are two major kinds of constraints on the capacity-building process—internal and external. Internally, the transition from one phase of the capacity-building process to the next is by no means a certainty. The upward spiral of capacity building is rarely—if ever—a regular, smooth flow. For example, a process might get off to an inappropriate start as a result of developing an idea that does not squarely address the problem. Later on in the spiral, particular people chosen for the activity may, for one reason or another, be unable to make use of the activity to bring about the desired change. Conversely, the appropriate people might be involved, but the activity may be wrongly designed or implemented.

The second kind of constraint is that imposed from outside the project activity. In Figures 8.2 and 8.3, the spiral starts well within the confines of the box, but as the idea develops into an activity and the stakes increase, the spiral begins to push against the outside forces. Sometimes, the outside forces can be so overpowering that they close in on the capacity-building activity and

---

Key Questions

1. What was the problem or issue? What triggered it? Who identified it? How?
2. How did the idea to address the problem/issue arise? Who raised it?
3. How was the idea transformed into a plan of action?
4. Was the planned activity congruent with the problem/issue? How so? How not? What resources were deployed and how?
5. Did the participants in activity "x" generate the knowledge, skills, attitudes, and behaviors necessary to strengthen their immediate workplaces (e.g., health posts, district hospitals) or community groups? If not, why?
6. Did the participants' peers in these organizations or community groups receive and adopt/adapt the knowledge, skills, attitudes, and behaviors generated in activity "x"? How? Or, if not, what happened?
7. Did changes take place in the organization or community as a result of the knowledge, skills, and attitudes generated in activity "x"? What changes? What implications (e.g., costs and benefits)? If not, why not?
8. How, if at all, did these changes become institutionalized in the organization or community?
9. How did the end users of the organization or community group benefit from the changes originally resulting from activity "x"?
10. What external factors impeded the capacity-building process? And how?
11. What has and can be done (and by whom) to counter these factors?
12. What external factors helped the capacity-building process? And how?
13. What has and can be done (and by whom) to take greater advantage of these factors?
14. What has to happen next to enable the objective of the activity to be met?

---

slow or stop its progress. Other times, the capacity-building process can be managed in such a way that the externally imposed constraints are reduced—that is, the spiral pushes the box outward.

The same external environment that poses constraints on a capacity-building process can also contain enabling factors that, if taken advantage of, can help the activity achieve its purpose. In this conceptual model, the relationship between the spiral and the box is dynamic—one can influence the other, and the nature and strength of this influence can change over time.

From this model emerges key questions to guide the evaluation team's inquiry within all streams of project activity. Questions used in this evaluation are included in the box above. Using the questions listed in the box as a guide, the HDP evaluators examined a variety of activities within each of the three project streams. They also considered the extent to which project activities reinforced each other and moved the HDP toward its overall purpose.

Table 8.1: Process Evaluation Schedule of Activities

Stage	Activity
I. PREPARATION span of time: 4 months amount of time: 70 (12%) person-days	Early Design Work (Canada)
	Design Workshop (Surkhet District)
	Design Workshop (Kathmandu)
	Development of Terms of Reference
	Evaluation Planning (logistics/document review)
II. ORIENTATION span of time: 2 weeks amount of time: 30 (6%) person-days	Orientation Conference (Kathmandu)
	Travel to Surkhet
	Orientation Conference (Surkhet)
III. INFORMATION GATHERING span of time: 2 weeks amount of time: 350 (62%) person-days	Generalist Physician Training (Kathmandu)
	Community Development (Surkhet)
	District Physician Training (Surkhet)
IV. SYNTHESIS & REPORTING span of time: 4 months amount of time: 110 (20%) person-days	Draft Findings Report
	Findings Workshop (Kathmandu) (Staff, Project Steering Committee)
	Calgary Advisory Committee Workshop
	Draft Final Report
	Stakeholder Review
	Final Report

Implementing the Process Evaluation

The tasks of the process evaluation were sequenced in four stages, as shown in Table 8.1. The table shows both the time span and the number of person-days required to carry out the set of activities in each stage. It indicates that the first and the last stages of the evaluation spanned the greatest amount of time, but that the information-gathering stage, while lasting only two weeks, required the greatest investment of person-days. Highlights of each stage are outlined below.

Stage I: Preparation

- *A half-day "think tank" session in Calgary*: This session was instigated by the Canadian coordinator and involved members of the Canadian Advisory Group and evaluation specialists. It yielded the initial concept paper with rationale, preliminary design considerations, and a rough timetable for the evaluation.

Core Evaluators

Project staff on both sides of the Pacific agreed upon a "core" team of four: a medical anthropologist and social policy analyst with a great deal of health research experience in Nepal; a physician, former dean of the IOM and one of the architects of the Generalist Physician Training Program; a physician currently working as the director of a community health development project in a sister organization; and an HDP research assistant based in Canada, with experience in participatory evaluation methodologies. In addition to securing the team of core evaluators, the project coordinator (Nepal) confirmed the participation of two resource persons, one from the Central Office of the Ministry of Health and one from senior management of the IOM.

- *Preparatory visit to Nepal by the evaluation coordinator:* The evaluation concept and plan were further developed participatorily with all levels of HDP staff in Nepal. The spiral model of capacity building, for example, emerged from a workshop with project staff in Surkhet District. The composition of the evaluation team was finalized, including locally recommended members. Timetable, logistics, community sites, and budget were decided. A final workshop in Kathmandu involving project staff, core evaluators, and key contacts from related institutions identified key issues for the evaluation and reached consensus on what the process evaluation should achieve for the project.
- *Terms of reference document developed*: Based on the output of the series of meetings and workshops in Nepal, this document guided the subsequent planning activities in the field.
- *HDP community development field staff took the idea of the process evaluation to the community and district health leadership*: Staff encouraged villagers at all three selected communities to build up their own ideas about evaluation on the basis that outsiders were coming to "learn" about their development experience. Discussion yielded ways that maximum numbers of villagers could be involved as a learning experience.
- *Creative compromises*: Balancing the requirement that all researchers have an opportunity to observe the same things within the available budget and time frame forced a compromise to interdisciplinary research. The solution: two subteams of core researchers—one subteam would focus on community activities, the other on district-level activities. The teams would meet as much as possible throughout the fieldwork in order to learn from the other team's observations and insights.

Community Participation

On the question of participation, field staff devised a plan to involve up to six villagers from each of the three VDCs as "counterpart evaluators." These villagers were to partner with the core evaluators for the two-day period that the core group was in their community. Similarly, HDP staff devised a plan to invite two key players from the Ministry of Health (Surkhet District) and the local development officer to be counterpart evaluators as well.

Process Evaluation: A Logistics Nightmare

" We discussed logistics . . . maximum number that might come; where they would sleep; number of sleeping mats; where they would eat; number of dishes; where and how to cook; availability of cooks; availability of water filters; what food and where to buy it; transportation of bedding and kitchen supplies; where people would wash so that the ground would not get muddy; where groups could meet to avoid direct sun; when meetings should be held to best fit in with the villagers' harvesting responsibilities . . ."
From the notes of the HDP community health nurse adviser

Stage II: Orientation

- *Orientation packages for the core evaluators*: Prior to convening in Kathmandu, each team member received an information package with terms of reference and assorted project documentation.
- *Two-day orientation and team-building workshop in Kathmandu*: The core evaluators, project staff (Surkhet and Kathmandu), and resource persons from the Ministry of Health and IOM closeted themselves with a trained facilitator. They reviewed the spiral model and the evaluation questions. They learned the basics of interdisciplinary team research and participatory appraisal techniques, clarified role expectations of the team and the staff, and practiced evaluation techniques in role plays of community and district health situations.
- *One-day orientation in Surkhet*: Evaluators, staff, and resource persons participated in another orientation/familiarization session with the counterpart evaluators from the community and the district health system. Icebreaking games and role playing enabled the counterpart "pairs" to

---

Orientation of Core Evaluators: Role Playing

The orientation to participatory appraisal included a role play. HDP staff became Nepali villagers sitting in a tea shop. The core evaluators and their interpreters (selected staff persons) were required to show up, order tea, and engage the patrons in a discussion of the vented stove— one of the key activities of the HDP at the village level. In participatory rural appraisal, this is called a semistructured interview.

---

become comfortable prior to working together in the community or district setting. The district group planned their agenda, while the community group further practiced interviewing skills.

Stage III: Information Gathering

The core evaluators spent two weeks collecting information. They met key government officials in Kathmandu, district officials, hospital and health post staff around Surkhet District, and villagers in three of the five participating VDCs. With the help of project staff, the team singled out key questions and usually designated one or two members to lead the questioning. Any interviews with high-level officials were formal and planned ahead of time. More informal techniques were used when meeting with villagers and health practitioners. All team members present for interviews took notes.

National and District Data Gathering

The district-focused evaluators:

- Met with nearly a dozen key informants within the Ministry of Health and National Planning Commission;
- Met with the faculty and students of the Generalist Physician Training Program at the IOM;
- Observed residents of the generalist training program performing surgery and conducting rounds;
- Talked with patients and outpatients of the hospital to find out how the presence of the residents was affecting service;
- Invited the residents to breakfast and asked them to comment on the training curriculum, the training sites, and their own career intentions;
- Went to the independent prenatal health clinic, and across town to the leprosy hospital and tuberculosis clinic, to find out how the HDP's district health collaboration strategy is viewed by other health organizations;
- Went to a primary health care center and to selected health posts and

---

Community Evaluation Agenda

1. Meeting with Counterpart Evaluators
2. Presentation of Social Maps
3. Community Walkabouts
4. Debriefing Evenings

---

sub–health posts to gain an impression of staffing and supervision, equipment and facilities, the supply and dispensing of drugs, and collaboration with community groups; and

• Held casual conversations with the users of health posts to hear their impressions of the facilities and service.

Community Data Gathering

The community-focused evaluators operated within a much more informal environment. Instead of meeting face-to-face across a desk or room, they met in circles and clusters under trees, in courtyards, or on the street. HDP community development staff in each village, responsible for initiating village-level planning for the evaluation, had agreed upon a common strategy during the preparation stage. As a result, the two- to three-day agenda was the same at each site.

Meeting with Counterpart Evaluators

The agenda opened with a half-day session with the counterpart evaluators. In this meeting, the counterpart evaluators spoke in depth about the evolution of the community development process and how they became involved. They displayed "social maps" portraying neighborhoods within the village and plotting the visible results of the community development process.

Presentation of Social Maps

The maps portrayed such features as latrines, vented stoves, irrigation projects, neighborhood water taps, beehives, bamboo plantations, reforestation zones, and health facilities.* The authors had signed their names at the bottom of each map. Some groups had made use of symbols in their maps and shown the actual number of households, latrines, stoves, and so on in a box at the bottom of the sheet. In others, every single house, stove, latrine, irrigation canal, water tap, and so forth was accurately represented. In one village, members of the neighborhood groups had taken the additional step of analyzing their maps from a "before HDP" and "after HDP" standpoint and presenting

---

* The maps were created by the villagers themselves using a participatory rural appraisal (PRA) technique, a user-friendly methodology for illiterate and semiliterate populations.

Table 8.2: Abridged "Before HDP/After HDP" Chart Prepared by Villagers from Babiyachaur

"Before HDP"	"After HDP"
Most people used thumbprint to sign name	90% of the people can sign their name
No vented stoves	210 households have vented stoves
No more than 4 latrines in village	50 latrines in use
Women were not permitted to attend group meetings	Mostly women participate in the meetings
Ordinary people (non–high caste) not accustomed to talking with outsiders	People feel comfortable talking with everybody
Ordinary people did not know about banking	All the banking papers are kept by the village groups themselves
Tailoring was done only by Damai caste	Anyone interested trains as a tailor
Moneylenders charged up to 60% per annum interest on loans	Villagers have their own savings and loan program (low interest)
Little contact with government and non-government service agencies	Organized for services of line agencies
No irrigation ditch for kitchen garden	Ditch for kitchen garden completed

the results on a separate flip-chart sheet. An abridged version of this chart is shown in Table 8.2.

The core evaluators used this information as a "springboard" for their community research. They huddled around the social maps with the counterpart evaluators and heard how the various activities unfolded—how the villagers identified the problems, arrived at a solution, found the resources, and organized themselves to carry out the work.

Community Walkabouts

Having analyzed the social maps, the evaluators and their community counterparts went on a "walkabout"—usually within the same neighborhood examined in the map. Along the way, team members stopped to talk with villagers active in the project, as well as those not involved. They sat in the middle of community-controlled forest conservation areas and learned about the measures taken by the community to curb deforestation. They stood in front of contaminated water sources about to be transformed into secure tap systems. They witnessed literacy classes in progress and asked the students about their lives, why they had joined these two-hour evening classes, and what they hoped would be different in their lives once they could read, write, and use numbers. And, upon invitation, the evaluators peered into kitchens to see the vented stoves and asked the owners why they had chosen to switch from the open fireplace to this new stove technology. In some households, they asked the opposite—why families had not chosen to adopt a vented stove or latrine.

Debriefing Evenings

Most nights, the community and district evaluators (both core evaluators and counterpart evaluators), as well as the resource persons, sat to go over the day's observations to glean insights. When possible, the community and district evaluators combined their debriefing sessions to keep each other apprised of the emerging picture of HDP capacity building. At times, the facilitator of the debriefing session (this responsibility shifted from person to person) encouraged the team members to relate observations to the spiral model. Often, particularly toward the end of the field research, this happened naturally.

The debriefing sessions set the stage for the next day's research. Participants would often become aware of gaps in knowledge and therefore plan to seek answers at the next opportunity. Sometimes, the district evaluators asked the village-level evaluators to gather health-related information from the village. In one situation, for example, the district evaluators asked the village-level evaluators to find out how villagers felt about the two-rupee registration fee charged by health post staff for every medical consultation.

Local Feedback Assembly

During the final day in each VDC, the evaluators ended their research with village assemblies. The purpose of the assembly was threefold:

- To seek verification and further analyze insights gained by the core evaluators while in the village;
- To give the counterpart evaluators an opportunity to ask questions of their peers about the progress of the locally organized groups and the value of their initiatives to date; and
- To share the impressions gained by the core and counterpart evaluators and reinforce the values underlying the community development effort.

In each of the three VDCs, more than 100 people came for the two-hour meeting, which combined small-group discussions with a plenary. The format for the small-group sessions emerged from outstanding questions or issues from the time spent in the village. Sometimes, the topics were thematic—for example, the changing roles of men and women, or agriculture and forests. Sometimes, the groups were drawn together by neighborhood affiliation for a broader discussion of the community development process as seen from that geographic vantage point. The spiral model of capacity building was not

Summary of the Surkhet District Debriefing

The district evaluating group performed a three-part skit; each part addressed a different aspect of the district health system—the hospital, the health post, and the Regional Training Centre. After the skit, the head of the district health post commented on the observations presented, concurring with the findings and stating that he worked with severe resource constraints. The village counterpart evaluators responded to the skit with their perspectives on the delivery of health services. They pointed to a lack of awareness among villagers about how to use medicine and the lack of trained staff at the health post; they stressed the need for a preventative emphasis, and noted the effect of the stove and latrine construction activities in helping villagers understand health issues.

The village counterpart evaluators performed a three-part skit to convey their experience with the community development process. Scene One was an early community meeting where the men and women would not sit in a circle despite the facilitator's urging. Most of the women covered their faces, speaking their names into their clothes. The men also had trouble saying their names. Scene Two opened with the men and women sitting in a circle. Each person stood up and clearly stated his or her name. They demonstrated that everybody in the circle could sign her or his name with a signature rather than a thumbprint. In Scene Three, the players recreated discussions around the formation of local savings and credit groups and illustrated their newfound confidence to stand up to moneylenders who charge high interest rates.

The meeting ended with an allegory about a musk deer that constantly went in search of a certain aroma, only to find that the aroma came from its own body. As the HDP's district manager put it in his closing remarks, "sometimes we don't realize our own strengths."

incorporated into the discussion with villagers. Rather, the presentations built upon the social mapping and other analysis already completed by the counterpart evaluators within the community prior to the core evaluators' arrival.

Stage IV: Synthesis and Reporting

Intrinsic to the design of the process evaluation is the idea that all stakeholder groups participating in design and research should also be part of a report-back process. Thus, in the VDC, the visit ended with the village assembly described above.

Prior to leaving Surkhet, HDP field staff organized a one-day debriefing meeting for all those participants who had attended the initial Surkhet orien-

---

Summary of Kathmandu Feedback Session

In preparation for this meeting, the core evaluators drafted mini reports—one for each stream of project activity and one for the HDP as a whole. These reports organized evaluation findings, insights, and constraints and enablers by the key questions originating with the spiral model of capacity building. This meeting was attended by all HDP program staff and managers, the representatives of the IOM, and the Ministry of Health. The reports were read over and discussed at the meeting, as were a series of draft recommendations.

---

tation two weeks earlier—the village counterpart evaluators, Ministry of Health officials, HDP staff, and core evaluators.

Another feedback session was held in Kathmandu, following which the evaluators revised the reports and used them as a basis for writing a draft document.

A presentation and feedback session was held in Calgary for the HDP Advisory Group and the Division of International Development. The draft was then circulated among project staff and CIDA for comment and action before being finalized in its current form.

Presentation of Major Findings

The evaluators concluded that progress in the capacity-building process has been uneven across the three streams of project activity—community, district, and physician training. The HDP has been more successful in stimulating "bottom-up" development with the VDCs than in stimulating "top-down" development with the Ministry of Health.

The spiral model is used to illustrate the degree of capacity building observed. Figures 8.4 and 8.5 provide a sample representation of the findings for the community development and the district health streams of activity. The spiral is positioned on the right-hand side of each figure. Indicators of capacity building are listed on the left-hand side, corresponding to the five zones of the capacity-building process—mobilization, planning and organization, learning, diffusion, and institutionalization. Those indicators written in plain bold text represent findings observed by the evaluators. Indicators written in italics represent other expected findings or situations that were *not* observed by the evaluators.

Capacity Building in the Community Stream of Activities

In the community stream, the evaluators found that initiatives are on the brink of sustainability and need short-term support to consolidate indepen-

Figure 8.4: Capacity Building Observed in the Community Stream of Activities

Indicators—Community Stream
- Change—social patterns
- Change—codes of conduct
- Established cooperative

- Replication
- Interaction effects
- External requests
- Expansion teams

- Access to new resources
- Technical skills
- Organizational skills
- Shifts in power

- Plans of action
- Cross-village discussion
- Gender and caste balance
- New use of resources

- Widening participation
- Inclusiveness
- Willingness to meet
- Individual curiosity

Figure 8.5: Capacity Building Observed in the District Stream of Activities

Indicators—District Health Stream
- *Replication by MOH*
- *MOH/NGO collaboration*
- *Policy change in MOH*
- *Change in management*

- *Spread in adoption of changes*
- **Identifiable "products"**
- **Requests for "products"**

- *Peer learning*
- *Follow-up application*
- **Skill development**
- **Congruent with need**

- **Collaboration with others**
- **Learner participation**
- **Priority need**

- **Joint vision and plan**
- **Work with the MOH**
- **Rapport-building time**

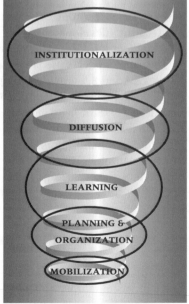

dent, proactive local organizations. The spiral diagram (Figure 8.4) documents the presence of indicators of capacity building in each zone up to and including institutionalization.

Evidence suggests that the community development process has:

- Heightened the level of confidence among villagers;
- Built a stronger sense of community identity;
- Created a vigorous democratic decision-making structure;
- Trained villagers in community leadership (e.g., problem solving, conflict resolution, and planning), and in a variety of technical skills (e.g., stove and latrine construction, beekeeping, forest conservation, literacy, and community banking);
- Attracted attention among increasing numbers of people within the VDCs (at the time of the evaluation, between a quarter and a half of all families across the three VDCs were active participants in community development activities);
- Enthused neighboring communities about the community development process (indeed, expansion from VDC to VDC has been influenced much more by villager demand than through promotion by project staff);
- Engendered new ways of thinking about personal health and hygiene, resource conservation, gender and caste relations, community organization, and the role of external development service providers (i.e., line agencies and NGOs); and
- Matured to a point where two of the three VDCs are ready to form their own independent associations.

External Factors Influencing Community Capacity Building

Following the spiral model, the evaluators noted the major constraints and enablers influencing the capacity-building process at the community level, for example:

1. *Ecological issues as an enabler.* Villagers are acutely aware of the disappearance of protective vegetation and soil erosion. Forestry groups, which have been established in all five VDCs, have established relationships with the Ministry of Forestry, designated zones for reforestation, planted trees, hired wardens, and established village bylaws (with enforcement) to control access and use. Villagers are also cutting back on their consumption of firewood, both because of the increasing scarcity of the resource and because of the lower fuel needs of the new vented stove.
2. *The country's political and administrative situation as both an enabler and a constraint.* The restoration of a multiparty democracy in 1991 with its commitment to decentralization created new openness toward local-level planning and management. However, embedded features of the political/administrative system continue to constrain the process, notably the lack

of readiness or ability of the line agencies, including the Ministry of Health, to respond to local participation.

3. *Long-standing economic conditions as a constraint.* The VDCs are located in food-deficit areas; those families that have not been able to grow enough food for themselves or find local work rely on work outside Surkhet, often in India. Lack of income undermines people's ability and time to participate in group discussion and inhibits risk taking. HDP field staff have approached this problem through microenterprise and savings and credit schemes.

4. *Local history and attitudes toward outside development organizations as a constraint.* The HDP has had to overcome a strong tendency among villagers to see the project as another "provider" of service. The rise and fall of participation levels in the community development process may be symptomatic of this tendency. As is typical of many projects, HDP staff have had to continually balance the need to engage villagers in their own problem solving with the need to achieve visible results/success, which in turn builds local support for the process.

Capacity Building in the District Stream of Activities

The evaluators found that the district management strengthening outputs, while well planned and received by the Ministry of Health and others, are not close to institutionalization. The spiral diagram (Figure 8.5) reflects the evaluators' observations that while there is some diffusion of learning as a result of project activities, there does not appear to be lasting change in the way the district health system functions.

In general, the HDP's district health initiatives have yielded:

- Successful activities designed to strengthen the District Public Health Office, such as annual report writing and the training of 140 traditional birth attendants affiliated with the health posts;
- Innovative and tested in-service training packages for all health post staff based on needs assessments—these packages have been used beyond Surkhet;
- Improved collaboration and coordination among regional and district health professionals and community-level staff;
- Efficiently functioning drug schemes in all health posts in the district; and
- A new district hospital facility.

Activities appear to have been carefully identified and implemented in collaboration with key Ministry of Health officials, as highlighted in the lower two zones of the spiral. However, the results of these activities have not, with the exception of the drug schemes, had a lasting impact on the Surkhet District health system. There has been very little diffusion of new skills, attitudes, or behaviors within the health system.

External Influences on District Capacity Building

External constraints clearly influenced the district stream of activities. The lack of diffusion in building institutional capacity can be attributed largely to the following factors:

- Frequent transfers of staff in and out of the district health system;
- Continuing scarcity of financial resources for health programming;
- Sweeping changes to the organizational structure of the Ministry of Health;
- A host of historical-cultural factors influencing the way the bureaucracy works; and
- Lack of skilled planning, given the limited resources available.

The evaluators concluded that, in view of transfer and appointment practices, it is unlikely that the gap between ministry policies and the implementation will be closed in the near future, and they recommended that the HDP reconsider the types of assistance that would be most fruitful in strengthening capacity building at the district level. In particular, the evaluators recommended that the project adopt methods for strengthening *local* management and staffing of health posts and the district hospital.

Reflections and Conclusions on Process Evaluation

The process evaluation methodology enabled the evaluators to look behind the visible outputs of the project—grassroots decision making, latrines, training curricula for health post staff—to find evidence of the HDP's capacity-building effect both on the communities and on the district health offices and facilities in this hilly, remote district of Nepal.

The methodology also encouraged the evaluators to appreciate the interaction effects both among individual project activities (e.g., savings and credit, literacy training) and between each of the three streams of activity (community development, district health strengthening, and generalist physician training).

Process evaluation allowed the team to identify indicators of capacity building in all three streams. It gave project implementers, from village to management level, exposure to evaluation as a relevant tool for quality control. It helped project stakeholders articulate a conceptual framework underlying the HDP—the spiral model of capacity building.

The following is a list of lessons learned from this first application of the process evaluation methodology. Lessons are arranged under the four characteristics of the methodology described earlier in the chapter.

Use of a Conceptual Model

- The model can be used to analyze a single activity, multiple activities, or the project as a whole.

- The narrower the scope of the analysis, the deeper the analysis.
- The team must be comfortable with all conceptual tools prior to fieldwork.
- Orientation is critical for building the team dynamic necessary for effective fieldwork and for understanding the conceptual model and translating it into a specific evaluation plan.

Reliance on Participatory Strategies

- The responsibility for evaluation design and management should be shared among stakeholders. If people know how they can contribute to the planning and management of the evaluation, and are keen on the exercise, they will offer their creative input. Participatory design and management, however, require good rapport and communication.
- People's participation in the process of evaluation itself builds individual capacity.
- Staff can offer a depth of understanding about subject matter.
- Staff can sometimes be put in compromising situations and might inhibit research activities and/or perceptions of nonstaff evaluators.
- Participatory evaluation is much less threatening than conventional evaluation, since it bridges cultures, staff with nonstaff, and local with external.
- Participation of local people as evaluators allows questions to be translated into village-level terminology and seems to increase the comfort level in the discourse that follows.
- Evaluators cannot assume that all stakeholders are able to analyze situations in a critical manner; some stakeholders are more analytical, others more descriptive—they should be allowed to complement one another.
- Evaluation teams should have a person designated as a process facilitator or manager to ensure that positive group dynamics are maintained.

Adoption of Participatory Appraisal Techniques

- Within a team, roles should be clearly delineated ahead of time. For example, are staff to be evaluators or resource persons? Who translates and interprets? Who leads off in the information-gathering session?
- It is important to critique one another's roles throughout evaluation.
- Evaluation team members should learn as much as possible about the others' strengths and weaknesses. In sharing responsibilities, the team should draw on member strengths.
- Everyone on a team should take notes.
- The team should keep a set of combined notes from debriefing sessions.
- Daily team debriefings and planning are *essential* to manage the tremendous amount of information that is collected.
- Evaluators should always refer to the conceptual model and accompanying questions when debriefing and planning for fieldwork
- It is important to make the team as inconspicuous as possible. Large numbers and "loud" presence get in the way of good information gathering.

- Accidental interviews are an important means of getting "backstage" information and a broader context for research findings.
- Social mapping is very valuable for collecting both quantitative and qualitative information from groups. Mapping is visual, participatory, and evocative.
- Using an existing body of information (e.g., a social map) can help focus inquiry.

Use of a Qualitative Approach
- Process evaluation is most effective if the methodology is designed for ongoing use from the outset of the project or activity.
- Process evaluation is a learning methodology; the more times it is practiced, the more competently it can be carried out.
- Process evaluation tends to make explicit what is known implicitly.
- Process evaluation is cost-effective if integrated into strategic planning and management of the project; otherwise it appears costly in terms of time and funds.
- Since project implementers are participants in the evaluation, the leap to planning and management is a small one.

The cycle of synthesis and reporting (which was repeated in Surkhet, in Kathmandu, in Calgary, and in the draft and final process evaluation reports) served to clarify the findings and facilitate the rapid implementation of changes in the management of the project. By the time the final document was issued, after one year, most of the recommendations had been addressed. In a sense, the earlier phases of the synthesis and reporting accomplished most of what was expected of an evaluation, while the final document serves as polished reference material.

Having used the process evaluation methodology once, the evaluators believe that it can be used repeatedly throughout a project. Each time the methodology is applied, either for ongoing monitoring (where the focus is on operational effectiveness) or for periodic evaluation (where the focus is on progress toward the project purpose), the framework evolves. This evolution occurs, over time, as conditions change and stakeholders learn about the effects of their capacity-building endeavors.

Costs of the Methodology

- Process evaluation involves a large number of individuals, from both the project setting and overseas. In the HDP, approximately twenty-seven people participated from Surkhet District (twenty from the communities, four from the district health system, and three from the HDP field office), eight from Kathmandu, and three from North America. It is estimated that the process evaluation took a total of 560 person-days to complete, an average of twenty days per person.

- The duration of the process evaluation is uncertain, as it depends on the readiness of the project staff and beneficiaries to fully participate alongside the external evaluators. In the case of the HDP, the exercise lasted twelve months from commencement of preparations in November 1993 to preparation of the draft evaluation report in October 1994. Intensive involvement lasted three months, from mid-January to mid-April 1994. As this first application of the process evaluation included the initial design work, subsequent applications would likely consume less time.
- Process evaluation is somewhat "messy," as it depends on the speed with which participation occurs—it cannot be rushed to meet the time lines of external evaluators. It may be as costly as a conventional evaluation or even more so, particularly when more individuals are involved and there is a higher total contribution of time. In the HDP evaluation, costs were comparable to those incurred by CIDA for regular end-of-project evaluations.
- In the absence of a conventional evaluation, the process evaluation methodology may have to be supplemented with surveys designed to provide information on items such as sources and uses of funds, audit procedures, allocation and costing of inputs, and authority and responsibility within the organization.

Benefits of the Methodology

- Process evaluation methodology supports the trend toward results-based management. It extends the emphasis beyond the traditional focus on outputs toward longer-term results. Process evaluation methodology helps managers gain maximum benefit from the interplay between action and reflection.
- The methodology is flexible enough to be used for short-term project monitoring and for long-term evaluation. It can inform the project of short-term operational issues as well as longer-term strategic issues. Put another way, it can be developed for use in measuring progress in relation to outputs, as well as progress in relation to the broader indicators of replicability and sustainability.
- Process evaluation is sensitive both to the concrete project outputs and to the less tangible human dynamics (individual and organizational change) that form the backdrop to the outputs.
- Because all of the primary stakeholders (those whose lives and work are directly affected by the interventions of the project) are active in the conduct of the process evaluation, it is relatively easy for recommendations that flow from the evaluation to receive full support and be quickly implemented. In the HDP, a number of the recommendations from the process evaluation were acted upon during preparation of the draft final report.

References

Bista, D. 1991. *Fatalism and Development: Nepal's Struggle for Modernization.* Calcutta: Orient Longman.

Davis-Case, D., ed. 1991. *The Community's Toolbox: The Idea, Methods and Tools for Participatory Assessment, Monitoring and Evaluation in Community Forestry.* Rome: Food and Agriculture Organization.

Freedman, J. 1994. "Participatory Evaluations: Making Projects Work." Technical Paper No. TP 94/2. Division of International Development, International Centre, University of Calgary.

Grandstaff, T. B., and D. A. Messerschmidt. 1993. "Manager's Guide to the Use of Rapid Rural Appraisal." Farm Management and Production Economics Service, Agricultural Services Division, Food and Agriculture Organization of the United Nations, draft.

———. 1995. *Manager's Guide to the Use of Rapid Rural Appraisal.* Bangkok: Food and Agriculture Organization of the United Nations.

Justice, J., H. Dixit, D. Harding, and P. Cox. 1995. "Process Evaluation of the Nepal Health Development Project: Final Report." University of Calgary, International Centre.

Messerschmidt, D. A. 1993. "Rapid Appraisal for Community Forestry: The RA Process and Rapid Diagnostic Tools." Institute of Forestry, Pokhara, Nepal.

———. 1995. *Rapid Appraisal for Community Forestry: The RA Process and Rapid Diagnostic Tools.* IIED Participatory Methodology Series. London: International Institute for Environment and Development.

Purdey, A. F., G. B. Adhikari, S. Robinson, and P. Cox. 1994. "Participatory Health Development in Rural Nepal: Clarifying the Process of Community Empowerment." *Health Education Quarterly* 21 (3): 329–43.

Robinson, S., and P. Cox. 1995. "Process Evaluation in Health Development: Tracking the Results of Capacity Building." Technical Paper No. TP 95/1. Division of International Development, International Centre, University of Calgary.

Robinson, S. A., P. Cox, I. G. Somlai, A. Purdey, and B. R. Prasai. 1997. "Process Evaluation: A Field Method for Tracking Those Elusive Development Results." *Canadian Journal of Development Studies* 18: 805–34.

———— 9 ————

Participatory Evaluation in Human Resource Development: A Case Study from Southeast Asia

Gary Anderson and Deborah Gilsig

Participatory evaluation is typically thought of as an overall attribute that any evaluation has to a greater or lesser extent. In reflecting on the concept of participation, we are inclined to believe that such a unidimensional characterization does not capture the complexity of many evaluations that have varied levels of participation by a wide array of stakeholders. Indeed, we feel that all evaluations have participation to some extent, and that the important thing is to analyze participation on each evaluation component. That is, the concept of participation is best understood in relationship to the various stakeholder groups in any evaluation, combined with a consideration of suitable levels of participation of these different stakeholders with respect to particular evaluation issues. In some evaluations there is equal participation from funders and beneficiaries; in other cases participation is delegated or unequal. When the purpose of evaluation is to extend the effects of the development project, equal participation has advantages, but when there is a focus on compliance, for example, unequal participation may better serve evaluation requirements. These differences suggest the need to define which forms and levels of participation are advantageous for particular issues and which are not appropriate. Furthermore, differential degrees of participation are consistent with aspects of contemporary evaluation thinking that emphasize the importance of stakeholder perspectives as they relate to the various evaluation questions (Guba and Lincoln 1989).

This chapter describes and analyzes our experience with a complex Canadian International Development Agency (CIDA) development project involving a dozen research and training centers in Southeast Asia and as many partner Canadian universities and colleges. It describes the evaluation and its methodology and concludes with a discussion of the implications of differential levels of involvement of different stakeholders in evaluation science.

The Southeast Asia Ministers of Education Organization

The Southeast Asia Ministers of Education Organization (SEAMEO) was founded in November 1965, for the purpose of promoting regional cooperation in education, science, and culture in its member countries. According to its charter, SEAMEO carries out this mandate in order to further respect for justice and the rule of law and for the human rights and fundamental freedoms that are birthrights of the peoples of the world. The organization has translated this vision of the benefits of peace, prosperity, and security through enlightened citizens into cooperative efforts in education, science, and culture.

Over the past thirty years, SEAMEO has focused on human resource development in the region through provision of short-term and long-term training courses, seminars, workshops, international and regional conferences, and information dissemination activities. Such programs are implemented through SEAMEO's twelve regional centers, which are located in various participating countries. There is a diverse range of specialization among the centers, from tropical biology and tropical medicine to educational innovation and technology, from science and mathematics to archaeology and the fine arts (see Table 9.1).

The SEAMEO-Canada Program of Cooperation in Human Resource Development

Since 1970, Canada has been involved in SEAMEO as one of five associate members, contributing financial and operational support that has averaged $1.5 million per year since 1985, when Phase I of the SEAMEO-Canada program of cooperation began. That year, the SEAMEO Pilot Project for Integrated Community-based Human Resource Development was launched under the financial assistance of CIDA. The five-year project (1985–1989) provided $9.5 million for regular program support and institutional cooperation.

Phase II of the program (1990–1995) provided a Canadian financial contribution of $7.1 million to SEAMEO in support of its regular training programs and to strengthen the institutional capacity of the SEAMEO centers and the organization's Secretariat (SEAMES). Project funds provided three main types of inputs:

- Financing for the regular training programs and activities of SEAMEO centers, thereby providing approximately 1,000 short- and long-term training opportunities;
- Institutional linkages that supplied technical assistance, training (in Canada and at the centers), equipment, and materials support in order to strengthen the institutional capacities of SEAMEO centers; and
- Canadian technical assistance to SEAMES to help develop its strategic management capacities.

Table 9.1: SEAMEO Regional Centers

SEAMEO Center	Canadian Partner	Specialization	Location
BIOTROP	University of Quebec at Rimouski	Tropical Biology	Indonesia
INNOTECH	Saskatchewan Institute of Applied Sciences and Technology	Educational Innovation and Technology	Philippines
RECSAM	University of British Columbia	Education in Science and Mathematics	Malaysia
RELC	York University English Language Learning Institute	Regional Language Center	Singapore
SEARCA	University of Guelph	Graduate Study and Research in Agriculture	Philippines
SPAFA	Collège Edouard Montpetit	Archaeology and Fine Arts	Thailand
TROPMED/ Indonesia	University of Manitoba	Tropical Medicine and Public Health	Indonesia
TROPMED/ Malaysia	University of Ottawa	Tropical Medicine and Public Health	Malaysia
TROPMED/ Philippines	Memorial University of Newfoundland	Tropical Medicine and Public Health	Philippines
TROPMED/ Thailand	University of Calgary	Tropical Medicine and Public Health	Thailand
VOCTECH	Humber College of Applied Arts and Technology	Vocational and Technical Information	Brunei Darussalam
RIHED	RIHED did not have a linkage partner	Higher Education and Development	Thailand
RTC	RTC did not have a linkage partner	Human resources development needs of Indochina	Vietnam
SEAMOLEC	SEAMOLEC did not have a linkage partner	Open learning and distance eduction	Indonesia

The funding to support SEAMEO regular programs was managed directly by SEAMES; however, SEAMES subcontracted certain lead Canadian universities and colleges to manage and administer institutional strengthening projects at SEAMEO centers.

The Evaluation

The evaluation discussed in this case (Universalia 1995) was conducted in the fifth, and final, year of the project and was intended to provide information to SEAMES, CIDA, its Project Advisory Committee (PAC), and the involved SEAMEO centers, the main general project stakeholders. In conjunction with its ongoing strategic planning efforts, SEAMES continually undertakes analyses of its work, so the evaluation was designed to provide information that could guide future SEAMEO capacity development. The design also had to account for the fact that the evaluation was being undertaken, in part, to fulfill the conditions of the agreement between CIDA and SEAMES and to provide accountability for CIDA's investment in the project. Hence, the challenge for the evaluators was to successfully mix the agendas of project understanding and compliance using a participatory methodology. The major evaluation questions and issues can be summarized as follows:

1.   To what extent did the project in general represent a sound development investment?
1.1 Did it have a sound rationale from the perspectives of CIDA and SEAMEO?
1.2 Was the project efficiently implemented?
1.3 What were its effectiveness and effects in developing organizational capacities of SEAMEO? Do these effects represent good value for dollar?

2.   To what extent did the institutional linkages help develop the capacities of the involved SEAMEO centers?
2.1 Did they help centers to understand their internal and external environments?
2.2 Did they help develop needed center capacities?
2.3 Did they contribute to center performance?

3.   To what extent was support for the regular SEAMEO training programs worthwhile?
3.1 What were graduates' perceptions of its efficiency, effectiveness, and effects in making specialists more competent in their jobs?
3.2 Did the investment in regular training programs improve their quality in a sustainable way?

Methodology

The approach involved various stakeholder groups in different levels of participation under the overall guidance and direction of the external evaluators from Universalia. Participatory evaluation methodologies were viewed as a learning process in which evaluation stakeholders gained a better perspective of the project and its relationship to the organization. We defined the participatory component of this evaluation as a process in which the various stakeholders worked with us, the independent evaluators, and contributed to defining the evaluation mandate, as well as participating in the data collection and analysis. The responsibility for producing the actual report, its conclu-

Table 9.2: Summary of Major Stakeholders and Their Roles

Stakeholder	Principal Role	Major Activities
CIDA	• Defining evaluation questions related to compliance • Receiving the evaluation report and acting on its recommendations	• Facilitating implementation of the evaluation • Providing data • Providing feedback on draft report
Project Advisory Committee (PAC)	• Acting as the mandated authority • Commissioning the evaluation and receiving its reports	• Approving the terms of reference • Discussing the draft report • Receiving and approving the final report
SEAMEO/ SEAMES	• Facilitating data collection • Assuming responsibility for data collection from training of graduates • Providing data • Assisting with interpretation of analyses	• Helping design training graduate survey questionnaire • Distributing and collecting surveys • Providing data on project implementation
SEAMEO Centers	• Participating and assisting in data collection • Providing data • Assisting with interpretation of analyses	• Helping design training graduate survey questionnaire • Distributing and collecting surveys • Conducting center self-assessments • Providing data on project effectiveness, effects, and impacts • Interpreting data on project effectiveness, effects, and impacts
Canadian Institutions (Colleges and Universities)	• Providing data • Providing feedback on draft report	• Providing data on project effectiveness, effects, and impacts, and implementation through interviews and Canadian Technical Assistant Questionnaire
SEAMEO Training Graduates	• Providing data	• Completing Regular Program Graduate Questionnaire

sions, and recommendations rested with the independent evaluators, with input from all stakeholders. The major stakeholders and a summary of their roles are shown in Table 9.2. All of the stakeholders took part in the process by providing data, and each of the stakeholders participated in one or more of the other evaluation activities: developing of the terms of reference, making

Table 9.3: Summary of Data Collection

Source of Data	Data Collection Instrument	Proposed Sample	Actual Sample as % of Proposed (Actual #)	
SEAMEO Centers	Center Self-Assessment Guide	12 centers + SEAMES	92%	(12)
	SEAMEO-CIDA Project Questionnaire	12 centers	100%	(12)
SEAMEO Center Staff Trainees	Center Staff Trainee Questionnaire	n/a		(56)
CIDA Project Team Leaders (PTLs)	Interview	Former & current PTLs	100%	(2)
Canadian Institutions	Telephone Interview	13 project heads	84%	(12)
Canadian Technical Assistants (TAs)	Canadian Technical Assistant Questionnaire	68 Canadian TAs	59%	(42)
Chairs of SEAMEO Governing Boards	Questionnaire for Members of SEAMEO Governing Boards	12	75%	(9)
SEAMEO Center General Program Trainees	Regular Program Graduate Questionnaire	1,000 former trainees	53%	(533)
PAC Members, SEAMES, CIDA	Numerous interviews were conducted to collect data on the functioning of the PAC, project management, etc.			

revisions to the work plan, developing data-collection instruments, collecting data, analyzing data, and discussing and suggesting revisions to the evaluation report. Table 9.3 presents the major sources of data for the evaluation, with the instruments used and the response rates obtained.

The Process

Planning

Although Universalia had a primary role in the preparation of the evaluation work plan, there was participation from many of the stakeholders in both implicit and explicit ways.

CIDA, through its standards, procedures, and manuals, provided the policy guidelines for the terms of reference and work plan. CIDA also reviewed both documents to ensure that the donor's needs and interests would be met.

In planning the participation of the various other stakeholders in the process, their relationship to the major evaluation questions had to be given careful consideration. Proactive participation of the project stakeholders was primarily related to project effects and impacts, designed to help the various stakeholders increase their mutual understanding of the project and its implications for the future, as well as to refine and develop center strategies. However, questions relating to project efficiency and effectiveness were designed to generate data to be used primarily to assess project compliance and to enable CIDA to make decisions on further funding. For these reasons, participation of the other stakeholders for these issues was limited to providing data and assisting with interpretation rather than with making judgments.

Development of Data-Collection Instruments

A number of instruments were developed for this evaluation, namely, questionnaires and interview protocols. They are listed in Table 9.3. However, two of the instruments deserve particular attention, as they required significant participation from some of the stakeholders at one or more level: the Center Self-Assessment Guide and the Regular Program Graduate Questionnaire.

The Center Self-Assessment Guide was developed to assist SEAMEO centers in understanding their center, its context, future directions, and needs. Universalia developed this tool using a framework we developed with the International Development Research Centre (IDRC) for institutional assessment (Lusthaus, Anderson, and Murphy 1995). This framework focuses on four dimensions: the environmental context of the institution, institutional motivation, capacity, and performance. The self-assessment tool developed by Universalia for this evaluation was a fifty-page guide that provided a procedure and content to assist centers in conducting a thorough self-assessment of their capacities and performance, and a conceptual framework for centers to help refine and develop. A draft of the guide was discussed with selected center directors and then modified to be more usable in the SEAMEO context.

Over the last few years, centers have been conducting follow-up surveys of their regular training programs. However, there was no coordination between the centers on these efforts, making aggregate data analysis impossible. As well, response rates to these instruments were very low (seldom over 20 percent), so the data collected had minimal usefulness. The centers all expressed an interest in developing a more effective, standard way of collecting data. The evaluation presented an opportune time to do so, as Universalia's expertise in instrument-building and data-collection techniques complemented the centers' knowledge of their information needs and understanding of the population. Universalia reviewed all of the existing instruments the centers had been using in the past and produced a draft questionnaire, using the latest research on evaluating training programs (see Kirkpatrick 1994). Universalia met with the center directors in small groups and worked together to revise the draft so that it was appropriate in terms of content, language, and culture. This cooperation resulted in better questions and allowed the centers to gain ownership of the instrument, which will help ensure its future use.

The process of participation in building the instruments was a lengthy but essential element of participation that built understanding of the participants' diverse perspectives. The use of words was troubling, as many phrases and ways of asking for information that were suitable in Canada were confusing to those from different backgrounds. Canadians are often concerned with counts and quantification, which may be inappropriate in other parts of the world. Even within Southeast Asia there are wide differences: Singapore and the Philippines use English in daily life, while other countries do not; people from Thailand are reluctant to express critical views openly; most Southeast Asians are concerned with people being able to save face. The challenge is to build data-collection instruments that respect diversity while not making them so general that the data generated loses its meaning.

Data Collection

As mentioned earlier, all of the stakeholders provided data for the evaluation. SEAMES/SEAMEO, the centers, the Canadian institutions, and the graduates from the regular training programs provided data that pertained to project efficiency (compliance) issues; the centers, Canadian institutions, and regular training program graduates also provided data that related to project effects and impacts; and data for project effectiveness issues came from CIDA, SEAMES/SEAMEO, the centers, the Canadian institutions, and the regular training program graduates.

In addition, the centers participated in proactive data collection. It was the centers' responsibility to send out and collect the Regular Program Graduate Questionnaires. One thousand questionnaires were distributed to individuals who had participated in one or more training programs between 1991 and 1993. Fifty-three percent of the questionnaires were completed and returned to the centers, which forwarded them to Universalia for preliminary analysis. This response rate surpassed, by far, previous data-collection attempts by the centers. Their involvement in the design and distribution of the instrument was a contributing factor to this success, because it ensured that the questionnaire was relevant and culturally and linguistically appropriate for the trainees; the participants responded well to something from an institution that was already familiar to them. Once again, we feel that this success, experienced firsthand by the centers, gave them ownership of the process and has enhanced the chances of continuation of this data collection by individual centers.

Completion of the center self-assessments involved major data-collection and analysis activities within each center. Each center mobilized an assessment team, ranging in size from three to thirteen staff members (three-quarters of the teams were composed of more than six members). Team members reviewed key documents, talked to people involved at different levels in the center, observed facilities and activities, and observed interactions between people in different contexts (classroom, meetings, and so forth). They discussed their observations and had to develop a consensus on the different issues presented in the self-assessment guide. The centers then sent the completed guide to Universalia. It was a complex process in which centers participated with varying levels of effort, and this variance was reflected in the depth and quality of data collected. Those centers that put significant effort into the self-assessment indicated to us that they had learned a lot about their organization in terms of future directions and needs. At least one of the centers plans to make this a regular activity.

Data Analysis

Data analysis occurred at a number of levels, with varying degrees of participation with the stakeholders. The completed Regular Program Graduate Questionnaires were forwarded from the centers to Universalia for preliminary analysis because Universalia has in-house expertise in qualitative and quantitative analysis. Universalia conducted statistical and content analyses, and partway through the evaluation presented the data to the center directors at their annual meeting. The evaluation was planned to coincide with this meeting because it was the major midpoint at which stakeholders could contribute to the analysis. At the same time, Universalia presented the data from the Center Staff Training and Canadian Technical Assistant Questionnaires. The group analyzed and interpreted the data together to build a collective understanding of what it meant. It was an interesting experience for all involved, including Universalia, as it clearly demonstrated the role culture plays in judgments. For example, how much "agreement" with a Likert-scale item is enough? Does the required level vary from country to country? How are differences interpreted? A puzzling finding to us was that, when asked whether they would like to return for additional training, the vast majority of the questionnaire respondents said "yes," but a further question revealed that they would prefer to do so in a different center. We found it impossible to understand why a person who valued training in a particular center preferred to return to a center that specialized in another field. We were inclined to consider the result negative, whereas the Southeast Asians did not. In participatory evaluation, the emphasis is on building shared understanding, and discussing such culturally based findings is a good means of doing so. Comparative levels of performance of different training programs also uncovered cultural differences, because Southeast Asians do not easily relate to data that make colleagues appear less good. Although comparisons between centers were made, they ended up being buried in an appendix of the final report because of such cultural concerns.

Universalia collected the completed center self-assessments, reviewed them, and prepared summaries of each one, with a short analysis of concerns and priorities. We reviewed these summaries with the center directors at their annual meeting, however, it was not done as a group activity. The summaries were treated as confidential to the evaluation team and to the respective centers. Center directors met, individually, with a Universalia team member to discuss the self-assessments. After the annual meeting, the center directors took the summaries back to their assessment teams for review. There was subsequent ongoing communication with those centers that had comments to make, to ensure that the resulting analysis was correct and acceptable to the center. It was decided at this time that the self-assessments would not be included in the evaluation synthesis report, although aggregate findings were embedded in it, thus leaving it a significant part of the evaluation owned exclusively by the participants themselves. Neither CIDA nor SEAMES received copies of the self-assessments.

Center participation in the analysis of another evaluation component was sought—the CIDA Project Analyses. Universalia prepared summaries and analyses of the effectiveness and effects of the project in building capacity within the centers through the linkages, Canadian technical assistants, and center staff training. We used data from the SEAMEO-CIDA Project Questionnaire, completed by the centers, as well as from the Center Staff Trainee and Canadian Technical Assistant Questionnaires. The analyses were shared with the center directors, confidentially, at their annual meeting. Ideally, they would also have been shared with the Canadian partners at this stage, but it did not prove feasible to do so during the summer months, so that step came much later. As with the self-assessment summaries, each center director reviewed the CIDA Project Analysis with his or her staff and sent Universalia comments for incorporation.

In most cases in which centers sent back revisions on both the self-assessments and the CIDA Project Analyses, their comments were informative and valid. The participatory nature of these two components was important because the centers' self-assessments and responses to the SEAMEO-CIDA Project Questionnaires allowed them to contribute their in-depth knowledge of both their individual centers and how the project had affected them. However, Universalia's critique and questioning of their data from a perspective that looked at the project as a whole ensured that the concerns of other stakeholders were reflected in the analyses, making them more relevant to all stakeholders of the evaluation.

Final Report

Two types of documents were produced as a result of the evaluation. Each center had produced its own self-assessment, which was supplemented by our observations and critique. These documents were confidential to the individual centers and were not presented to all of the stakeholders.

The second major written output from the evaluation was the final evaluation report. It consisted of a synthesis document and three volumes of appendices. It was presented, in its draft form, to the PAC for discussion and review. At that time we learned an important lesson about the need to circumscribe roles of the involved stakeholders. As it turned out, the PAC had invited center directors and also project heads from Canadian institutions. It was the first time the latter group had been involved in more than providing data for the evaluation. Although some of the data and findings were familiar to the PAC and center directors because of their participation throughout the evaluation, none of the separate stakeholder groups had seen the overall analysis of the external evaluator, and most felt that their perspectives had been overshadowed by those of other stakeholders. In particular, most of those who had benefited from the project considered the results overly negative and much too centered on developing capacities that participants had agreed to initially but had difficulty achieving, rather than activities that may have been successful in isolation but did not contribute to capacity development in a sustainable way.

Evaluation Findings

The final evaluation report presented a number of findings related to the questions the evaluation set out to answer.

The project had been designed essentially as a continuation of previous practice (Phase I) supported by the CIDA context at the time of its inception. However, no in-depth needs assessment was done at the beginning of Phase II, and thus the design supported some components in inappropriate ways and missed opportunities to be more strategic. In addition, the context in which this project was conceived had changed dramatically over the five years of its implementation—changes in Canadian foreign policy and development assistance, social and economic developments in Southeast Asia, and SEAMEO's transition into a truly regional organization and the related changing roles of the centers. All of these changes significantly altered the continuing soundness of the rationale of such a project.

Although the project appears to have been effective in producing its intended outputs, achieving these outputs did not ensure realization of the purpose of the project: institutional strengthening. Effectiveness of project management was also limited for similar reasons—weak project design, inefficient management processes, and a lack of initiative by major players to take leadership and adapt the project in order to make it more effective in achieving its purpose.

The evaluation found that the successes of the linkage partnerships in building capacity in the centers varied widely. The choice of partners and their degree of compatibility played a large role in determining the success of the linkage. Another factor was the large turnover in project staff, including center directors and heads at the partnering Canadian institutions (eleven of the former and six of the latter have been replaced since the beginning of the project). Additionally, weaknesses in the project design limited the effectiveness of the linkages. However, institutional needs assessments in the individual centers may have compensated for the weak design and would have more clearly identified the individual needs of each center.

Overall, the responses of the regular training program graduates were quite positive. However, there were significant differences across centers. It also became evident that, with a few exceptions, the regular training at the centers was supply-side programming and was not highly relevant to the participants' jobs (the main exception being TROPMED/Philippines, which was very demand oriented and, with help from the linkage project, brought telemedicine technology to the islands). Although the project's investments into regular program training added some sustainable quality in a few of the centers, Canadian technical assistance and funds in this area served primarily as input substitution.

Results of the Evaluation Process

We feel that this evaluation, with its participatory components, built capacity within SEAMEO in two important ways. First, the process appears to have given the stakeholders a much deeper understanding of their organization (SEAMEO as a whole) and how it could link to Canada's development interests. This was reflected largely in the center directors' discussions about a possible Phase III of the CIDA project. In these discussions, which followed the evaluation process, the concepts are more demand driven than supply oriented. The thoughts are more strategic and present a thematic cut across centers, as opposed to support for centers as individual units. A more competitive or selective process for funding is also being considered by the center directors, reflecting an understanding that funding may not be available for all centers and will not be provided to be used for input substitution.

Second, it helped to build evaluation capacity. Some of the centers plan on using the self-assessment tool (or an equivalent) on a regular basis. A few of the centers are using the information gained from this process in their strategic planning. The centers' participation in the development of the questionnaire, data collection, and analysis for the regular training component gave them ownership of the process, and the success (higher rates of return and useful data) has encouraged them to continue using the instruments for future training reaction assessments.

Implications and Conclusions

When Is Participation Legitimate?

The major premise of this chapter is that the extent and nature of participation depend on the purpose of that participation. The case study illustrates one way of conducting a participatory evaluation when the concern is both to continue the development process and to evaluate project compliance. In the approach used, the evaluation partners had considerable freedom in some demarcated areas and limited input in others. This evaluation attempted to structure participation of the stakeholders with their varying interests in and degrees of concern about the evaluation issues in mind.

Essentially, the SEAMEO evaluation had three sets of issues that intersected with the legitimate concerns of the stakeholders—compliance, self-analysis, and understanding the effects on others. Compliance, in our view, is primarily the concern of the donor and requires an external and objective review in order to ensure accountability as demanded by donor policies and realities. This concern focuses on how well the project has been implemented and its effectiveness and effects as a way of enabling the donor to judge whether it has been a good investment from the donor's perspective. Thus, in donor-assisted projects, the benefits of involving beneficiaries in the generation of knowledge through participatory evaluation need to be balanced with the donor's separate need for accountability. This may be a Western paradigm, but it is a real one. In a context of severe fiscal constraint, donor governments and their publics are often skeptical of investments in distant projects, and self-reports may be an insufficient basis on which to continue project funding. The public demands accountability, and only an independent evaluation suffices. In contrast, if the goal is to engage beneficiaries in sustainable development, then full participation may be a better route.

The case incorporated what was actually an embedded evaluation: the center self-analyses. These complemented the ongoing strategic planning activities of the centers and were clearly an area where the centers owned the process and the data. They learned from the exercise, and they were able to decide whether or not it was in the center's interest to share it. The approach we used was similar to that incorporated in an impact evaluation of CIDA's project to construct a Natural Resources College in Malawi (Anderson 1989). In that evaluation project, a dozen senior faculty in the college worked with us to improve their knowledge of and skills in research methods and then applied this to the collection and analysis of data from college alumni employed throughout the country. The college development project had been completed several years before, so there was no need to revisit issues of compliance. The focus in that evaluation was on finding out the impact of the college graduates in rural development in the period since graduation, and it was useful for researchers from the North and from the South to help one another in understanding the answer to this complex question. Although all involved evaluators were keen to find out what had happened, few of the college personnel had been involved in the construction phase, so their concern with impact did not conflict with their role in execution of the project. Not so with the SEAMEO project, which stressed compliance as well as understanding. The answer to the evaluation questions in the SEAMEO case reflected directly on the performance of those who had been involved in compliance, so there were some aspects of the SEAMEO evaluation that were not considered part of the evaluation mandate of those from the involved centers and Canadian institutions. In both the Malawi and SEAMEO cases, we worked with project beneficiaries to develop a shared and mutually understood methodology that the local participants then implemented. They, not we, were the custodians of knowledge, and we benefited only to the extent that they were willing to share.

The third aspect, understanding the effects of the general training programs, was a legitimate concern of both SEAMEO and the donor, but from differing perspectives. The survey study of training graduates was an aspect in which the centers stood to benefit from knowing how their training was being received. The donor also had a legitimate concern, because the project had invested in this component. However, the center's concern was essentially formative, while the donor's was summative—the centers wanted to know how to improve the training; the donor wanted to know whether the training that had been delivered had made any development difference. The findings were positive from SEAMEO's perspective but negative from CIDA's. SEAMEO needed cash to continue conducting general training activities. This is an understandable need, and the CIDA project had succeeded in providing financial resources to this end in an efficient way. Efficiency, however, is but one concern. In this case, CIDA's investment did not further CIDA's interest in building sustainable local capacity for relevant training. Indeed, as the external evaluators concluded, support of the regular training component may have had overall negative effects because it postponed a strategic decision about the nature of this training that SEAMEO would have to make once the flow of donor funding was reduced. The perspective of the involved Southeast Asians was that this component served their needs and should be continued; however, the donor was concerned with developing sustainable capacities, not with providing money as a substitution for local inputs. In other words, the beneficiaries wanted resources with few conditions, while the donor wanted accountability for its agenda of sustainable development. Under such circumstances, the investor's perspective dominates, so it is the investor that needs to make the judgment on the value of continuing such a project component.

It is fundamental to participatory evaluation that those involved in the project or organization being evaluated are recognized as the "key custodians of knowledge" (Freedman 1994, 3) about the endeavor being evaluated. There is little doubt that the perspectives of such participants are valid for assessing effects and impact on them and their organizations, but there is considerable doubt that these stakeholders are able to pass judgment on many aspects of compliance. Any group, with the help of suitable data, is capable of assessing whether deliverables were in fact delivered and of judging whether they were provided in a timely way, but it is the investor, not the beneficiaries, that can say whether the investment met the investor's needs. Thus, the answer to questions about the development investment are fundamentally grounded in the purpose of the investment and how different stakeholders value different outcomes.

How Should Participation Be Shared?

Equal leadership is inherent in equal participation, but when there are differing areas of legitimate concern, participation is inherently unequal. This approach is not shared by everyone, as it reflects Rigg's (1991) contention that attitudes toward participation mirror the concerns participants have about top-down versus bottom-up management. Our main conclusion is that evaluators need to ensure that the various roles and responsibilities are well understood. Freedman (1994) notes the advantage of using existing groups in participatory evaluation. In this case, there were several different groups involved. However, the level of collective learning experience within each group varied widely, and those who had more experience gained more from, and contributed more significantly to, the evaluation. The PAC meets only once a year as a group and therefore had a limited role. The Canadian institutions have never met collectively, and it is for this reason that their participation was limited to providing data. Within each center, systems were already in place for group working and learning: The internal Strategic Planning Groups built upon their existing procedures by using the Universalia/IDRC framework on organizational capacity and performance to conduct a self-analysis of their centers. At the next level, the center directors worked collectively to link the results of individual self-assessments to an analysis of the whole organization and the relationship of the CIDA project to it. The center directors often meet as a group and are becoming a strong unit. Their collective involvement in instrument development and data analysis was very useful to the evaluation and increased their learning in the process.

One of the lessons we learned was the advisability in future work of this type of clarifying the roles of and demarcation between the groups. If each group of participatory evaluators knows what it is responsible for and how its work relates to that of other groups, then the results may come together more easily. In this case, we encountered difficulty when some groups tried to expand their roles to exert their influence at other levels. There were several noteworthy instances. First, we initially thought of including the center self-assessments as part of the overall evaluation report. However, the center directors made us realize that the self-assessments would be more candid and have more impact on the concerned centers if they were confidential to each center. We changed the initial plan and kept our feedback and the final self-assessment reports confidential between us and the center directors, and, in at least a couple of instances, these self-assessments had considerable impact on individual centers. Another example involved the PAC, which is a small group of individuals who have an arm's-length relationship to the centers and the Canadian universities and colleges. When the draft report was presented, however, all the center directors and several Canadian university project heads were present. While these guests were in fact observers, they raised questions about why they had not been consulted in advance on the overall conclusions. The overall conclusions were, of course, the legitimate concern of only the smaller PAC.

The notion of creating a common body of knowledge (Freedman 1994, 57) is a good one, but it is not necessary that every group of participants be involved in collecting all the information or even that people endorse the perspectives of the other groups. Once the information is shared, at least people can challenge it and, with supportive group processes, can use it to build their understanding of how others act on the common knowledge.

Goulet (1989) refers to participation being seen either as a goal or as a means. If it is intended to do nothing more than help in the analysis, it may represent yet another example of the dominant group exploiting the intended beneficiaries. If it is viewed as a legitimate extension of the development project, then it may be an excellent way to empower beneficiaries in a sustainable way.

Do the Costs Justify the Benefits of Participatory Evaluation?

The costs of participatory evaluation are structured differently from those in expert models. One difference is the requirement for a substantial investment in planning, training, and coaching. It allocates resources to the means of evaluation rather than applying resources directly to the tangible outcomes. While this may have greater long-term impact, it is clearly an investment in the future and needs to be understood as such, including the necessity for a longer period of time for the evaluation process to take place. Another difference is the cost of the time demanded of participants. It takes more of their time because they are involved, and also because they are typically involved in group processes that are inherently time-consuming. The dollar value of an investment in participatory evaluation may not appear any greater than that in expert evaluation, but the overall costs to society when people's time is included are undoubtedly much more.

The benefits are in building participants' capacities to understand the development efforts in which they are involved. Because capacity development is a lengthy and incremental process, the growth in human capacity is difficult to evaluate, but a growth in capacity is essential if beneficiaries are to assume control over their own destinies. Perhaps the solution is in viewing participatory evaluation as a legitimate part of the development project rather than as a separate component not generally charged to programming. If viewed in this way, then it could begin earlier, could legitimately demand participant time, and could itself be judged for its development impact rather than for its contribution to donor knowledge.

References

Anderson, G., ed. 1989. "Natural Resources College of Malawi: Impact Evaluation." Report on the Participatory Component of the NRC Evaluation. NRC, Lilongwe, and CIDA, Hull.

Freedman, J. 1994. "Participatory Evaluations: Making Projects Work." Dialogue on Development, Technical Paper No. TP94/2. International Centre, University of Calgary, Calgary.

Goulet, D. 1989. *Participation in Development: New Avenues*. Oxford: Pergamon Press.

Guba, E. G., and Y. S. Lincoln. 1989. *Fourth Generation Evaluation*. Newbury Park, Calif.: Sage Publications.

Kirkpatrick, D. L. 1994. *Evaluating Training Programs: The Four Levels*. San Francisco: Berrett-Koehler Publishers.

Lusthaus, C., G. Anderson, and E. Murphy. 1995. *Institutional Evaluation: A Framework for Building Organizational Capacity for IDRC's Research Partners*. Ottawa: IDRC.

Rigg, J. 1991. "Grass-roots Development in Thailand: A Lost Cause?" *World Development* 19 (2/3): 199–211.

Universalia. 1995. "Evaluation of SEAMEO-Canada Programme of Cooperation in Human Resource Development, Phase II." Universalia Management Group, Montreal.

——————— 10 ———————

Participatory Evaluation: Offering Kenyan Women Power and Voice

Bonnie B. Mullinix and Marren Akatsa-Bukachi

R esponsive, clear, and action-oriented evaluation usually addresses and balances three key questions and can be encapsulated as follows: *Who* wants to know *what* for *what purpose*?* As the many different whos, whats, and whys pull the evaluation process in different directions, it is often the voice of the client, beneficiary, or target participant that gets lost. In the rush to gather information and assess program impact, the needs and voices of donors and project implementers generally overpower those of the actual participants, and important information is lost.

This chapter provides the opportunity to discuss how this voice can be brought back into the process. In doing so, it addresses the definition, purpose, impact, and potential of participatory evaluation. To add implementation issues into the mix, the chapter also supplies an outline of a training program designed to provide field-workers with the skills and experience to facilitate participatory evaluation with women's groups.

What Is Participatory Evaluation?

Let's start this exploration with a definition provided by one of the Kenyan participants at the end of the second participatory evaluation workshop. In response to the question What is participatory evaluation? she wrote: "It is a democratic approach [for] examining the values, progress, constraints, and solutions of individuals, groups, or group activities by involving all people. It recognizes and values the subtle contributions of grassroots people, and grassroots workers plus the communities. And believes that all human beings are capable of receiving, and coming up with ideas which may be used to make

This paper was first presented at the Sixth Annual Conference on Ethnographic and Qualitative Research in Education, University of Massachusetts, Amherst, 1994. The paper was a product of input by the staff of the YWCA of Kenya through many workshops facilitated by Bonnie Mullinix.

* Dr. David Kinsey, Center for International Education, University of Massachusetts, Amherst, developed this structure in the early 1980s to help move beyond "why" (the classic third question) and have participants in evaluation address how they hope to utilize findings.

better their socioeconomic status—but as long as they are empowered to know and believe that they can be and are in control of their destiny."

While some may wish to polish or modify this definition, it is offered here because it captures several key aspects of participatory evaluation that make it different from traditional evaluation practices. It also reflects both the impact of the training program and the existing philosophical orientation of the guiding organization (the YWCA of Kenya).

What Makes Participatory Evaluation Different?

As captured in the above definition, participatory evaluation has certain characteristics that set it apart from evaluation that assigns a role to participants. These include:

- *Origin of purpose/questions:* Evaluation questions emerge from the interests and priorities of the participants.*
- *Extended usefulness/application:* Participants develop an understanding of the purpose and importance of evaluation and the ability to conduct meaningful evaluations.
- *Skills development:* Through participation in the evaluation activity, participants develop the ability to collect, analyze, and act on information.
- *Locus of control:* Involvement in participatory evaluation activity empowers participants to take responsibility for assessing and articulating the impact a project has had on them according to their priorities.

Basically, when done properly, participatory evaluation promotes empowerment, confidence, self-esteem, and independence.

A Context for Exploration and Application

Utilizing participatory evaluation requires a commitment to and understanding of the purpose and benefits it can bring to both a project and an organization. As a membership organization that balances the needs of its members against the requirements of donor agencies, the YWCA of Kenya is such an organization. It has struggled for many years with the failure of traditional evaluation mechanisms to adequately identify and address the impact of its programs. Established guidelines often dictated that the impact of a project be measured by the degree to which it affected the financial status of its participants. The collective experience of the staff of the YWCA of Kenya at village,

---

* The term *participants* refers to the women and men involved in and most directly affected by a project. As participants in the participatory evaluation process, field-workers are able to contribute concerns and questions from the NGO/donor community (provided they do not dictate and drive the procedure).

branch, and national levels told them that there was much more going on, and that donor focus and time frames were often too narrow to accurately capture the true impact of projects on women and their groups. Given the need to define its actions based on member input and the general support for institutional development provided by the United States Agency for International Development, the YWCA chose to explore participatory evaluation as a strategy for capturing some of this lost information. In articulating its rationale for this selection, the YWCA cites the need to identify what its members (not donors) believe to be important, as well as the desire to share the skills and capacity to conduct evaluation activities with the women.

A Structure for Implementing Participatory Evaluation

In order to adopt participatory evaluation as a key evaluation strategy, several things needed to happen:

1. Field-workers and YWCA staff needed to have the opportunity to explore what evaluation was in general, and what participatory evaluation was in particular.
2. They needed to reflect on and structure mechanisms for sharing what they had learned with members of women's groups.
3. They needed to spend time in the field conducting participatory evaluation.
4. If impact was to be measured, this activity would need to span at least two years.
5. If women were to appreciate the value of evaluation, activities had to be useful from the start.

In response to these requirements, a two-year scheme was structured. This began with a training workshop for field-workers and staff with a focus on evaluation as a needs assessment and planning tool. This workshop incorporated a three-day village-based training and evaluation exercise with three separate women's groups. The training introduction was designed by participants as a participatory activity that could help explain the purpose and importance of evaluation and have participants reflect on their group needs and possible action plans. Role plays, skits, case studies, and small-group activities provided effective mechanisms for generating understanding and ideas from within the group. From these initial ideas, the women generated questions and designed and carried out a research and evaluation activity to gather information and determine which course of action might be most beneficial to the group. This phase of the activity provided participants with an introduction to process and skills and a practical understanding of what participatory evaluation is and how it works.

The second phase of the activity took place a year later and focused on consolidation of skills and conduct of an impact evaluation. Participatory evaluators (trainees) designed participatory reflective processes utilizing memory-activation mechanisms (materials, reports, stories, and photographs from the year before) that allowed participants to fix a reference time in their minds. This collective experience and memory made it possible for them to look back on activities that had happened over the past year and consider the changes that they saw in their group, families, communities, and themselves. The resulting discussion of impact was both broad and powerful.

Training Support for Implementation

The following is an overview of the information and activities included in the Participatory Evaluation Training Workshop Series and field activities.

First Participatory Evaluation Training Workshop

The first workshop on participatory evaluation was an eight-day workshop for branch and national-level staff of the YWCA of Kenya and three women's groups in the Mombasa region. As it was considered to be the first in a two-part series of workshops, it focused on establishing a participatory evaluation practice that could be monitored and completed in nine to twelve months' time.

This first workshop then, maintained and met the following objective: to orient participants to evaluation in general and participatory evaluation in particular through training, discussion, and practical application of techniques. By the end of the workshop, participants had

1. Discussed definitions, purposes, and types of evaluation;
2. Listed the steps in evaluation and dimensions of evaluation;
3. Identified guidelines for conducting evaluation;
4. Discussed issues surrounding participatory evaluation;
5. Described a variety of evaluation tools and discussed their relative advantages and disadvantages;
6. Developed and implemented a participatory evaluation activity with a women's group;
7. Identified key issues and components of an evaluation plan for the YWCA of Kenya; and
8. Experienced a range of evaluation techniques and shared and evaluated their own experiences during the workshop.

Second Participatory Evaluation Workshop—Impact Evaluation

The second workshop on participatory evaluation was a five-day follow-up workshop for branch and national-level staff of the YWCA of Kenya and three women's groups in the Mombasa region. As the second part of the two-part series of workshops, it focused on helping the members of the women's groups to be able to assess and articulate changes in their group, individual, family, and community lives and identify the impact of group activities after twelve months.

The second participatory evaluation workshop had the following goals and objectives: to allow participants to conclude their exploration of participatory evaluation, identify field-generated indicators for success, determine reporting structures and mechanisms, and generally consider the importance of participatory evaluation as a tool for planning and impact assessment. By the end of the workshop, participants had

1. Conducted participatory evaluation follow-up with women's groups that had participated in the 1992 activities;
2. Utilized women's opinions as a basis for identifying indicators for evaluating impact;
3. Explored and utilized mechanisms for assisting in memory activation and access;
4. Developed a process for helping women's groups to collect, record, and analyze information that will allow them to evaluate group activities;
5. Determined guidelines for keeping staff journal entries and utilizing these for evaluating subtle indicators; and
6. Developed a basic format for and a written sample of evaluation reports.

Reporting Participatory Evaluation Findings

The primary products of the participatory evaluation activities were reports on the participatory evaluation of women's groups. The following format for participatory evaluation reports was produced by participants based on their field experience and data collected.

1. Introduction
   • Rationale/reason for evaluation
   • Description of methodology
   • Review of previous evaluations & findings
2. Background information on group to include
   • Location: division/district/province
   • Year when started
   • Membership
   • Year when joined YWCA
   • Other points of interest (as related by the group)
3. Summary/recommendations
4. Members' backgrounds to include
   • Age
   • Social status
   • Family size
   • Economic status

- Marital status
- Religious affiliation
5. Leadership structure
6. Group activities
   - Programs/projects/social, economic, educational activities
7. Resources/assistance provided
   - Technical assistance
   - Financial assistance
   - Educational assistance
     a) Trainings/seminars/workshops organized by
        - YWCA
        - Other governmental organizations/nongovernmental organizations (NGOs)
     b) Exchange visits/programs
8. Impact of activities (social/economic/educational/political)
   Benefits to group
   - Dividends
   - Soft loans
   - Merry-go-round
   - Training
   - Individual savings
   - Sharing ideas
   - Fellowship/moral support
   Benefits to individuals
   - Income (for business/self)
   - Promotion of business
   - Improved standard of living
   - Improved self-confidence
   - Status in/recognition by community
   Benefits to family
   - Increased income to family
   - Support from group
   - Improved standard of living
   Benefits to community
   - Service to community (committee membership)
   - Voting
   - Community support/role models
9. Group levels
   - Where they are now (present)
   - Where they were (past)
10. Future plans
    - For existing programs/projects
    - For new programs
    - For technical skills—trainings/seminars
11. Comments/observations

Evaluating Participatory Evaluation

Obvious questions arise about the comparative benefits and disadvantages of participatory evaluation versus traditional evaluation. Some of the more critical questions revolve around time to carry out an evaluation, the quality of the information collected, the training support required for evaluators (or evaluation assistants), and the readiness of participants. Since the YWCA had recent experience being trained in and conducting a traditional evaluation exercise, there was a direct basis for comparison that is used to highlight the generalized categories of concern.

Time. While it would seem that participatory evaluation may take more time, when compared with the time needed to administer individual questionnaires or interviews to a significant number of participants, initial appearances shift. For example, teams of two to three YWCA field staff spent an average of twenty to twenty-four hours with between nine and sixteen women collecting information about the group, its members, and its activities. A more traditional impact evaluation was carried out by two field staff and required contact with roughly five to six members of the women's groups on an individual basis, representing roughly fifteen to eighteen hours (one to one and a half hours initial interview plus one to one and a half hours impact interview). While many other issues exist, actual time and information coverage per participant were more effective in the case of participatory evaluation.

Quality of Information. Questions of methodology and validity come into play when considering which type of evaluation may be more effective. Basically, participatory evaluation offers the opportunity for participants to generate, collect, and analyze data as a group. By handing control for questioning and data collection to the participants and group, some of the information on individual members may be lost, but other rich and equally important information is invariably found. The quantitative data so highly prized in traditional evaluation methodologies may diminish slightly in the beginning, but the qualitative stories that emerge offer striking images that cannot be found in the numeric summaries resulting from structured questionnaires and interviews. It is the blending of the qualitative images with the quantitative data through participatory evaluation strategies that lends credibility to the data collected.

Given serious time constraints, the YWCA participatory evaluation teams were never quite able to collect and record a large amount of information on individual member status. They were, however, able to gather a large amount of group information as well as individual vignettes that were valuable and unanticipated. Following the field activity, YWCA evaluation team members were given a copy of the impact assessment questionnaire that had recently been developed for use with women's groups. They found that they could easily complete 80 to 85 percent of the questionnaire, missing only certain financial details that are best gleaned from records. (Visitors who heard the women's one- to two-hour presentations on their evaluations of their groups were able to complete 30 to 50 percent of this questionnaire.) Venturing well beyond the confines of this questionnaire, the participatory evaluation process generated information on sociocultural benefits that were prized by the women and in keeping with the YWCA mission and goals as well as those of empowerment and development.

Training Required. At a minimum, traditional evaluation mechanisms require training in interview techniques and occasionally questionnaire design and/or administration. Training in facilitation of participatory evaluation is undoubtedly far more involved. Participatory evaluators must develop and maintain a deep understanding of what evaluation is in general and what participatory evaluation is in particular. With this understanding, they must be immersed in the process and allowed adequate time to reflect upon their experience.

The YWCA found that in the region where all field staff and branch staff had participated, participatory evaluation activities had been started with other women's groups. Where only the branch secretary had been trained, no such activities had been carried out. This was not surprising; it merely highlighted the fact that participatory evaluation cannot be explained but must be experienced if it is to be understood. During the training workshops, it took a role play/simulation, two pre-field simulations of the implementation experience, and actually carrying out a participatory evaluation activity in the field before participants truly had an understanding of and feel for the process of facilitating participatory evaluation. Once in place, these skills and abilities translated nicely to other locales and remained in tact over the course of the intervening year.

Readiness of Participants. The ability of a group to take responsibility for self-evaluation requires a certain level of collective maturity. Conducting an evaluation and implementing a needs assessment and project planning evaluation activity can be done by a group as soon as it can be identified as such. To conduct an effective impact evaluation, the group must have advanced beyond initial stages of group development, as outlined in the model below.

Levels of Development for Women's Groups*

Level One   *Unformed*—The group is not formed and lacks structure. Different people with different ideas have come together. They do not know how to work together. They are not able to identify their problems.

Level Two   *Formed*—The group is formed, leaders are chosen, and roles are assigned, but the group is not sure what to do. People still have different ideas but have not identified their needs. Leaders believe they "know it all," and members do not know their roles.

---

* This framework was developed by Tototo Home Industries, Mombasa, Kenya, and was utilized and adapted by the YWCA of Kenya over years of fieldwork with women's groups throughout Kenya.

Table 10.1: Development Progress of Women's Groups

Women's Group	Group Level		Participatory Evaluation for	
	1992	1993	Needs Assessment/ Project Planning	Impact
Case 1 (Ganga)	Level Two formed	Level Five interdependent	Successful	Successful
Case 2 (Itambiya)	Level Five/Six inter-independent	Level Six independent	Successful	Successful
Case 3 (Mwaleni)	Level Three/Four dependent-reactive	Level Two/Three formed-dependent	Successful	Unsuccessful

Level Three *Dependent*—The group believes that it cannot accomplish anything without help from the outside. Most of the members are able to identify their problems but believe that action is not their work but the duty of the leaders. They are not free to discuss their problems.

Level Four *Reactive*—The group has identified its problems, it has even started a project that is running well, but suddenly it encounters difficulties and the members blame one another. They even blame the person who introduced the project.

Level Five *Interdependent*—The group works well with field-workers or advisers. From time to time it may need technical advice on how to expand the project. The problems are being solved. Projects are successfully started. The work of the group is shared.

Level Six *Independent*—The group and its leaders work well with minimal outside assistance. They can identify and solve their problems and carry out projects. They are also able to identify and properly utilize outside assistance. The work of the group is shared. They can even train others.

This framework provided a mechanism for observing group progress and identifying necessary preconditions for participation. The results of the participatory evaluation exercises in relation to group development are shown in Table 10.1.

Although groups that are just barely formed (as low as level two—possibly one) can master the skills necessary to lay the groundwork for a project, conducting a participatory impact evaluation requires that the group have cohesion and some level of collective experience and history (minimum level four). Further, it was found that the participatory evaluation process directly assisted the Case 1 group in progressing quickly from level two to level five in the group development framework.*

---

* Case 3 regressed from a level three/four to a level two/three due to a series of external interventions, including the substantial and uncoordinated provision of external funds from several donor agencies.

Building in Evaluation Capacity—Transfer of Responsibility and Control

As one participant put it when defining and explaining what she understood about participatory evaluation: "With some training and in the long run, the process [of participatory evaluation] is supposed to become in-built so that the members are able to carry out the evaluation on their own even without help from an outsider."

This is certainly a goal of participatory evaluation: the sharing of skills and the establishment of a capacity for self-evaluation. By identifying this as both goal and priority, the YWCA is looking at slowly establishing among its women's groups the ability to periodically undertake self-directed impact evaluations. In the coastal region, there are now at least three groups that can tell visitors how to carry out participatory evaluation and describe changes in their group and the impact that participation in their women's group has had on their lives, their families, and their communities. The power of the presentations by the women and their ability to evaluate their projects and their personal and group projects were inspiring. They offered a view of an alternative structural and organizational future worth striving for.

The long-term advantages, power, and potential of participatory evaluation make it an important strategy to consider. It has the ability to provide a rich data source that grows from the women's voices and leaves them with the skills to evaluate their own projects. While traditional evaluation often removes information and leaves little of use behind, participatory evaluation gives voice to those most immediately affected by a project or program. The more voices we are able to bring into this choir, the louder and clearer will be the message they are able to share, and the better the chance that we will be able to hear it.

——————— 11 ———————

Participatory Internal Monitoring and Evaluation in Water Projects: A Case Study from Ghana

Andrew J. Livingstone

The Ghana Water and Sewerage Corporation (GWSC) Assistance Project commenced in 1990, funded by the Canadian International Development Agency (CIDA) and the government of Ghana (GOG). The project's scope is to establish community and district-based management of small urban water supplies throughout northern Ghana, concentrating upon fourteen towns in the first phase, 1990 to 1998. The main objectives of the project are to establish and train fourteen effective local-level water management boards; rehabilitate the fourteen small urban water supplies, emphasizing low-cost appropriate technology; and strengthen GWSC and increase its capacity to promote this shift to community management of water supplies.

The project is implemented by GWSC, a large, relatively centralized parastatal agency of the GOG. Technical assistance is provided by a Canadian Executing Agency (CEA), Wardrop Engineering Inc., using expatriate and Ghanaian advisory personnel.

External monitoring by CIDA of the project's activities has taken place since inception, with a two-person team visiting the project, usually twice a year. Through staff interviews and observation of project reports and publications, the external monitors have identified deviations from the project's planned implementation schedule, issues to be addressed to mitigate obstacles and delays, and constraints affecting project implementation. External monitoring has essentially served to measure compliance of the project's performance to planned activities and outcomes.

Project management realized that many of the project's activities are breaking new ground in northern Ghana. There are no precedents for community management of small urban water supplies upon which to draw. District-level management structures are at an early stage of development, and recently introduced decentralization policies by GOG demand considerable capacity building at the local level. Women's roles in water supply management decision making, while significant in some areas, are generally proscribed. The GWSC is under considerable pressure to transform itself into an economically viable agency, managed on a commercial basis.

Faced with this large degree of uncertainty, and subject to rapid and often unpredictable changes in conditions, project management identified the need early on to establish an effective internal monitoring and evaluation mechanism. The desire was to learn by doing: measure the appropriateness, effectiveness, and sustainability of key project activities; and identify modifications to activities and new initiatives needed to reach optimal outcomes. It was realized that, to achieve a reliable measure of project performance, internal monitoring and evaluation would need to be a fully participatory exercise, involving the project and all stakeholders at all levels.

Methodology

Internal monitoring and evaluation are planned to take place annually, in the March–April period each year from 1993 to 1998. A work plan is developed to determine which project activities to focus on annually. The work plan comprises four distinct stages: data collection at the community level; data collection at the institutional level; data analysis and report preparation; and presentation of a report and discussion of the recommendations with project management to prepare an action plan for the coming year.

The monitoring methodology is based on internal monitors conducting participatory discussions and semistructured interviews with key individuals and groups at both the institutional and the community level. During these interviews, open-ended questions are asked relating to the perceived effectiveness of project activities. Specific questions are targeted according to the individuals or groups being interviewed. Responses to questions are recorded to highlight the key elements of each response, positive and negative opinions and impressions, and suggestions and questions raised by the interviewees. In 1993, fifty-eight persons were interviewed at the community/district level, and forty persons at the institutional level, providing a rich source of data.

Data collected from interviews and from secondary sources are analyzed using a qualitative matrix for each objective. Each matrix consists of a set of criteria of effectiveness, posed as questions, which are established in reference to the activities being monitored. In each matrix, monitoring data are used to assign a rating against each criterion, depending on the positive or negative responses to the question posed. Comments are provided to clarify responses, constraints, and sources of enhancement to effectiveness.

Changes in effectiveness from one monitoring period to another will be identified by comparing the ratings assigned in each matrix for each objective. Changes of a positive nature will be reflected by higher scores or ratings, and conversely, changes of a negative nature will be reflected by lower scores or ratings. Activities that are stalled, with no change from one evaluation to another, or with a consistently ineffective score or rating, will also be identified.

The knowledge gained from the analysis of data is integrated to develop recommendations and short-term action plans to improve project effectiveness.

A baseline report resulted from a five-week initial mission conducted in March and April 1993. The mission was conducted by a four-person team.

Objectives

It was decided to focus upon three main areas of project work that are the primary determinants of sustainability and effectiveness. These areas are community management, human resource development, and gender development. Internal monitoring and evaluation objectives were established

- To evaluate the appropriateness and sustainability of the project's community management strategy;
- To evaluate the effectiveness of the project's training activities; and
- To evaluate the sensitivity of the project to gender equity issues.

An annual work plan is developed for internal monitoring and evaluation. Initially, the 1993 work plan concentrated upon establishing baseline parameters for future comparison. The case study presented here is primarily a description of that baseline. In subsequent years, annual work plans will concentrate upon measuring changes in appropriateness, effectiveness, and sustainability against the baseline data.

Process

Three matrices were developed against which project performance in the three areas identified in the objectives could be gauged.

Data were collected primarily from participatory discussions and semistructured interviews at the community/district level and at the institutional level by a four-person monitoring team. The team was chosen to reflect not only the subject areas of monitoring (such as training, community management, and gender issues) but also a gender and perspective (Canada/Ghana) balance.

During a three-week period, qualitative data were collected from the community and institutional levels by a participatory process and from secondary data sources, such as project reports and papers. The team then processed and analyzed the data to collectively formulate responses to the questions posed by the normative criteria. Once consensus within the team was reached, scoring of the matrices was undertaken.

Scoring, while being subjective and qualitative, is internally consistent, in that it indicates the collective perception of project performance from all data sources. The scoring system used is based upon Table 11.1.

The total score for each of the three matrices then reflects the overall performance of the community management strategy, the training activities, and the sensitivity of the project to gender equity issues.

Table 11.1: Normative Criteria Scores

		Score:
Answer to question is :	No	
	Generally No	1
	Partly	2
	Generally Yes	3
	Yes	4
		5

Results of 1993 Baseline Mission

The matrices used for the preparation of the 1993 internal monitoring and evaluation baseline report are presented in Figures 11.1 through 11.3. Analyses were conducted for the major elements that constitute the main project component being evaluated.

Community Management

Under the community management strategy, representativeness, decision making, communications, planning capacity, interrelationships, and sense of achievement were analyzed. Overall, the project's community management strategy has been partly appropriate and sustainable to date and scored 68 within a possible range of 21 to 105.

There is a coherent understanding and agreement among Water and Sanitation Development Boards (WSDBs), district government, and GWSC on the principles contained in the strategy. WSDBs have a clear vision of their role in enabling the process of community management, and individual WSDB members generally have a clear picture of their specific roles and responsibilities. Linkages and interactions between WSDBs and GWSC have improved substantially, and GWSC's customer relations have benefited considerably. To date, planning water supply rehabilitation has been the main achievement of WSDBs. Plans prepared reflect community needs, desired service levels, and affordability and are generally appropriate and potentially sustainable. Significant consideration has been given to operation and maintenance requirements in the preparation of rehabilitation plans.

Although a framework for operation and maintenance involving both GWSC and WSDBs has been developed, both GWSC staff and WSDB members need a clear definition of their roles and responsibilities in operation and maintenance. GWSC's ability to effectively participate in community-managed operation and maintenance is constrained by weak accounting and billing procedures and by inadequate financial management and control systems.

Figure 11.1: Matrix for the Evaluation of the Appropriateness and Sustainability of the Project's Community Management

1.	Community management activities are planned and designed in a flexible way?	Score 4

Comments: At various levels of the project, there is a coherent understanding and agreement on the broad objectives of the community management strategy. Different communities are interpreting these objectives differently, an indication of the level of flexibility in the strategy.

2.	Community management capacity in GWSC is developing and evolving effectively?	Score 3

Comments: Considerable improvement in the awareness of the community management process within GWSC. Senior management are especially convinced that community management processes are new additions to their corporate culture, which until recently was dominated by an engineering bias. This process appears to be conceptualized at the senior management level, but staff at the operational level have not fully understood community management.

3.	Community management activities are systematically supervised and reported?	Score 3

Comments: Well-coordinated system of supervision and reporting at the project level. Concern is that project is developing a vertical system, with WSDBs likely to depend more on project staff and requirements rather than on community and district-level institutions, such as District Assemblies. Reporting and supervision are not happening at the district level, although some WSDBs have established a feedback mechanism with the community.

4.	Community management activities are planned and coordinated incrementally?	Score 4

Comments: Communities are practicing an incremental approach, starting with their role in planning water system rehabilitation, collecting operation and maintenance (O&M) funds, WSDB training, etc. The WSDBs have a clear vision of what they will do after rehabilitation, but they will need a lot of assistance to enable them to achieve this vision.

5.	Effective linkages exist between project and GWSC?	Score 3

Comments: At the regional management levels, these linkages are strong. At the level of operational staff, linkages between CEA and counterpart staff are weak. At the community levels, GWSC station managers and operators feel alienated from the process of community management. Communications occur between project community liaison workers and GWSC at the community level, but linkages are not strong.

6.	Effective linkages exist between GWSC and communities?	Score 4

Comments: Linkages have improved considerably since WSDBs were inaugurated. Relations between GWSC and communities have been further enhanced by the designation of GWSC counterparts to community liaison teams. Most of these are revenue collectors, whose community relations skills have improved through WSDB and related training.

7.	WSDBs are representative?	Score 3

Comments: For the most part, membership reflects various sections of the communities. In a few cases, functional requirements and literacy levels have resulted in fewer members representing community interests on the WSDBs, thereby diminishing the WSDB's representativeness.

8.	WSDBs are effective?	Score 4

Comments: In nearly 90% of the WSDBs, there is a clear understanding of their role and responsibilities. Decision making is organized and responsive to community expectations. In just one WSDB was there a serious leadership problem.

9.	Design and planning are WSDB-led and reflect community needs?	Score 4

Comments: Generally so. However, the participation of women in planning has been limited by the traditional and cultural limitations.

10.	Roles and responsibilities of WSDB members are clearly defined?	Score 4

Comments: Clear definition and understanding of roles and responsibilities. Most literate members of the WSDB are eloquent and able to function in their capacities. Illiterate WSDB members are not being assisted by other members to execute their roles and responsibilities fully.

11.	Community management activities have an effective feed-back mechanism?	Score 3

Comments: Feedback is happening between the WSDBs and the community. Women WSDB members participated in a two-way process, sending information to the community and transmitting community needs and information back to the WSDB. More often the men would only pass on information on WSDB decisions to the community. Most District Assemblies are not being informed of progress and constraints of WSDBs.

12.	Engineering site inspections are being cooperatively performed involving GWSC and community members?	Score 3

Comments: In over 75% of the cases, this is happening consistently. However, in a few cases, WSDBs have been bypassed as work has proceeded on technical aspects of the water system.

13.	Rehabilitation options and alternatives are being proposed that embody least-cost appropriate technology and renewable energy sources wherever possible?	Score 3

Comments: There is a perception that these issues are being incorporated in the conceptual design of the community water systems. However, there is little understanding of the rationale, other than financial cost, of these considerations. Issues of technology choice and renewable energy sources are not presently being related to overall cost considerations.

14.	Conceptual and detailed designs are appropriate and sustainable, and fully reflect community input?	Score 4

Comments: For the moment, only conceptual designs have been completed for some communities. These have incorporated community input and feedback fully, with both men and women participating.

15.	Operation and maintenance requirements are being fully analyzed and planned for in rehabilitation designs?	Score 4

Comments: Most communities understand that this is the basis of the six-month O&M commitment fee required. Where inappropriate or unsustainable O&M requirements arise, community leaders are able to reject these and start the process again. Not all community members fully understand the basis of these O&M requirements. This ignorance is more apparent among women in sections of the community where men are perceived to be responsible for decisions about payment.

16.	An operation and maintenance policy and procedures have been developed and implemented for various degrees of community-managed rehabilitated water systems?	Score 2

Comments: These are in the community management strategy, but neither GWSC nor the WSDBs fully understand their implications.

17.	Tariff and supply/service pricing policies are being developed by GWSC to support community management?	Score n/a

Comments: Currently being planned.

18.	The GWSC water sales and customer relations programs are being strengthened and enhanced?	Score 4

Comments: By implication, the involvement of GWSC counterparts on the community liaison teams has greatly enhanced the community animation skills of these personnel. Since most are in the water sales and revenue department of GWSC, performance in these areas has improved, with less conflict with community members and customers.

19.	The GWSC accounting and billing systems are being strengthened and enhanced?	Score 1

Comments: Perception is that the project has neglected this aspect of the project to date.

20.	Existing systems and procedures for financial management and reporting in GWSC are being assessed and analyzed?	Score 3

Comments: These have been incorporated into the Commercial Optimization Program, but concern lingers that the lack of a full- or part-time CEA adviser could seriously limit the pace of work in this area.

21.	GWSC financial management and control systems are effective?	Score 2

Comments: The general perception is that financial management and control systems in GWSC are adequate; but these are presently not fully utilized, hence effectiveness is limited.

22.	Recommendations for improvements in the financial management of GWSC are being made?	Score 3

Comments: Under consideration and ongoing review.

INDIVIDUAL SCORES

No (1)	*	(1)
Generally no (2)	**	(4)
Partly (3)	*********	(27)
Generally yes (4)	*********	(36)
Yes (5)		(0)

TOTAL SCORE	68/105

APPROPRIATE AND SUSTAINABLE?		
NO	PARTLY	YES
(21)	(63) [68]	(105)

Figure 11.2: Matrix for the Evaluation of the Effectiveness of the Project's Training Activities

1.	A GWSC training database has been established and is periodically being updated?	Score 2

Comments: According to the Training Program Progress Report, a database was established during Phase II of the training-of-trainers program. No one in the field mentioned this. Other forms of reporting reflect the rudiments of a database; no conscious efforts to synthesize these into a coherent and active database were observed.

2.	Job analyses have been conducted and a methodology prepared for future analyses by GWSC?	Score 2

Comments: See above.

3.	Tasks and skills analyses have been conducted and a methodology prepared for future analyses by GWSC?	Score 2

Comments: See above.

4.	Training equipment and supplies have been obtained and will provide for ongoing training within GWSC?	Score 3

Comments: Equipment and supplies have been obtained but are not being used in Upper East and Upper West because the training rooms are not ready.

5.	A procedure for selecting GWSC trainees has been developed and implemented?	Score 2

Comments: Trainees were selected for the training-of-trainers course. Criteria and procedures for selection of all trainees are not known.

6.	Training-of-trainers is being conducted, and will result in a sustainable training capacity within GWSC?	Score 2

Comments: A training-of-trainers course has been conducted once in a series of four workshops. Presently most training occurs as a result of a training request from the project. These trainers do not appear to understand the process or have the confidence and knowledge to develop training independently in response to a training request. The morale to initiate on-the-job training (OJT) was low until appropriate incentives were instituted. There is a concern that these incentives may not lead to a sustainable training capacity within GWSC.

7.	A GWSC technical training plan has been developed, and a methodology prepared for updating, expanding, or otherwise changing the training plan?	Score 2

Comments: Modules have been developed, but an overall training plan has not been articulated.

8.	On-the-job performance indicators have been developed and have been institutionalized within GWSC?	Score 1

Comments: No evidence of on-the-job indicators being developed. Chances of OJT and related performance indicators being institutionalized within GWSC are presently low in view of the fact that incentive schemes for OJT activities are presently not part of GWSC policy.

9.	GWSC trainee and training learning aids have been developed, and GWSC's capacity for developing additional aids has been enhanced?	Score 3

Comments: Trainers were trained in this area, but capacity to develop additional aids is weak.

10.	Training evaluation is taking place, and is linked to the methodology for developing future training plans?	Score 3

Comments: Generally all training is being evaluated at the end of each training activity. However, evaluations are not being linked to future training needs. Periodic post-training and performance evaluation is presently not happening. The implications of post-training evaluations for future training plans are not perceived by many respondents.

11.	Training of GWSC staff in rehabilitation procedures for existing equipment is being conducted?	Score 3

Comments: Limited to OJT.

12.	Training of GWSC staff in installation procedures for familiar and innovative types of equipment is being conducted?	Score 3

Comments: Limited to certain individuals in the northern region. No coherent plan to transfer this knowledge to other regions.

13.	A methodology for the preparation of inspection reports of installations by GWSC staff is being developed?	Score n/a

Comments: Not started.

14.	WSDB employees (operators, mechanics) are receiving on-the-job training by GWSC trainers?	Score n/a

Comments: Presently WSDBs do not have any employees and have not as yet assumed direct management of any water systems.

15.	A commercial and financial training plan has been developed for GWSC and a methodology prepared for developing future training plans?	Score 4

Comments: The Commercial Optimization Program outlines these plans, and the financial and commercial staff have been duly involved in the process. Concern has been expressed about the training philosophy and the fear that this training plan may not adequately meet the human resource development needs of the financial and commercial section.

16.	Performance of commercial and financial personnel is linked to performance in other parts of GWSC effectively?	Score 2

Comments: Status of commercial and financial staff is still relatively low in GWSC. Their services are not valued as much as engineering staff. Their morale is low.

| 17. | GWSC commercial and financial training is effectively being conducted? | Score n/a |

Comments: Plans are under way and known. Actual implementation has not started.

| 18. | A management and supervisory training plan has been developed for GWSC and a methodology prepared for developing future training plans? | Score 3 |

Comments: Plans have been developed, but the process is not well understood by the managerial staff.

| 19. | A plan for institutional strengthening and capacity building for GWSC management, supervisory, and administrative personnel is being developed? | Score 3 |

Comments: Plans to build capacity are being developed by the project. This process is not being institutionalized at GWSC.

| 20. | GWSC management and supervisory training sessions and activities are being developed, resources identified, and materials prepared? | Score 3 |

Comments: Yes, limited. Training in computerization has been implemented. The perception is that the training was too short and too limited to strengthen GWSC's management, supervisory, and administrative capacity.

| 21. | GWSC management and supervisory training sessions are been conducted effectively? | Score 3 |

Comments: Positive comments have been received about project sensitization activities, but there was no reference to these as management and supervisory training.

| 22. | Progress is being made on encouraging GWSC to interact with other sector groups in community management activities and issues? | Score 4 |

Comments: Interaction has been quite high. This has resulted in increased creditability, increased community tolerance, and increased revenue for GWSC. Concerns were expressed about the expense of this increased interaction and the long-term sustainability of this activity.

23.	WSDB training plans have been developed and a methodology prepared for developing future WSDB training plans?	Score 4

Comments: Initial WSDB management training has taken place. There is a methodology developed for future WSDB training plans. There was an overwhelming concern expressed by GWSC that WSDB training must be an ongoing process.

24.	Public awareness training has been developed and a feedback mechanism developed for monitoring and modifying public awareness training?	Score 4

Comments: Public awareness training resulted in increased support for WSDBs and a corresponding increase in O&M collection. Informal feedback of public awareness training was reported by WSDB members.

25.	Community (WSDB and public) training sessions have been organized and developed effectively?	Score 4

Comments: Community training sessions have largely been developed within the community liaison team, with GWSC participating mainly as trainers.

26.	Community (WSDB and public) training sessions are being conducted and supervised effectively?	Score 4

Comments: Training sessions have been planned and conducted effectively. Concern was expressed about language of instruction in WSDB management training. This has interesting implications for the project. Most trainers are literate in English, while many WSDB members are literate in their local language and may understand English but not write it. Public education is conducted entirely in the vernacular, and extensive translation and taping have been undertaken by the project.

27.	GWSC and communities have effectively interacted and cooperated during program training activities?	Score 3

Comments: The process of interaction has been initiated. GWSC is now more sensitive to community needs and community sentiments. GWSC trainers participate in programming training activities, but the effects of these interactions on cooperation with the community are still rather minimal.

28.	Progress is being made on building capacity within GWSC for community development, participation, and management activities?	Score 3

Comments: There is increasing understanding at GWSC on incorporating community preferences in water systems design. This increased capacity is more evident at the senior management level than at the operational staff levels.

INDIVIDUAL SCORES

No (1)	*	(1)
Generally no (2)	*******	(14)
Partly (3)	***********	(33)
Generally yes (4)	******	(24)
Yes (5)		(0)

TOTAL SCORE	72/125	

EFFECTIVE?		
NO (25)	PARTLY (75) [72]	YES (125)

Figure 11.3: Matrix for the Evaluation of the Sensitivity of the Project to Gender Equity Issues

1.	Women's water supply and related needs are being addressed by specific project activities?	Score 4

Comments: Through women's participation on WSDBs, women's water needs are considered in the design of water systems.

2.	WSDB composition ensures adequate representation for women?	Score 3

Comments: Representation on the WSDB is limited to income-earning women, who are in the minority (e.g., food sellers, pito brewers). In areas where women are predominantly subsistence farmers, the needs of employed women are still considered first.

3.	WSDB decision making reflects due consideration of women's water supply and related needs?	Score 3

Comments: Decision-making processes reflect the WSDB's perception of the community needs for water—not necessarily women's water supply needs.

4.	District government is supportive of women's participation in community management?	Score 4

Comments: District governments feel that women's participation will enhance the performance of WSDBs but do not know the full implications of involving women in decision making.

5.	Water service levels and water tariff structures in community plans have been decided primarily by women?	Score 2

Comments: The WSDBs decided water service levels and tariff structures, occasionally in consultation with the community, not necessarily or specifically with women.

6.	Community women have been effectively provided with hygiene education and sanitation training?	Score 3

Comments: Women have a general idea of hygiene and sanitation but do not practice. Training in water systems generally needs to include health and hygiene education.

7.	Women WSDB members have been effectively trained in water supply operation and maintenance?	Score n/a

Comments: Training has not begun in this area, as yet.

8.	Women WSDB members have been effectively trained in water supply financial management and administration?	Score 4

Comments: Women WSDB members are involved in this training.

9.	Women WSDB members have been fully involved in developing the WSDB constitution and bylaws?	Score n/a

Comments: As yet, this process has not begun.

10.	GWSC regional/district staff are sensitive to gender equity issues?	Score 2

Comments: When questioned, staff know that there are gender differences in whether men or women pay for water. Generally they observe that women are ones who pay. The staff do not understand the gender implications of this, other than the fact that through women, GWSC gets paid.

11.	Training for GWSC staff has involved women staff members or women from other projects?	Score 4

Comments: For computer training, four out of thirty-seven staff members trained were women. In relation to the gender situation regarding staffing positions of GWSC, this is not unexpected. For management training, women from other projects have been involved.

12.	Institutional-strengthening and sector linkage activities within GWSC have stressed the importance of the role of women?	Score 3

Comments: The importance of the role of women's responsibility in fetching and providing water is well known at GWSC. Hence, the practical needs of women to obtain water are being stressed. The implications of meeting these practical needs and the impact on the strategic needs and the empowerment of women are not being analyzed.

13.	Women or women's groups have been approached to assist with project mobilization, planning, and training activities?	Score 3

Comments: Apart from the community-based women's groups that are represented on the WSDBs, there are few external linkages with other women's groups.

14.	Project communication and information provision activities especially target women as well as men?	Score 3

Comments: To the extent that the community at large is being targeted, then women are informed. However, women's workload and time constraints do not appear to be considered in designing public awareness training schedules.

15.	The degree of women's participation in the project is being monitored and evaluated?	Score 2

Comments: The implications of the project on different levels of gender awareness, the needs of women , and the context in which these needs can be met are not generally being addressed at the present time.

INDIVIDUAL SCORES

No (1)		(0)
Generally no (2)	***	(6)
Partly (3)	******	(18)
Generally yes (4)	****	(16)
Yes (5)		(0)
TOTAL SCORE	40/65	

EFFECTIVE?		
NO	PARTLY	YES
(13)	(39) [40]	(65)

Training

With the project's training activities, analyses were performed on both GWSC in-house training and community/district-level training, linkages developed, and collaborative arrangements forged. Overall, the project's training activities have been partly effective to date and scored 72 within a possible range of 25 to 125.

With the development and approval of a commercial optimization program, which includes a comprehensive training plan for GWSC financial and commercial staff, there is a degree of optimism that this component of the project is now receiving attention. WSDB management training has generally been effective and well organized and has resulted in more positive interactions between GWSC staff as trainers and WSDB members. Public education, delivered primarily by WSDB members and community groups, has been well received, although it has only recently been initiated. Increased support for WSDBs and increased rates of operation and maintenance deposit collection as a result of public education have been reported.

Technical and administrative training appears to be weak. GWSC lacks an effective training database, and there is little or no evidence of job, task, or skill analyses being performed. There does not appear to be any established procedure for selecting GWSC trainees, and no on-the-job training performance indicators are in place. Overall, the training-of-trainers exercise has been poorly understood by GWSC staff at all levels, and no overall technical and administrative training plan exists to provide guidance. At this point, there is little chance of institutionalizing on-the-job training within GWSC, and therefore it is not considered to be a sustainable effort as currently formulated.

Gender Sensitivity

Concerning gender equity sensitivity, analyses were performed for the achievements with GWSC and the project staff, and with community/district and other government staff and individuals. Overall, the project is partly sensitive to gender equity issues and scored 40 within a possible range of 13 to 65.

Women, primarily through WSDB membership, have participated effectively in water supply rehabilitation planning and design. Women WSDB members have received significant training in financial management, administration, water utilization, hygiene, and sanitation. The district government is very supportive of women's involvement on WSDBs. GWSC staff training has made a conscious effort to include women participants, particularly for management and supervisory training sessions.

WSDB decision making does not always reflect community input, and as such does not necessarily reflect adequate prior consultation with community women. Regional and district GWSC staff are generally unaware of gender equity issues, especially the impact of water tariff, billing, and collection practices upon community women. Women's participation in project activities is not being comprehensively monitored.

Issues

Following analyses of the data and scoring of the matrices, the internal monitoring and evaluation team identified an array of issues that had emerged up to 1993:

1. WSDB members should be fully involved in any work being done by GWSC on the community water system, no matter how small the work is. This level of involvement will increase the credibility of WSDB members and give the assurance that rehabilitation of the system has started.
2. Objectively verifiable achievements should be established for project activities in community management. These would include the ability of a WSDB to mobilize and prepare for community management, preparing a successful rehabilitation design, collecting and managing funds for the operation and maintenance deposit, and sustaining the management of operation and maintenance.
3. The project training coordinator should concentrate on establishing a training database by conducting a job analysis for each staff grouping, developing an inventory of the tasks done and skill levels currently held

by staff members, and comparing the gap that exists between the two. Based on the training needs identified, a training course could then be developed for each staff member.

4. The job descriptions for GWSC trainers should be modified to recognize their increased job responsibilities for providing training.

5. Quarterly job task performance evaluations should be developed, for both trainers and trainees, to monitor actual outcomes of increased skill levels achieved by on-the-job training.

6. The project should continue to provide ongoing skills training for GWSC trainers, based on training needs identified in these quarterly evaluations.

7. Training on the community management process should be provided at the district and community level for GWSC staff.

8. A communications strategy must be developed to more effectively transfer information between the project and field-level and operations staff.

9. A plan should be developed to communicate the overall project training program to project staff, trainers, GWSC staff, and WSDB members.

10. Within the communications strategy, a public relations plan should be developed, for both internal and external audiences, to link the commercial/financial sector to the continuing viability and maintenance of an effective water system.

11. The project's training plans must be transparent and communicated widely to increase the understanding that training can occur in nonformal as well as formal learning.

12. Project data should continue to be compiled in a gender-disaggregated manner so that the degree of women's and men's participation in the project can be monitored and evaluated from the perspective of both practical and strategic gender needs.

13. Project staff should consult more frequently with women's groups in order to increase staff understanding of gender roles in the community and to assist in identifying appropriate gender-awareness training activities.

14. Women could be trained and/or hired to fill the water sales/customer relations positions within GWSC.

15. Gender differences in payment for water should be monitored and evaluated on a continuous basis to ensure that the financial inputs required at the community level do not have a differential and/or detrimental impact on women.

16. A gender training session should be developed that examines the role of women and men on the WSDBs and on the role of women and men in the supply of water to the community.

17. Mechanisms to include community women in the decision-making process (such as the active involvement of women's groups or meeting with women separately) must be developed and monitored to ensure that community women's water needs are incorporated into the water systems.

18. Public education programs should be designed to influence men's and

women's attitudes with regard to the roles men could play in the health and hygiene activities within their families and in the community generally.

19. Women and/or women's groups must be encouraged to assume the responsibility for management of operation and maintenance fund collection, tariff collection, and all financial management matters of the WSDBs.
20. Any training provided by the project to district and community organizations should incorporate awareness of gender issues and skills in gender analysis.
21. The project should continue to expand opportunities for women's participation in decision making and leadership and to seek methods to increase men's participation in the areas of health and hygiene.

Recommendations and Action Plan

These issues were presented to project management, and a round-table discussion then formulated the following recommendations for action:

Project Management

• Improved communications are needed between project management and project/GWSC regional and district staff concerning project strategies, objectives, plans, and activities.
• More information is required on the project's technical training and management/supervisory training plans and activities.

Community Management

• Improved linkages are needed between WSDBs and district government.
• Strengthening of district governments is required, especially in the areas of community management, gender development, and planning.
• Strengthening of WSDBs is required, especially in the areas of gender development, decision making, and communications.

Interim Stabilization

• Improved responsiveness to technical water supply problems in the communities is required.

Technology Demonstration

• A better understanding of appropriate, low-cost technology is needed by the WSDBs that will manage this technology.

Technical Training/Upgrading

- Training coordination must concentrate on revitalizing the training of trainers, establishing and maintaining a database, developing individual staff training plans, and monitoring trainer and trainee performance.

Financial/Commercial Upgrading/Training

- The sense of alienation from the project expressed by regional financial and commercial staff must be overcome.

Management/Supervisory Upgrading/Training

- A clearer explanation of the formal and nonformal components of the management and supervisory upgrading and training activities is required.
- Gender development training must be incorporated into management and supervisory training activities.
- Management training plans for individual staff should be developed.

A tangible result of these recommendations, developed by consensus between the monitoring team and the project management, was an action plan for 1993–94 that aimed at both modifying existing activities and identifying new or additional activities. This action plan was then incorporated into project work plans at all levels.

The internal monitoring and evaluation process is to be continued until the end of the project. The 1993 baseline report produced by the internal monitoring and evaluation team provided a clear picture of the performance and effectiveness of the project to date. The three main activities of the project—community management, training, and gender equity promotion—had been only partly appropriate, effective, and sustainable so far. The need to and the means to improve project activities were clearly delineated, in a broadly participatory manner.

Modified and new project activities subsequently initiated by the 1993 action plan were evaluated in 1994 as to their appropriateness, effectiveness, and sustainability, using a similar methodology and following a similar process as in the 1993 exercise.

———— 12 ————

Rose Hall Ten Years Later: A Case Study of Participatory Evaluation in St. Vincent

Patricia Ellis

Over the last two decades, a great deal of attention has been paid to increasing people's participation in the development process. Attempts to achieve this have given rise to the use of more participatory approaches and to the development and use of a participatory methodology. This methodology is used to involve ordinary people at the micro level in urban and rural communities in research and training and in the planning, implementation, and evaluation of community development programs and projects.

In the Caribbean, many development activists, project officers, extension workers, and adult educators are using the participatory methodology, but with varying degrees of competence and effectiveness. The Women and Development Unit (WAND) of the University of the West Indies uses this methodology in all of its programs. Since its inception in 1978, it has developed and refined the methodology and has not only acquired a great deal of experience, skill, and competence in using it but also trained a number of individuals in nongovernmental organizations (NGOs) and at the community level in how to use it.

Between 1981 and 1983, WAND experimented with the participatory methodology and used it to test a model of "bottom-up" development based on people's participation. One result of this experiment was that people in the "pilot" community developed skills and attitudes that enabled them to work in a way that increased their own participation and that of others in the process of personal and community development.

At the end of the experiment in July 1983, the Community Coordinating Committee carried out its own participatory evaluation of the pilot project. Through this evaluation, they obtained information on community members' views about the impact of the project on the community and generated data that they used to plan new programs for the following year. In addition, the evaluation provided an opportunity for members to gain additional skills and to increase their competence in doing participatory evaluation.

Eight years later and ten years after its implementation, the Rose Hall Working Group decided to undertake a major internal community-based participatory evaluation of the project. This case study describes that evaluation and provides evidence to show how ordinary people can, through the use of the participatory methodology, become empowered and motivated to participate in and take control of their own development.

Background

The Pilot Project for the Integration of Women in Rural Development (commonly called the Rose Hall Project) was an initiative of WAND. It was implemented in 1980 in the small rural community of Rose Hall (population approximately 1,200) in the island of St. Vincent in the Caribbean. Among its original objectives were:

1. To develop a model of "bottom-up" development through the use of a participatory methodology to assess community needs and to plan, implement, and evaluate community programs and projects.
2. To engage rural women in a process of development through which they would
   • examine their economic and social contribution to the development of the community;
   • develop their desire and their ability to take leadership and decision-making roles in their community; and
   • generally improve the quality of their own lives and that of their community.

Although the main emphasis of the project was the development of women and their "integration" into the development of the community, it was conceived as a community development project and encouraged the participation of men as well as women in the various project activities that emerged.

From its inception, stress was placed on the active participation of community members in all aspects of the project, and the initial project activity was a community-based three-week workshop in participatory needs assessment, program planning, and evaluation (March 1981). While a core group of about six community members participated full time and gained skills in doing participatory research, participatory planning, and participatory evaluation, several other community members also participated in some of the workshop sessions and activities.

Early in the life of the project, the Rose Hall Community Working Group was elected by the community and given the responsibility of managing the project and coordinating project activities. During the first ten years (1981–1991), the Working Group, using and building on the knowledge and skills gained in the initial workshop, designed, implemented, managed, and sustained a number of community projects that have resulted in the achievement of a significant degree of self-reliance within the community. Through a series of Working Group meetings, ongoing community-based education and training workshops, and community meetings, they have been able to motivate community members to achieve higher levels of self-confidence and to increase their participation in the process of community development.

In November 1991, the Working Group and the community organized a Week of Celebrations under the theme of Reflect, Rejoice, and Renew to mark the tenth anniversary of the project. As part of these activities, the Working Group invited WAND and the original project coordinator (the author) to facilitate consultations within the community as a way of evaluating the first ten years of project activity and of planning for the future development of the community.

Evaluation Questions and Issues

Prior to the evaluation, the Working Group identified a number of questions to which the members wanted answers. They believed that the evaluation would not only provide them with answers but also generate useful information and critical insights that they could use to plan for the future development of the community. These questions were:

1. What have been the major achievements of the project?
2. What conditions and factors have contributed to these achievements and to the development of Rose Hall over the last ten years?
3. In what ways has the project affected the lives of individual community members and the life of the community as a whole?
4. What major problems and setbacks has the Working Group faced in implementing the project?
5. How has the Working Group developed as an organization, and how can it become more financially self-sufficient?

Evaluation Objectives

The objectives of the evaluation were to provide an opportunity for members of the Rose Hall community to:

1. Review what had happened in Rose Hall over the last ten years as a result of the project.
2. Reflect on and analyze the process and outcomes of the project, and assess its impact on the lives of individual community members and on the community as a whole.
3. Begin to develop a new plan for the future development of Rose Hall.

Development Issues

Given these objectives, the evaluation also sought to identify how some key development issues had been addressed within the project. Among these were:

1. Change and development at the individual and community levels;
2. Participatory development and people's participation in the development process;
3. Leadership, power, and empowerment;
4. Community self-reliance; and
5. Women, gender, and development.

Methodology and Design

The experiences, wishes, and decisions of the Working Group influenced both the evaluation design and the methodology used. In keeping with its philosophy of people's participation in the development process and its use of a participatory methodology to achieve this, the Working Group indicated that the evaluation should include a series of consultations with various community groups. Group members also agreed that these consultations should focus on reflection/evaluation and renewal, projection, and planning and were adamant that they did not want a "quick and dirty" or "rushed" job. Because neither the evaluator nor the members of the community were able to devote a single block of time to the evaluation exercise, a decision was made that the evaluation should take place over an extended period. However, while evaluation activities were planned and implemented mainly at times when the evaluator was available, they had to be negotiated with community members, and particular activities took place when the latter were available.

There were disadvantages as well as advantages to designing the evaluation in this way. For example, while the entire exercise took much longer to complete and to document than if it had been done all at once, more people in the community were able to participate in the evaluation and planning processes. The Working Group was also able to take time to engage in serious reflection and to analyze various aspects of its work, and to immediately use some of the outcomes of evaluation activities to improve or reorient existing community projects.

Data Collection, Analysis, and Interpretation

Several methods were used to involve various groups and individual community members in providing, analyzing, and interpreting data in order to assess the effects and outcomes of the project, and in identifying components of a new development plan for Rose Hall. Methods used included community workshops with different groups and a regional workshop, project committee meetings, informal interviews, and discussions.

A variety of techniques were also used to engage community members in a process of reflection, analysis, visioning, and planning. Among these were small- and large-group discussions, role plays, skits, song and poetry, story-telling, drawing, photographs, and frameworks for evaluating and reorienting existing community projects. These methods were used to collect data from a number of key individuals and groups in the community and generated a large amount of rich data, most of which were qualitative. Data provided by both individuals and groups and generated in workshops and community meetings were constantly fed back to them for collective analysis and interpretation. This process allowed data to be sifted through a number of different eyes and then further analyzed as new and different meanings emerged from a wide variety of perspectives.

Data were also analyzed and interpreted by the evaluator. Her analysis was informed not only by events that took place during the evaluation but also by her knowledge of the Rose Hall community and her understanding of the context within which the project and the evaluation took place.

Process and Outcomes

In keeping with the wishes of the Working Group, and based on discussions between them and the evaluator, evaluation activities were designed to ensure and facilitate active participation of a wide cross section of community members in a process of reflection/evaluation, renewal/projection, and planning.

Workshops

Workshops were the most common method used throughout the evaluation. A total of eight one- and two-day workshops were held with members of the Working Group (three workshops); young people between the ages of twelve and thirty (two workshops); and members of the coordinating committees of four community projects—the preschool, the bakery, the adult education program, and the chemical shop (one workshop). In addition, several residents participated in a three-day workshop on money management and fund-raising for community groups and in a weeklong regional workshop on the theme of communities organizing for self-reliance. Young and old, women, men, and children participated in the workshops. In all, about two hundred people were involved in evaluating their experiences in project activities over the last ten years and in contributing to plans for the future. In addition, as is common practice in Rose Hall, a number of children sat in and participated in many of the workshop sessions.

During these workshops, different groups of people:

1. Shared, reflected on, and analyzed their experiences of participating in project activities and identified the ways in which their lives had been affected by their participation and by the project.

2. Identified and discussed the factors that were responsible for the achievements and success of the project and those that created problems and setbacks.
3. Assessed the project and identified ways in which the community had benefited from it.
4. Evaluated each community project and agreed on actions that needed to be taken to improve it.
5. Did a critical analysis of the operations of the Working Group and made suggestions for increasing its capacity and capability to manage the community projects and the development process.
6. Identified components of a new development plan for Rose Hall and additional activities that should be implemented to meet the present needs of individuals in the community and to solve present community problems.

In those workshops that dealt with effect and impact of the project (e.g., Working Group self-reliance, young people), valuable information and insights emerged from life stories, skits, and individual and group drawings and from small- and large-group discussions. Data were also generated from one-to-one interviews, informal discussions, and a practical research activity carried out during the workshop on self-reliance and analyzed and interpreted by workshop participants.

In workshops, members of coordinating committees and executive members of the Working Group used a framework for evaluating community projects developed by the evaluator to do an in-depth evaluation of each of four community projects. The data and insights produced by this activity were used to reorient and/or improve the way in which the projects were functioning.

The workshop on money management and fund-raising facilitated by the evaluator and a financial analyst provided an opportunity for those who participated to assess the financial position of the various community projects and of the Working Group. The bakery was used as a case study, and an in-depth

Table 12.1: Participation in Evaluation and Planning Workshops

WORKSHOPS	Female	Male	Total
Working Group	84	22	106
Young People	29	26	55
Coordinating Committees	17	4	21
Fund-Raising	25	8	33
Self-Reliance (Reg.)	17	7	24
TOTAL	172	67	239*

* In many cases, the same persons participated in more than one workshop.

financial analysis enabled participants to see and to appreciate the need for proper record keeping; for budgeting, management, and planning; for putting structures, systems, and procedures in place; and for rules and regulations. They also began to understand the difference between undertaking projects solely to provide services as part of a process of social development and undertaking community projects that are viable and profitable economic enterprises. The need for more in-depth discussion of this issue was also recognized. In addition, participants identified and explored a variety of ways in which money could be generated and/or obtained to finance the Working Group, the existing community projects, and additional activities that had been identified in the new plan.

The workshops with young people and the workshop on self-reliance gave birth to a development plan. The participants in both of these workshops were young people between twelve and twenty-five years of age. Through drawings, interviews in the community, and small- and large-group discussions, these young people identified some of the "new" problems now facing them and the community as a whole. Among these were relationships between youth and older people and between young men and young women, lack of recreational facilities for youth, unemployment, lack of discipline, need for more and different types of education programs (e.g., skills training, family life education), and need for guidance and counseling. Through a visioning exercise, they identified a number of programs, projects, and activities that, if implemented, would enable Rose Hall to become an even more self-sufficient and self-reliant community and would translate their vision for the future of Rose Hall into a reality.

Six young men and four young women participated in the regional workshop on self-reliance. Like the first workshop in 1981, this was sponsored by WAND and brought together representatives from intermediaries and communities in six other countries. The workshop was the first step toward preparing a new generation of leaders in Rose Hall to ensure continuity and sustainability of the project. Workshop activities provided these young people with opportunities to:

1. Understand the philosophy, principles, and concepts that underlie and inform the project, e.g., holistic, integrated, self-reliance, empowerment, sustainable.
2. Obtain firsthand, accurate information about the history of the project from older members of the Working Group.
3. See how the participatory methodology was and can be used to promote, encourage, facilitate, and ensure participation of community members in the community development process.
4. Gain some practical skills in participatory evaluation by planning and carrying out a community investigation that produced information about the effect and impact of project activities on the lives of individuals and on the community as a whole.

5. Identify some of the problems with which the community is presently faced, some of the needs that must be met, and some of the issues that the Working Group should attempt to address.
6. Begin to discuss some of the critical issues that are important to the continuity of the project, e.g., new leadership, management, and accountability both within the Working Group and within each project.
7. Identify activities and programs that should be undertaken in the next five years.
8. Discuss and agree on the role that, as young people, they can play in the future development of their community.

Workshops were an effective strategy for facilitating a great deal and a high level of participation by community members in the evaluation process. They produced a large quantity of rich qualitative data and deep insights. They engaged people in a process of reflection, critical analysis, and thinking that generated many fresh, creative, and innovative ideas that form the basis of a new development thrust in Rose Hall and will influence its direction in the next five to ten years.

Project Committee Meetings

As a follow-up to the workshop with project committee members, meetings were held with the preschool and adult education committees. In both of these meetings, the information generated by the evaluation framework was used to develop a draft plan for improving the management and operations of the preschool and an outline of a new adult education program.

In the case of the former, the committee identified structures, systems, and procedures that needed to be put in place, and in the latter, a decision was made to refocus on adult literacy and nonformal adult education programs and to reduce the emphasis on academic examination courses for General Certificate of Education O Level and Caribbean Examinations Council examinations.

Community Meetings

Throughout the life of the project, community meetings were used as a mechanism for ensuring community participation; for engaging a wide cross section of community members in the process of policy formulation, decision making, and problem solving; and for giving support to the initiatives of the Working Group.

Two community meetings were held, and over one hundred women, men, and children participated. During these meetings, participants relived the first ten years of the project through:

1. A display of personal objects that held special memories and meaning for them, during which they talked about their involvement in and

experiences of project activities. Objects included gifts received in the first Christmas exchanges, souvenirs collected when they participated in workshops/conferences in other parts of the world (e.g., Ghana), agricultural produce, and uniforms made by the sewing project. Participants shared with one another the particular events that their object represented and the reasons why these had been of significance in their lives.

2. A display of photographs of women in Rose Hall and of events and activities occurring over the life of the project. Discussion of these photographs reminded participants of the role that women, some of whom had since died, played in the community and of their contribution to the success of many of the community projects.

3. The telling of personal stories by several participants, which gave insights into the lives of the storytellers and revealed how the project had motivated them and had contributed to positive changes in their lives and relationships. Of particular interest was the presence and participation of several children who had been the first pupils of the preschool in 1983 and of their parents. Their comments, stories, and testimonies were concrete proof of the positive effect and impact of the project on the lives of individuals in Rose Hall.

4. Several dramatic skits that highlighted problems being experienced by existing projects, such as the bakery, and showed how these had been or might be solved. They also demonstrated a variety of approaches to problem solving and provided examples of arriving at decisions through discussion that leads to consensus.

Interviews and Informal Discussions

Throughout the period of the evaluation, the evaluator held informal discussions and interviews with a number of individuals in the community. These provided information on the ways in which the project had affected people's lives, on their views of how it had impacted the community, and on what changes should be implemented now so that it might continue to contribute to the development of the community.

Information collected in this way corroborated, expanded on, and reinforced information that was generated by other methods. However, the most significant fact that emerged from these interviews and discussions was that "the project had touched the lives of every man, woman, and child in Rose Hall," that "everybody in the community has benefited either directly or indirectly as a result of the project," and that "Rose Hall is a better place because of the project."

In addition, many people were convinced and made it clear that, while there had been many tangible and visible outcomes (e.g., the Community Centre), the intangible benefits (e.g., self-confidence, self-esteem, caring, sharing, love, more harmonious male-female relations, decrease and almost total disappearance of domestic violence and wife beating) were by far the most important achievements of the project.

More in-depth interviews and discussions with key members of the Working Group provided opportunities for them to reflect on the group's development from one with a loose structure with a facilitating role to one with a more formal structure (chairman and secretary) and responsibility for managing a number of community projects and a complex community development process. They also discussed critical issues affecting the group's capacity and capability. For example, roles and responsibilities of officers, leadership and the importance of teaching young people to take on leadership roles, the group's image and credibility, and loyalty of group members. Concerns were also expressed about the changing composition of the group, about relations among group members, and about the level of commitment of some members. Some members also observed that while many of those who had benefited directly from the project (e.g., opportunities to further their studies) were active members of the group, others did not seem to feel that they should "give back something" to the community by taking responsibility for some of the activities that were now being undertaken by the group.

These informal interviews and discussions provided opportunities for individuals to "air their views" and enabled the evaluator to probe beneath the surface and to uncover deep feelings and sensitive emotions. The range of opinions expressed, the variety of perspectives, and the many deep insights gained enriched the evaluation process and its outcomes.

The exercise in participatory evaluation provided an opportunity for community members to examine and discuss how some key development issues had been addressed within the framework of the Pilot Project. The workshops with the Working Group, with youth, and on organizing for self-reliance were particularly useful in generating information and insights on the following issues.

Development and Change

Both the purpose and the expected outcome of development is change. Within the Rose Hall project there was a significant amount of change at the individual and community levels. Some of the major changes identified during the evaluation were:

At the Individual Level

- Improvement in the way people relate to one another: "more love and caring," "more respect for each other," "more willing to listen and to cooperate."
- Broadening of horizons and aspirations—seeking out and making use of opportunities for continuing higher education, including university education, for self and children.
- Change in male-female relations.

- Greater motivation to pursue personal goals.
- Increase in skills, including technical, interpersonal, and analytical skills.
- Increase in awareness and knowledge.
- Qualitative change in the quality of life.
- Increase in self-confidence, self-esteem, and self-worth.
- Change in the way people now approach problems and do things, e.g., in a more planned and systematic way.
- Change in attitudes.

At the Community Level

- Change in the physical appearance of the community because of construction of new concrete buildings—the Community Centre, large houses.
- Improved standard of living through introduction of new facilities, technology—telephones, TVs, videos, water in homes, etc.
- Upgrading of housing—move from wooden to concrete.
- New facilities—preschool, bakery, Community Centre.
- Successful development projects.
- Increase in community togetherness, cooperation, cohesion, and commitment to the development of the community.
- Greater community spirit and sense of pride among community members.
- Greater and more effective use of community structures for implementing community projects and for facilitating and enabling the process of development.
- Emergence of a common goal linked to a shared value system based on caring and cooperation.
- Ongoing project activity over an extended period.

These and several other changes were identified by every method used during the evaluation, and they were all seen as indications that development had taken place in the community. More in-depth discussion and analysis of some of the major changes revealed the developments that resulted from the changes, the type of development they brought about, the new problems and needs they gave rise to, and the implications for future development.

During the workshops, in-depth discussion and analysis of some of the major changes caused participants to ask some critical and relevant questions. Attempts to answer these led participants to identify other important issues related to facilitating and bringing about change that will result in development that enables self-reliance, ensures empowerment and equity, leads to benefits of development initiatives, and addresses the variety of needs of different groups in the community and that the community can manage and sustain.

For example, when they looked at the changing landscape, some remarked that the increase in the number of big concrete houses, though a positive sign of improvement in the living standards of some, may be seen as the emergence of "a new elite." Others felt that an increase in the number of these houses could mean less land being available for agriculture or backyard gardening and could lead to competition for land between housing and agriculture. This led to a discussion about the difference between modernization and development and to questions about the kind of development that is sustainable and the aspects of development that should be sustained.

Related to this is the question, on which aspects of development should emphasis be put, and when? During the early stages of the Rose Hall project, a great deal of emphasis was put on the areas of personal development and social development. This provided the basis and the foundation on which other aspects—physical/infrastructural, political, and economic—of development could take place. It also equipped and prepared community members so that they were enabled, empowered, and motivated to engage in and take responsibility for other aspects of their community's development.

Consequently, community activity in the early years was concentrated on education and training, meeting of needs, and provision of services (e.g., workshops on community organizing and mobilizing, and community meetings to decide what would meet identified needs and to provide services to the community, e.g., sewing project, preschool). These were followed by projects that sought to provide and improve physical facilities and to improve the standard of living (e.g., Community Centre, new houses, chemical shop). Later still, there was a shift to more and to larger and organized economic activities designed not only to meet community needs but also to generate income and profit (e.g., food preservation, bakery). The emergence of the latter has resulted in new challenges for the Working Group and for the community, especially in areas of management, accountability, and balancing economic social benefits within the context of community development programs and projects. As a result of this evaluation, initial steps were taken to enable the community to face and deal with these issues as the project continues.

Another issue that surfaced concerned the benefits of development programs and projects. Questions were asked about who benefits and how from these activities, and about the extent to which the benefits were equitable. Some held the notion that persons with a certain level of education and a certain status, and family members and friends of key persons in the project, might have benefited more than others in the community. There was also a feeling that this could have a negative effect on community organizations and on future development efforts.

A review of the developments that had taken place in Rose Hall over ten years also raised issues about management of the development process and about sustaining it. Among these were the fact that the Working Group had met every week for ten years and had shifted over time from a small, informal, and loose structure to a larger group with a more formal structure; the increase in the number, type, and size of the projects implemented; and the increasing complexity of the development process. These all created the need for a coordinator and manager rather than a community facilitator, as in the first ten years, and for the development of specific criteria for selecting such a person.

One other issue that assumed a great deal of importance as the evaluation proceeded was that of the involvement of youth in the development of Rose Hall. It is significant to note that many of the young people who were involved in these evaluation workshops had "grown up with the project," and some of them had participated as young children in several project activities. They felt not only that they had positive roles to play in the community's development but also that development efforts should make serious attempts to meet their needs and help them solve the problems they are facing. They stressed their need for employment, for training in skills, for guidance and counseling, and for recreational and entertainment facilities, including a disco. They realized the difference between these needs and those identified ten years earlier when the project began, and the importance of looking within development projects at the specific needs of particular groups within a community, at how community needs change, and at how new needs emerge as "development" takes place.

Discussions on these issues not only served to assess the current position but also enabled those who participated to appreciate the complexities of development, to identify some new areas of need, and to recognize the importance of equipping community members with new knowledge and skills that would enable them to manage the process more efficiently and effectively.

Participatory "Bottom-Up" Development

It is now widely accepted that people's participation in the development process is crucial to the successful achievement of development goals. However, it is important to recognize that people's participation in the process of development depends on many factors. Among these are respect for people, a belief in their value and a recognition that each person can make a valuable contribution, and acceptance that people have the desire and the right to manage their own affairs and to make decisions that affect their lives. The way in which people participate, however, is determined by the existence of democratic structures and mechanisms in which they can participate, and by the extent to which they are equipped with the knowledge, skills, and attitudes they must have if they are to participate actively in their own development and that of their society. It is therefore important to carefully examine and analyze who is participating in what activities and for what purpose—in short, what kind of participation has taken place, and with what results.

As residents of Rose Hall evaluated the project, they provided overwhelming evidence that over the life of the project there had been an extremely high level of participation by community members and that this had been responsible for the success of the project and for the type of development that had taken place in the community. There are several reasons for this. From the inception, the primary focus was on the development of people, and a large number of educational and training workshops were organized on an ongoing basis to facilitate this. The emphasis in many of these workshops was on personal development and interpersonal relations, including gender relations, group building, and teamwork. Other workshops enabled those who participated to improve technical skills as well as skills in reflection, critical thinking, and analysis. The use of a participatory training methodology in these workshops also provided practical experience in and a deeper understanding of the "process of participation."

Participation had also been made possible by the creation of democratic structures (e.g., Working Group and project committees) and other mechanisms (e.g., community meetings, project coordinators) that encouraged and facilitated participation of a wide cross section of community members not only in planning, implementation, and evaluation of community projects and activities but also in problem solving and decision making. In terms of the latter, consensus was usually arrived at through a participatory process in meetings of the Working Group and in community meetings.

During the evaluation, some concern was expressed that in recent times there had been a gradual shift from participatory to more centralized decision making by and within the Working Group, and that there was a need to "go back to having community meetings more regularly" to ensure participation of a large number of people in this process.

Both the type and the quality of participation of people of Rose Hall in their own development and in that of their community demonstrated that with appropriate and relevant training people can be motivated and equipped to participate actively in the development process. More than this, however, it shows that space and opportunities must be created to allow people to participate, and that structures and mechanisms must be put in place to enable them to do so.

Leadership and the Use of Power

One of the objectives of the pilot project was to motivate and encourage women and to increase their ability to take on leadership and decision-making roles. There can be no doubt that this objective has been achieved.

In Rose Hall, women are in the forefront and in control of the management of the development process. They not only hold more leadership positions than do men, but they are perceived to be community leaders by most, if not all, of the community members. At the same time, these women leaders have operated in such a way that the concept of "shared leadership" has become a reality in Rose Hall. By encouraging other women to accept responsibility for specific projects, activities, and tasks, by sharing their own experience and knowledge, by "letting go" of their power and control, the original two or three leaders have empowered other women and have enabled them to become leaders in their own rights.

Consequently, it is women who hold positions of power in formal community structures. They are executive members of the Working Group, they are coordinators of subcommittees and of community projects, and it is mainly they who are involved in making decisions and implementing projects that will be undertaken in and by the community. It is women too who represent the community and its interests in national, regional, and international fora.

Because of the way in which women leaders in Rose Hall have used their power and authority, and because of the extent to which they are in constant dialogue and consultation with the entire community, questions about who is the leader, power conflicts, and leadership struggles have been few. However, when these did surface, they were dealt with effectively and satisfactorily through a process of consultation and dialogue.

The issue of new leadership surfaced quite early in the evaluation process, and the need to prepare "a new generation of leaders" became an important topic for discussion among both older and younger members of the community. Workshops with the youth and their participation in the workshop on organizing for self-reliance provided young people with opportunities to examine and explore their ideas on the leadership roles they might play in the community. Several young people expressed their willingness to undertake such roles, and some agreed to function as a "watchdog group" to monitor project activities and to work with the Working Group to implement some of the suggestions made in the evaluation exercise.

Community Self-Reliance

Community development projects are one strategy for enabling communities to achieve and sustain self-reliance. Within and as a result of the pilot project, the community of Rose Hall not only achieved a significant degree of self-reliance but has been able to sustain a particular type of development in which the development of people is the central concern.

Evaluation workshops helped community members to focus and reflect on how this had been achieved and how it could be maintained and sustained in the future. It was recognized that many project activities had been successful (e.g., the building of the Community Centre, the preschool, and the adult education program) because the community had been able to mobilize its internal resources, the most important of which was its people. Everyone agreed that the commitment, willingness, ability, and skills of community members, and the harnessing of these for the development of the community, had been the single most important reason for the success of the project.

At another level, the issue of dependency and interdependence was brought up, for example, the need for financial resources and for technical assistance from outside the community, and the role of intermediary agencies such as WAND. In terms of the former, the initial funding came to an end in 1983, but given the initial success of the project and the skills that the Working Group members had acquired, they were able to submit project proposals and to get additional funding. At the same time, the group was able to obtain small subventions from government. However, in more recent times, such funds have been slower in coming. In the area of technical assistance, the community has been able to access technical expertise not available in the community from a number of governmental and nongovernmental agencies. It is important to note that assistance was identified and requested by the community if and when it decided that it needed help. This precedent was established early in the project when the Working Group members declared that "WAND could not tell them what to do, but that they would let WAND know what they wanted it to do and when."

This self-determination on the part of the community members emerged out of their ability and confidence in identifying their goals, problems, and needs; in exploring alternative solutions; and in mobilizing the internal and external resources they needed to arrive at and implement their own solutions.

Those who participated in the evaluation realized that at this point in the community's development it was important to think more seriously about the internal resources available and about the type of external assistance that might be needed to increase self-reliance and to sustain the project.

Women, Gender, and Development

Even though one of the main objectives of the pilot project was "the integration of women in rural development," from the beginning, the community insisted that "men should not be left out." As Working Group members reflected on the early years, they remembered the men's initial negative reaction to the project's emphasis on the development of women. They also remembered their own concern about the fact that only a very small number of men were participating in project activities.

They realized how consciousness-raising workshops had helped them to become more aware of themselves as women and of their capabilities and had increased their self-awareness, self-esteem, and self-confidence. They pointed out, too, that through workshops that focused on interpersonal and male-female relationships, men and women had become more aware of factors that determined their behaviors and their interaction with other women and with men.

They singled out the workshop on the role of men in development of Rose Hall (1983), emphasized its importance, and stressed yet again that this had been a turning point in male-female relations in the community. They confirmed that both men and women had grown to respect and appreciate each other's point of view and had developed skills in problem solving and conflict resolution, and that couples were now more apt to deal with family problems through discussion and negotiation rather than through confrontation and argument.

In addition to workshops held in the community, several women from Rose Hall have participated in national, regional, and international workshops on women in development and on gender. This exposure has not only increased their understanding of women's condition worldwide but also helped them to better understand their own experience of discrimination and oppression. It has helped them to understand the links and relationship between the events of the macro level and the reality of their lives at the micro, community level. As a result, they became more aware of their rights and of the need to organize and to work with other women and with men to improve their own situation and that of other women.

Several people related personal experiences of positive changes in their relationships with their partners or spouses. One man testified that men "no longer beat their wives"; another agreed that "it does not make sense to beat my wife, we now sit down and discuss things together." Others declared that "the community would deal with any man who beats a woman." Later in the evaluation process, one response to a question about violence against women did suggest that there might still be a man or two who beats his wife. On the other hand, it is true that there are many more examples of both young and older men who are playing a greater role in and taking some responsibility for child care and child rearing, and who also are willingly doing their share of household tasks.

These phenomena are concrete evidence of a significant change in gender roles and relationships, in the sexual division of labor, in decision making within families, and in beliefs, attitudes, and expectations about appropriate gender roles.

The question of men's participation in community projects and activities was again raised during the evaluation. Attempts to increase their participation had been made in 1983, and the workshop on the role of men succeeded in getting about forty men to participate in a discussion of this issue. Following this, several men did become involved and did accept some specific responsibility by becoming members of project committees, but their numbers have again decreased.

However, there are a number of young men who have shown interest and who are involved in some of the community projects. For example, the new secretary of the Working Group is a young man, but he is experiencing difficulty in functioning effectively. In addition, his tendency to hold on to power and to use it in an autocratic way is in conflict with the way the group operates and is cause for concern. He was reluctant to participate in evaluation workshops in which these problems were being discussed. There is still a need to find ways of getting more men involved in and willing to contribute to the development of the community.

At the same time, attention must also be paid to the participation of younger women in the project. During the evaluation, both the young women and the young men who participated in the workshops expressed their willingness to become more involved in the Working Group and to take on leadership roles. The challenge for the Working Group now is to plan and organize training activities to prepare this new generation of young female and male leaders who can work together to continue to sustain the development of Rose Hall.

Unlike many who are responsible for and involved in development projects, the people of Rose Hall do not have any fears about evaluation; rather, they welcome it, request it, and do it regularly. In their hands, evaluation has become a useful tool that works to their advantage. Members of the Working Group especially have developed skills in evaluation and research and, more specifically, in coordinating participatory evaluation.

The ten-year evaluation provided yet another opportunity for people in Rose Hall to participate in assessing and defining their own development. Through it they have been able to recreate and relive the history of the project and to:

- Systematically analyze and reflect on their community, identify indicators, and assess the project's effect and impact on their lives.
- Make judgments about the operations of the Working Group and its efficiency.
- Gain deeper insights into and understanding of the complexity of development.
- Generate new knowledge about individuals and groups in the community and about their goals, aspirations, needs, and concerns.
- Begin to identify new development goals and to develop a five-year plan for their community.
- Show yet again that ordinary people do have the ability and can successfully carry out evaluation research and can use the results to plan future development programs that respond to and meet their needs.

This participatory evaluation of the Rose Hall project was an example of people's participation in their own development. During the evaluation, by analyzing activities and processes in which they had participated, community members were able to identify the causal relationship between changes in their attitudes, behavior, and relationships; the process of development; and the achievement of self-reliant, sustainable community development. The evaluation provides concrete evidence of how community development at the micro level can give meaning and can inform and clarify our understanding of development theory and concepts. It shows how empowerment and change can not only become alive and real but can become a way of living and doing for ordinary people.

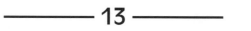

13

"We Need to Rebuild This House": The Role of Empowerment in Evaluation of a Mexican Farmers' Cooperative

Elizabeth Whitmore

Several years ago, I was asked to be the evaluator for Phase I of a project to assist dairy goat farmers in developing a cooperative. This co-op was located in a small village near the U.S.-Mexico border.* The project was designed to be participatory, and those involved wanted the evaluation to be consistent with this.

A major goal of the project was to "revitalize community life by increasing participation levels."** There were two sets of objectives, one involving concrete tasks, the other related to increasing social participation in the cooperative. The latter would be accomplished by involving local farmers in establishing the co-op as a viable commercial venture. To achieve this, the proposers chose a participatory action research approach as the most appropriate methodology, and they

---

* Why me, a middle-aged, white "Anglo" woman from an eastern Canadian city who knows nothing about goats, you might well ask? They needed someone who knew how to do a participatory evaluation and could also speak both English and Spanish, and I qualified on both counts. There are many such evaluators in Central and South America, of course, where participatory action research and evaluation are well established. I was recruited by one of the unilingual anglophones leading the project, however, and the networks he was using may have been limited. He did indicate that he had made some unsuccessful attempts to find a Mexican evaluator. In addition, they may have actually wanted someone from the U.S. or Canada. One of the objectives was also "to meet the challenge of Third World scholars who say that First World social scientists cannot create methods of inquiry and service that are responsive to the basic needs of people in isolated communities characterized by social and economic depression."

** The project proposal states a major goal as the "identification of characteristics that can lead to successful long-term operation of cooperatives. These could include such topics as sustaining a participative organization beyond Phase I, building local and long-range networks for information sharing, continuing education, ownership in decision-making processes, peer review, etc." Later, the project is identified as an opportunity to mount "a community revitalization project that will offer income and employment opportunities to enable small farmers to stay on the land with their families and to earn a decent living while rebuilding social institutions to make them responsible to the needs and aspirations of the citizens" (Project Proposal, p. 4).

wanted the evaluation to be consistent with that approach. My job as evaluator of Phase I of the project was to assess the degree to which the co-op had achieved this goal.

History and Context

The Sinombre Valley, located on the border of the United States and Mexico, is approximately forty miles long.* Many of the people in the area farm for a living, and while a few large irrigated farms are prosperous, the majority of small farmers are unable to earn a living from working their land. The village of Sinombre (with an estimated population of 200) is located on the banks of the Rio Grande.

The people of Palomas (the village located directly across the river) and Sinombre form a culturally homogeneous community, interrelated through intermarriage and a common heritage. This community has a unique and valuable cultural heritage, for more than half the residents can trace their ancestry to original Spanish settlers who arrived over 300 years ago. All of the farmers, and all but three of the total families, are of Mexican or other Latin American or Native American origin.

Life in the Sinombre Valley is difficult, especially economically. It is a struggle to make a living from the land, and there are few other local means of supporting oneself or a family. Unemployment and underemployment levels are high, and two-thirds of the families live below the poverty line. In order to find work, many residents are forced to migrate to the cities, or they are restricted to seasonal labor. These workers are often forced to leave their families behind without any means of support for months at a time. Lack of economic resources is coupled with other familiar problems (including poor housing, isolation, low educational levels, hopelessness, and so forth).

Yet people are deeply rooted here—this is home—and are willing to work hard to develop a viable economic base in their community. Dairy goat farming is one promising alternative. The environment and climate are well suited to goats, it is a labor-intensive operation, and there is potential demand for goat and milk products. Many farmers already raise goats and are familiar with such an undertaking. A dairy goat cooperative would engage in small-scale production and marketing of goat's milk products (cheese and candy). Local farmers would supply raw materials to a producer-owned and -operated factory to be built in Sinombre, directly benefiting twenty families and indirectly benefiting an area population of thousands. The danger is the liquidation of a potentially viable rural community by large commercial interests, such as has already taken place in neighboring Miraflor, where over 90 percent of the farmland is owned by two corporate farms.

---

* The names of locations and people have been changed for reasons of confidentiality.

The Farmers' Co-op

In August 1990, Father James, a missionary of the Episcopal Church and resident of Sinombre since 1984, and Dr. Albert Smith, a retired sociologist and experienced goatkeeper living in a nearby town, teamed up to write a proposal (to the Department of Agriculture) for Phase I of this project. This was to be a six-month preliminary phase during which information would be gathered and a beginning made toward building the cooperative. It was anticipated that further funding would be sought to complete the project. Phase I was funded from June to December 1991.

The opportunity presented by this project was to mount a community revitalization project that would offer income and employment opportunities to enable small farmers to stay on the land with their families. This would allow them to earn a decent living and to rebuild the social institutions that meet the needs and aspirations of the citizens.

Objectives of the Project

As stated earlier, there were two sets of objectives for Phase I, one involving concrete tasks, the other related to increasing social participation in the cooperative. Specifically, the concrete tasks were to:

1. Identify and recruit potential milk producers;
2. Raise funds;
3. Establish a model herd;
4. Assist members in developing family herds;
5. Develop a delivery system for getting milk to the factory and a marketing system for distributing the product; and
6. Build a small factory for production of cheese.

The social participation objectives were to form a cooperative and strengthen the involvement of local people in its operation and to do the research necessary to develop the products. (The emphasis was to be on participatory methods in which residents of the area and outsiders were to work in partnership.)

Project Evaluation

My initial proposal involved two site visits—one as the project was beginning, and a second toward the end of Phase I.* I had proposed that an evaluation committee of local people be formed, and together, we would set up the evaluation design. I would then work closely with them (albeit long distance) over the next few months as they gathered the data. During the second visit,

---

* Limited funds restricted me to a maximum of two visits.

we would analyze the data and draft a report, in consultation with the people in the village. After my first visit, it was clear that this plan was not going to work out.

As the outside evaluator, I went to Sinombre for two days. I found that not only had there been no discussion of the evaluation at the co-op meetings, and therefore members had no idea what this was all about, but also the local people had no idea who this strange white lady was, how I got there, or what an evaluation was all about. My first meeting with one of the Anglos consisted of two hours of vitriol against the other; the second, with the other Anglo, echoed the sentiment. Their initial partnership had obviously broken down. There was disagreement on just about every issue, from how to raise goats to the roles of members and leaders, though both did acknowledge that the project had pretty much ground to a halt and needed help. On top of this, I was quietly told (by one of the women) that it would be inappropriate for me, as a female, to talk with the men in the village. This was not an auspicious beginning!

I recruited the (male) outside facilitator who was there at the time,* and with his help, I was able to talk with a number of the villagers. They reported that they really didn't know what was happening, for the two project directors (the Anglo men) were fighting and couldn't get along at all. Even though the funding (for Phase I) from the government had been approved, there appeared to be no progress in getting the cheese factory going, so people were suspicious. They wondered who was getting the money. The co-op meetings were conducted in English, so most people had stopped attending, since they could not understand what was going on. The facilitator, who had been in more regular contact with the situation, confirmed these impressions.

One conclusion was clear—that the conflict between the co-directors was seriously inhibiting the progress of the project and that people in the village felt basically left out. Their expectations were certainly not being met.** I concluded that the local people needed to take control of "their" project if it was to achieve any of its objectives. Otherwise, I feared that it would fail and they would be worse off than before—poorer, feeling more inadequate and hopeless, and ineligible for further funding because of this project.

So I was left with the question of how, or indeed whether, one could do a participatory evaluation under such circumstances. But at this point, I had no choice but to proceed and figure out a plan for my second visit.

---

* There were two outside consultants for this project, myself as the evaluator and a facilitator who was to be available as needed. He had made several visits to Sinombre by the time I made my first visit and was thus somewhat familiar with the problems.

** I wrote an interim report with a set of recommendations for change, including that a truly democratic process be established in the co-op, with meetings conducted in both Spanish and English, and that high priority be given to the building of a cheese factory, which would represent a tangible sign of progress and be a place where people could sell their milk and/or be employed. I also arranged for a local evaluation team to be set up to work with me over the next few months in planning the evaluation.

Theoretical Background

Participatory evaluation (PE) has been discussed in the literature for more than fifteen years now (Cousins and Earl 1992; Fernandes and Tandon 1981; Feuerstein 1986; Hall, Gillette, and Tandon 1982; Reason and Rowan 1981; Rugh 1994). Its principles are incorporated in the discourse on participatory research (PR), which defines itself in contrast to conventional approaches.*

Maguire (1987) summarizes the emergence of participatory research from three sources: radical critiques in international economic development assistance, adult education as empowerment, and the growing challenge to the dominant social science paradigm (chap. 3). Much of the literature, up until recently, has come from sources in Latin America, Africa, and Asia.** The origins and philosophical foundations have been well explicated elsewhere and thus do not need to be elaborated here (Hall 1975, 1981; Hall, Gillette, and Tandon 1982; Maguire 1987; Tandon 1981).

The basic definition of participatory research as combining three activities—investigation, education, and action—also forms the basis for conducting PE. Three types of change are envisioned as integral to the process: development of a critical consciousness for both the researcher (or evaluator) and participants, improvement of the lives of those involved in the process, and transformation of basic social structures and relationships (Maguire 1987, 29).

A number of basic assumptions underlie participatory approaches to research and evaluation:

- Inquiry is not neutral, but is socially constructed. Research and evaluation are political processes. Someone gains from the process and products of inquiry.
- Science is a cultural product; it is not context free. What is investigated and how it is implemented are grounded in the historical, cultural, political, and economic context within which it is conducted.
- Experts are not the only ones who can create valid knowledge. Ordinary

---

* There is a great deal of debate around naming, reflecting lively ferment in the field. Terms include participatory action research (PAR), which emphasizes the action as well as the research aspect, action research, ideological research, community-based research, empowerment research, and collaborative research. Many group such approaches under "alternative paradigm" and include feminist research in this.

** There has been a particularly vital debate in the last several years, documented in *Collaborative Inquiry,* a newsletter edited by Peter Reason from the University of Bath, England. Those from the South—Latin America, particularly—focus on collective aspects of change and the importance of critical analysis and structural transformation. Northerners—exemplified in the U.S. by William Foote Whyte and the group at Cornell University—use the term PAR. Their focus is more on linking research to action, but there has been little critical analysis of the economic, social, or political context. The notion of fundamental structural transformation disappears in the process. The fear is that once again, Northerners will appropriate the method and transform the discourse to suit the purposes of dominant societies.

people are capable of generating knowledge that is as important and as valid as that produced by more highly structured and scientific processes.

* Knowledge or information is a potential source of power, and as such, it ought not to be the exclusive domain of dominant institutions.

Working collectively is a particularly important aspect of participatory research and evaluation. Fals-Borda (1987, 338) suggests that gathering information as a group "provides a social validation of objective knowledge which cannot be achieved through individual methods based on surveys or field work. In this way confirmation is obtained of the positive values of dialogue, discussion, argumentation and consensus in the objective investigation of social realities."

From a PE perspective, addressing issues of power relations and empowerment of less powerful groups is an inherent and explicitly stated part of the process. Empowerment is not only a legitimate aspect of evaluation; indeed, issues of power are present in all evaluations whether a participatory approach is used or not (Whitmore 1994). "The distribution of power determines WHOSE ideology, interests and information will be dominant" (Weiss 1983, 239). Someone gains power through an evaluation, however neutral we might pretend to be. What subtle (and not so subtle) processes are at work in our choices of design, whom we work with, whom we include and exclude? Whom do we choose to focus on, and what are the implications? PE is "characterized by widely shared collective power . . . the people become agents of social action and the power differentials between those who control and need resources is reduced through participation" (Fernandes and Tandon 1981, 5). The question is thus not whether certain individuals or groups are empowered, but whom is the evaluation really for, and why? Becker's (1970) question, posed so many years ago to sociologists, "whose side are you on?" is equally applicable to evaluation.

Empowerment is a term that has long been used, abused, and now seems co-opted. What began as part of the civil rights movement in the United States, with its emphasis on collective rights and action, has been refocused more recently, especially by business and management interests, into a wholly individual activity. In this discussion, I would like to return to the original meaning, summed up by Baker-Miller (1983): empowerment, in short, is a series of attacks on subordination of every description—psychic, physical, cultural, sexual, legal, political, economic, and technological (cited in Simon 1990, 28).

Empowerment is not something one does "for" or "to" someone else, however. "Empowerment is a reflexive activity, a process capable of being initiated and sustained only by the agent or subject who seeks power or self-determination. Others can only aid and abet in this empowerment process. They do so by providing a climate, a relationship, resources and procedural means through which people can enhance their own lives" (Simon 1990, 32).

These philosophical principles formed the foundation of what I intended to do in the evaluation of Phase I.

Back to Sinombre

The local evaluation team never did get formed, and I continued to have no alternative but to communicate through the co-directors, particularly Dr. Smith, who sent me minutes of the co-op meetings, copies of the newsletter he was editing, and other information about what was occurring. I was basically forced to plan pretty much in a vacuum, though I did have the support of the outside facilitator.* As it turned out, he had been asked to facilitate a co-op meeting just before the evaluation, so he would be on site at the same time I was.

My second visit (in January 1992) occurred after the project was officially over (as far as funding was concerned). I planned to be at the site for four days, during which I hoped to conduct the evaluation with members of the co-op as a collective. I arranged through the treasurer that members would be paid for their time and expertise. Both co-directors fully supported the idea and seemed eager to participate in the process. This was the plan; here's what actually happened.

Day One. The first day was taken up entirely by a membership meeting, which I sat in on as an observer. This meeting was facilitated by the outside facilitator, whom they trusted and respected. This was key to keeping the conflicting parties under control and the process reasonably productive. Some ground rules were established, one of which was that everything would be in both Spanish and English—spoken and written.

At the end of the day (when everyone was tired and needing to leave to tend their herds), I was given five minutes to explain my role and what I wanted to do. Not the beginning I had planned! I hurriedly explained what I planned to do and why I felt that a collective process was essential. I said that I could interview them separately and individually, go away, and submit a report, but I felt that this would not accomplish much and would certainly be of no use to them.**

Subsequently, the facilitator and I met privately with the two co-directors and confronted them about the destructiveness of their conflict. Both could agree that it was not good for the organization.

Later, with the help of the facilitator, I developed a careful strategy to involve all the members in a process of evaluating first the stated objectives of the project (the easy part) and then the functioning of the Co-op itself.

Day Two. The next morning, a few people showed up, but not enough to proceed. The local members went off to round up others, and within an hour, we

---

* He had made one further visit during the fall and was in sporadic contact with the co-directors. We were, however, able to pool our understandings of the situation.

** Another part of the context that should be noted is that I was paid $400 a day (a huge amount by local standards). This served to increase the suspicion of me by local people.

had a solid representation of community people (all male, however, except for two, the secretary, and the wife of a member).* I reiterated the rationale for an evaluation and together we set some guidelines for how we would work together.** The facilitator then set the context, reviewing his involvement and discussing the contributions of key actors in positive terms. The intent was to set a positive tone and to reframe their diversity as a strength.

I began by dividing them into small groups and asking each to assess one of the original (concrete task) objectives. What had been accomplished for that objective, and what remained to be done? They needed to own what they had done (which was actually quite a bit) and to agree, as a group, on what still needed to be accomplished. They reported back, and all was recorded—in both languages—on flip charts. By the end of the first day, they reported feeling amazed at how much they had actually done and left with a sense of excitement and optimism. Participants felt that they were clearer about what had happened and understood better what needed to happen from here.

Again, privately, the consultant and I met with the two co-directors, in a last effort to see whether they could work positively together. The short answer, we concluded afterwards, was no. They were simply too different, and too much had already been said and done to repair the damage. This only reconfirmed my conviction that the local people needed to take control of the co-op if any progress was to be made.

Day Three. Today, we were to look at the structure and functioning of the co-op, a touchy subject, to say the least. This discussion would probably affect the future of the organization, positively or negatively.

I began by asking them, individually, to think of two things in response to the question: What do you need an organization for? (Why have one at all?) I presented examples—"We don't need an organization to have goats. We do need an organization to . . ." (I could not ask them to jot these down, for some could not write or read). I then asked them to think of two things that most got in the way of doing these things (better). They shared their responses as a group (and again, all was recorded on flip charts).

I then divided them into small groups to discuss one time when a decision had been made and they liked how it was made. In the large group, we shared these and discussed how decisions are normally made in the co-op. Again in small groups, I asked, "What most concerns you about the way most co-op decisions have been made?" Responses included "most didn't agree but went along anyway"; "inadequate (or devaluation of) participation in decisions";

---

* There was a total of about twenty-five people at this evaluation. About half were villagers (male); the others were primarily Anglos involved in the project in one way or another. As stated, including myself, there were about four to six women involved at various points during the process.

** Guidelines included logistics, everyone should have a chance to speak, no interruptions, listen for the positive, no blaming or personal attacks, everything would be translated, and the bilingual people would all share in this task.

"all participation should be respected and valued"; "disregarding formal decisions (not following through)." In the ensuing larger discussion, it became clear that one thing that was needed was a training session in decision-making strategies.

Day Four. Everyone was there and ready to go.* Moving from the previous discussion, today we examined the structure of an organization by looking at what positions are needed and their tasks and functions. Again, they worked in small groups, responding to specific questions (e.g., what do you expect of a president? A secretary? A treasurer? A model herd manager?). The purpose was to clarify expectations and guide people in their positions, not to tell the present occupants what they had done wrong. The discussion nearly came unstuck when one faction (led by Anglo #1) attacked the other, whose leader (Anglo #2) could not attend that day.

We then spent time planning for the future in specific terms: what needed to be done, by whom, and when. This was an attempt to establish an open process in which everyone knew what was supposed to happen and how. They agreed upon decision-making procedures in which all would participate and that there had to be consensus for action to be taken.

Finally, I reviewed with them a wide range of my own impressions and conclusions (which had been written out on flip charts). I was free to say out loud what everyone knew but could not articulate publicly. We checked those that they felt were valid and either modified or eliminated those that were not.

We ended with a round: the most important thing you have learned in these past three days is. . . . Some reported learning what an organization is and what the duties of officers were; others stated that it's good to clear up the confusion when things go wrong. One summed it up by saying: "we need to rebuild this house."**

We celebrated with a barbeque—goat, of course.

Issues and Dilemmas

A number of questions arise from this experience that exemplify the dilemmas inherent in participatory approaches to evaluation.

1. Participatory evaluations focus more on the process than on the production of a final, technically sophisticated report. This has certain implications.

As the evaluator in this situation, was my role simply to document the outcome? I question whether this would have been useful to anyone. In fact, it

---

* It should be noted that on this day, two young women were present, daughters of one of the members. Both were bilingual and literate and were of great assistance with translating and recording. Dad just beamed with pride!

** At the end of this session, one of the local leaders jumped up from his chair and ran over and gave me a hug. This from someone I was barely allowed to speak to in my first visit!

might have made matters worse. At the very least, it would have been another outsider making negative judgments about the local situation, reinforcing the sense of despair people had about efforts to improve their lives.

When an evaluator becomes involved, she or he influences the situation and the people in it. That is a given. Focusing on outcome, in fact, involves a process (of talking to people, of "measuring" something, of deciding what the results mean), however "objective" we'd like to think it is. By deciding to focus on process, the evaluator makes a deliberate decision to assist the actors in reshaping the situation. This takes a great deal of skill and discipline, for intervening in power relationships is tricky, and people, especially those with less power, can get hurt. It can be a dangerous game, one fraught with potential conflict. But whatever we do involves either reinforcing the power of those who already have it or encouraging those with less power to assume more responsibility. We ought to make our choices explicit (see Whitmore in progress).

The emphasis on process has implications for the evaluator's role. She or he becomes an enabler responsive to the needs of those involved, working with "the moment" to assist people to express themselves openly and effectively (see Barndt 1989). It becomes very different from the traditional role of "impartial" outside technical expert, and we have not been trained to do this, which means that our educational institutions need to shift their emphasis. I am not saying that we could or should eliminate our technical training and expertise. Far from it. I'm suggesting that we need to put this in a context and understand its political implications. Once we do that, we must change our role.

2. There are severe limitations to short-term, one- (or two-) shot site visits at the best of times, but especially when one emphasizes the process. Ideally, there is an ongoing relationship, with the evaluator working closely with a cross section of the stakeholder population over time. Building trust is key to this process, and doing it in a short period means that the evaluator is severely limited in what she or he can accomplish. Indeed, one can condense only so much the normally long-term process of creating trust. I was forced to focus, in this instance, on what could be done in a few days and recognize the limitations.

Such short-term work reflects a model predicated on "objective" assumptions in which an outsider can or should come in and accurately assess a situation. It does not take into account the complexity of cultural, class, racial, or gender differences and the subtle and unseen resistance of powerless people to such "experts" (Gaventa 1980; Hooks 1984; Whitmore 1994).

In hindsight, I would not attempt such an evaluation again. I don't think that PE can be done short term; PE needs to be built in from the very beginning of a project, and the process takes time and sustained contact. For example, there wasn't any time to engage participants in formulating the evaluation questions, much less in the process of elaborating the evaluation design. All this is part and parcel of good participatory work.

Short-term work does not allow for follow-up either. Even though there was a shift from day one to day four in terms of trust and empowerment, however limited, how long it would or could last is another question. Whatever impact might have been made by the process described is likely to have been undone by those with power who are likely to benefit most from the status quo.* The best that can be hoped for, in this case, is that the facilitator may be in a position to follow up and that he can somehow build upon the alliances built during the evaluation.

In the end, a PE approach does not work with an organization that is not participatory. If a group or organization operates in a participatory fashion, an evaluation that uses PE will be consistent and it will be relatively easy to act on the results. If the group operates in a more hierarchical or dictatorial or paternalistic manner, the impact of a participatory evaluation is likely to be minimal. The issue in this case was power, and though the Anglos espoused participatory rhetoric, the actuality was seen as "divisive." Noblitt and Eaker (1987, 22) note that "authoritarian and/or disruptive strategies are necessary for successful network change under conditions of substantial power imbalance." While I was neither authoritarian nor disruptive, the structure of the process was deliberately designed to engage those with less power. And I did take enough control of the process so that the Anglos, and particularly the co-directors, could not dominate.

In such a situation, an evaluation will either reinforce the already divided relationships or help to mobilize members to change the situation. How much the villagers were able (or wanted) to act to take more control of the co-op remains to be seen. An idea was planted, and if it germinates at all, it will do so slowly and with plenty of nurturing.

3.   There are limitations on how familiar an outside evaluator can be with the local culture and how much she or he will be trusted. As an Anglo white

---

* This is exemplified by my well-intentioned attempt to give them control of the money earmarked for the evaluator's fee. In meeting with several local (Hispanic) leaders, they decided that the money would be put toward the training of local people. This included such things as assisting a number of local people to go to GED classes, paying for the consultant/facilitator to do a two-day workshop on leadership and decision making, and getting bookkeeping training for the treasurer.

Though the two co-directors agreed in principle with this plan, it broke down when they refused to co-sign the check that would have turned the money over to the co-op. By this time, there were two different organizations, and neither would allow the money to go to the other's group. So they sent the money to me, which meant that by the time both the U.S. and Canadian governments took their tax bite, and I deducted the cost of expenses incurred in trying to arrange this long distance, there was very little money left over. Though I had warned them of the tax implications of my receiving the money, I suspect that the local people felt betrayed once again by a promise unfulfilled. Both Anglo men ended up angry with me, so they have likely reinforced this feeling. I am not present to rebuild the trust developed during the time I was there.

person, my relationship with them was burdened with the legacy of colonialism, no matter how sympathetic I might have been. The degree to which someone like me could be a role model for them is limited, and this restricts what the process can achieve. In addition, I am an academic, worlds apart from a group of illiterate goat farmers. Though we worked well together and the immediate response was most positive, I cannot pretend that the class barriers were not a factor in our interaction.* Issues of race, class, and gender are rarely addressed in evaluations yet operate everywhere. This situation was no different; it just had its own unique set of circumstances.

The whole question of gender and the issues raised by our differences were exemplified by my not even being allowed, at first, to talk with the men. Though we all relaxed after a while, our worlds were very far apart on how we saw the role of women. It could hardly be concluded that the community was learning to work democratically when half the population was excluded (Maguire 1987, 57). Maguire (1987, 57) points out that the machismo factor is a major obstacle to women's participation in community projects and concludes that "we need more insight into how researchers have dealt with machismo." I did raise the issue of including more women in the co-op and made a point of recognizing the contribution they were already making, but I did this carefully, understanding that if I pushed them too far, I would undo whatever little progress we might make on this and other fronts. Being an outsider can be an advantage; as a woman not dependent on local males, I was free to raise issues that local women could not.** Maguire (1987, 69) notes the complexity of this issue, raising the question, "how can (PR) be culturally sensitive and yet not collude with oppressive sexist policies and practices which are frequently defended as culturally appropriate or traditional?"

One major objective of this project was to "revitalize community life and increase participation levels." Evaluating such an objective by inviting community members to participate is entirely consistent with this. Increasing participation levels should, by definition, be empowering. One of the problems with the word *empowerment,* however, is precisely that it has been increasingly used to co-opt participants into working harder to achieve someone else's goal.*** In the same way, participatory action research and evaluation have become trendy and are being used by many organizations and groups to give

---

*   The co-directors kept introducing me as Dr. Whitmore, which they may have seen as respectful and appropriate to my role as "expert" (or perhaps it was even hostile), but which I saw as reinforcing the barriers between the participants and myself.

** Mbilinyi (1982) discusses the role of the outsider who could articulate what the local women had told her because she could not be intimidated or silenced by dependence on a local male.

*** To be more productive in a business setting, for example.

people the illusion of participation. Governments call it participatory when they "consult" with the public about policy changes; business uses focus groups for marketing research and calls it participatory. Neither is based on an ideology of real empowerment, that is, the achievement of power by those who do not have it.

In this case example, I was asked to do a participatory evaluation, ostensibly by the co-op members, but actually, as I found out, quite unilaterally by one of the co-directors. The original proposal (which he had primarily written) did indeed envision using a participatory action research approach in developing the products, but it became clear in the evaluation that this vision became a problem when his own power was threatened. I was then seen as "divisive" and "intrusive."[*] I suspect that this is not an unusual situation, for as participatory evaluations are indeed intended to intervene on the side of those with less power, those with power in a given situation are bound to resent it.

It's important not to romanticize "the community" or pretend that "the people" or the powerless are always right. Such an attitude is naive and quite unrealistic. What is needed is a collaborative relationship in which all parties are able to contribute their understanding and knowledge in an atmosphere of respect and mutuality. Such a relationship is formed only when all members share a deep respect for the abilities, characteristics, and culture of one another. In this situation, such a relationship did not exist. The situation here was perhaps classic in that outsiders, however well intentioned, dominated the process in the paternalistic belief that the villagers could not do it themselves. As one Anglo concluded in the final meeting: "I'm so impressed with these people. They are much more intelligent than I thought!"

Sjorberg (1975, 45) states that "researchers must do more than accept the categories of the system when they carry out their research. . . . We must formulate research orientations that emphasize the development of alternative structural arrangements that transcend some of the difficulties inherent in the present-day social order." "Evaluators" can be substituted for "researchers" in this statement, for the issues are the same. Empowerment is a role that evaluators play. As stated earlier, "they do so by providing a climate, a relationship, resources and procedural means through which people can enhance their own lives" (Simon 1990, 32). The evaluator clearly provides a climate, establishes a relationship (with stakeholders), brings resources and procedures to the process. The question becomes, to what ends? And for whose benefit?

---

[*] This was stated in a letter to me from Dr. Smith, ironically, after the organization had split into two factions, each led by one of the co-directors.

References

Barndt, D. 1989. *Naming the Moment: Political Analysis in Action.* Toronto: Jesuit Centre for Social Faith and Justice.

Becker, H. 1970. Whose Side Are You On? *Social Problems* 14: 239–48.

Cousins, J. B., and L. M. Earl. 1992. "The Case for Participatory Evaluation." *Educational Evaluation and Policy Analysis* 14 (4): 397–418.

Fals-Borda, O. 1987. "The Application of Participatory Action Research in Latin America." *International Sociology* 2 (4): 329–47.

Fernandes, W., and R. Tandon. 1981. *Participatory Research and Evaluation: Experiments in Research as a Process of Liberation.* New Delhi: Indian Social Institute.

Feuerstein, M.-T. 1986. *Partnership in Evaluation: Evaluating Development and Community Programmes with Participants.* London: Macmillan Publishers.

Gaventa, J. 1980. *Power and Powerlessness: Rebellion and Quiescence in an Appalachian Valley.* Chicago: University of Illinois Press.

Hall, B. 1975. "Participatory Research: An Approach for Change." *Convergence* 8(2): 24–32.

———. 1981. "Participatory Research, Popular Knowledge and Power: A Personal Reflection." *Convergence* 3: 6–19.

Hall, B., A. Gillette, and R. Tandon, eds. 1982. *Creating Knowledge: A Monopoly?* New Delhi: Society for Participatory Research in Asia.

Hooks, B. 1984. *Feminist Theory: From Margin to Center.* Boston: South End Press.

Maguire, P. 1987. *Doing Participatory Research: A Feminist Approach.* Amherst, Mass.: Center for International Education.

Mbilinyi, M. 1982. "The Unity of 'Struggles' and 'Research': The Case of Peasant Women in West Bagamoyo, Tanzania." Pp. 102–42 in *Fighting on Two Fronts*, edited by M. Miles. The Hague: Institute of Social Sciences.

Noblitt, G. W., and D. J. Eaker. 1987. "Evaluation Designs as Political Strategies." Paper presented at the annual meeting of the American Educational Research Association, Washington, D.C.

Reason, P., and J. Rowan, eds. 1981. *Human Inquiry: A Sourcebook of New Paradigm Research.* New York: J. Wiley and Sons.

Rugh, J. 1994. "Can Participatory Evaluation Meet the Needs of All Stakeholders? A Case Study: Evaluating the World Neighbors West Africa Program." Paper presented at the annual meeting of the American Evaluation Association, Boston.

Simon, B. L. 1990. "Rethinking Empowerment." *Journal of Progressive Human Services.* 1: 27–37.

Sjorberg, G. 1975. "Politics, Ethics and Evaluation Research." Pp. 29–51 in *Handbook of Evaluation Research*, edited by M. Guttentag and E. Struening. Beverly Hills, Calif.: Sage.

Tandon, R. 1981. "Participatory Research in the Empowerment of People." *Convergence* 14 (3): 20–27.

Weiss, C. 1983. "Ideology, Interest and Information: The Basis of Policy Decisions." Pp. 213–45 in *Ethics, the Social Sciences and Policy Analysis*, edited by D. Callahan and B. Jennings. New York: Plenum.

Whitmore, E. 1994. "To Tell the Truth: Process, Quality and Working with Oppressed Groups in Participatory Approaches to Inquiry." Pp. 82–98 in *Participation in Human Inquiry*, edited by P. Reason. Thousand Oaks, Calif.: Sage.

———. In progress. "The Ideology of Evaluation."

Further Reading

Books

Chaudhary, A., and R. Tandon. 1984. *Participatory Evaluation: Issues and Concerns*. New Delhi: Society for Participatory Research in Asia.

Clark, N., and J. McCaffrey. 1979. *Demystifying Evaluation*. New York: World Education.

Edwards, M., and D. Hume, eds. 1996. *Beyond the Magic Bullet: NGO Performance and Accountability in the Post–Cold War Period*. West Hartford, Conn.: Kumarian Press.

Fals-Borda, O., and M. A. Rahman, eds. 1991. *Action and Knowledge: Breaking the Monopoly with Participatory Action-Research*. New York: Apex Press.

Fernandes, W., and R. Tandon, eds. 1981. *Participatory Research and Evaluation— Experiments in Research as a Process of Liberation*. New Delhi: Indian Social Institute.

Fetterman, D. M., S. J. Kaftarian, and A. Wandersman, eds. 1996. *Empowerment Evaluation: Knowledge and Tools for Self-Assessment and Accountability*. Thousand Oaks, Calif.: Sage Publications.

Feuerstein, M.-T. 1986. *Partners in Evaluation: Evaluating Development and Community Programmes with Participants*. London: Macmillan.

Guba, E. G., and Y. S. Lincoln. 1995. *Fourth Generation Evaluation*. 2d ed. Newberry Park, Calif.: Sage.

Maguire, P. 1987. *Doing Participatory Research: A Feminist Approach*. Amherst, Mass.: Center for International Education.

Marsden, D., and P. Oakley, eds. 1990. *Evaluating Social Development Projects*. Development Guidelines No. 5. Oxford: Oxfam UK.

Marsden, D., P. Oakley, and B. Pratt. 1994. *Measuring the Process: Guidelines for Evaluating Social Development*. Oxford: Oxfam UK.

Nelson, N., and S. Wright, eds. 1995. *Power and Participatory Development: Theory and Practice*. London: Intermediate Technology Publications.

Park, P., M. Brydon-Miller, B. Hall, and T. Jackson, eds. 1993. *Voices of Change: Participatory Research in the United States and Canada*. Toronto/Westport, Conn.: OISE Press/Bergin and Garvey.

Selener, D. 1997. *Participatory Action Research and Social Change*. Ithaca, N.Y.: Cornell Participatory Action Research Network, Cornell University.

Smith, S. E., D. G. Willms, with N. A. Johnson, eds. 1997. *Nurtured by Knowledge: Learning to Do Participatory Action-Research*. Ottawa/New York: International Development Research Centre/Apex Press.

United Nations Development Programme. 1997. *Who Are the Question-makers? A Participatory Evaluation Handbook*. New York: Office of Evaluation and Strategic Planning.

Journal Articles and Technical Reports

Beaulieu, R., and V. Manoukian. 1996. "Institutional Changes and Mainstreaming of Participatory Approaches: Background Paper." Prepared for a meeting of the Inter-Agency Working Group on Participation at the World Bank, Washington, D.C.

Bhatnagar, B., and A. Williams, eds. 1992. "Participatory Development and the World Bank—Potential Directions for Change." World Bank Discussion Paper #183. World Bank, Washington, D.C.

Chambers, R. 1995. "Paradigm Shifts and the Practice of Participatory Research and Development." Pp. 30–42 in *Power and Participatory Development: Theory and Practice*, edited by N. Nelson and S. Wright. London: Intermediate Technology Publications.

Chaudhary, A., S. Dhar, and R. Tandon. 1989. "Report of International Forum on Participatory Evaluation." International Council for Adult Education and Society for Participatory Research in Asia, New Delhi.

Cousins, J. B. 1996. "Consequences of Researcher Involvement in Participatory Evaluation." *Studies in Educational Evaluation* 22 (1): 3–27.

Cousins, J. B., and L. M. Earl. 1992. "The Case for Participatory Evaluation." *Educational Evaluation and Policy Analysis* 14 (14): 397–418.

Feuerstein, M.-T. 1988. "Finding the Methods to Fit the People: Training for Participatory Evaluation." *Community Development Journal* 23 (1): 16–25.

Isham, J., D. Narayan, and L. Pritchett. 1996. "Does Participation Improve Performance? Establishing Causality with Subjective Data." *World Bank Economic Review* 9 (2): 175–200.

Knowledge and Policy: The International Journal of Knowledge Transfer and Utilization (special double issue on participatory evaluation of development programs and porjects) 10 (1/2) (1987). Guest Editors: F. Harry Cummings, Wm. C. Found, and Terry Smutylo.

Mosse, D. 1994. "Authority, Gender and Knowledge: Theoretical Reflections on the Practice of Participatory Rural Appraisal." *Development and Change* 25: 497–526.

Rebiens, C. 1995. "Participatory Evaluation of Development Interventions: The Concept and Its Practice." Working Paper No. 4, Department of Intercultural Communication and Management, Copenhagen Business School, Denmark.

Manuals and Tool Kits

Freedman, J. 1994. "Participatory Evaluations: Making Projects Work." International Centre, University of Calgary, Calgary.

Gosling, L. 1993. "Assessment, Monitoring and Review Toolkits." Save the Children Fund, London.

Mebrahtu, E., ed. 1997. *Participatory Monitoring and Evaluation: An Introductory Pak.* Brighton: Institute of Development Studies, University of Sussex.

Narayan, D. 1993. "Participatory Evaluation: Tools for Managing Change in Water and Sanitation." World Bank Technical Paper No. 27. World Bank, Washington, D.C.

Narayan, D., and L. Srinivasan. 1995. "Participatory Development Tool Kit: Training Manuals for Agencies and Communities." World Bank, Washington, D.C.

World Bank. 1996. *The World Bank Participation Sourcebook.* Sustainable Development Department, Washington, D.C.

Bibliographies

Johnson, S. 1994. *Participatory Research: A Selected Annotated Bibliography.* Ottawa: International Development Research Centre and Norman Paterson School of International Affairs, Carleton University.

McPherson, S. 1995. "Participatory Monitoring and Evaluation: PRA Bibliography." *PRA/PLA Notes*. International Institute for Environment and Development, London.

Rietbergen-McCracken, J., ed. 1996. *Participation in Practice: The Experience of the World Bank and Other Stakeholders*. Washington, D.C.: World Bank.

Organizational Resources

Africa

GAS Development Associates Ltd.
Contact: Sulley Gariba
P.O. Box 16208
Accra, GHANA
Tel/Fax: 011-233-21-777-582

MWENGO
Contact: Ezra Mbogoro
P.O. Box HG
817 Highlands
Harare, ZIMBABWE
Tel/Fax: 263-4-722-363

Asia

Participatory Research in Asia
Contact: Rajesh Tandon
45, Sainik Farm, Khanpur
New Delhi, INDIA 110 029

Freedom from Hunger
Campaign/Action for Development
Food and Agriculture Organization
Contact: Kamla Bhasin
55, Lodi Estate
PB No. 3088
New Delhi, INDIA 110 003

Bangladesh Rural Advancement
Committee
Research and Evaluation Division
66 Mohakhali Commercial Area
Dhaka 1212, BANGLADESH
Tel: (8802) 884180-7
Fax: (8802) 883542

Europe

Marie-Thérèse Feuerstein
Consultant
49 Horton Street
London W8 7NT,
UNITED KINGDOM
Fax: (171) 937-1039

Institute of Development Studies
Contact: John Gaventa and
Robert Chambers
University of Sussex
Brighton BN1 9RE,
UNITED KINGDOM
Fax: (1273) 621202/691647

International Institute for
Environment and Development
3 Endsleigh Street
London WC1 HODD,
UNITED KINGDOM

Latin America/Caribbean

Instituto de Estudios Politicos
Universidad Nacional
Contact: Orlando Fals-Borda
Bogota, COLOMBIA
Tel: 571-368-1579
Fax: 561 -368-7471

Latin American Council for Adult
Eduction (CEAAL)
Contact: Jorge Osorio
Rafael Canas 218
Casilla 163-T
Santiago, CHILE
Tel: (562) 235-2532
Fax: (562) 235-6256

International Institute of Rural
Reconstruction
Apartado Postal 17-08-8494
Quito, ECUADOR
Fax: (593-2) 443-763

Pat Ellis and Associates
Contact: Patricia Ellis
No. 15 Sandford
St. Philip, BARBADOS
Tel/Fax: (246) 423-8115

North America

Centre for the Study of Training,
Investment and Economic
Restructuring
Carleton University
Contact: Ted Jackson
Social Science Building
1125 Colonel By Drive
Ottawa, Ontario
K1S SB6, CANADA
Tel: (613) 520-2600 Ext. 8241
Fax: (613) 520-3561
E-Mail: edward_jackson@carleton.ca

International Centre
Contact: Sheila Robinson and Philip
Cox
University of Calgary
2500 University Drive NW
Calgary, Alberta
T2N 1N4, CANADA
Tel: (403) 220-7700
Fax: (403) 289-0171

International Development Research
Centre, Evaluation Unit
Contact: Terry Smutylo
250 Albert Street
Ottawa, Ontario
K1G 3H9, CANADA
Tel: (613) 236-6163
Fax: (613) 583-0815

The World Bank
Contact: Deepa Narayan
1818 H Street, N.W.
Washington, D.C. 20433, USA
Tel: (202) 473- 1304
Fax: (202) 477-0541

The Fielding Institute
Contact: Peter Park
1313 Richards Alley
Wilmington, Delaware 19806, USA
Tel: (302) 427-7804
Fax: (302) 427-9314
E-Mail: ppark<104446.513
            compuserve.com

Department of Adult Education,
Community Development and
Counselling Psychology
Contact: Budd Hall
Ontario Institute for Studies in
Education
University of Toronto
252 Bloor Street West
Toronto, Ontario
MSS 1V6, CANADA
Tel: 416-923-6641 Ext. 2410
Fax: 416-926-4725
E-Mail: bhall@oise.utoronto.ca

International Council for Adult
Education
Contact: Lalita Ramdas
720 Bathurst Street
Suite 500
Toronto, Ontario
MSS 2R4, CANADA
Tel: 416-588-1211
Fax: 416-588-5725

World Education
Contact: Bonnie Mullinix
210 Lincoln Street
Boston, Massachusetts 02111, USA
Tel: (617) 482-9485
Fax: (617) 482-0617

Useful Websites

Institute of Development Studies, University of Sussex, Brighton, United Kingdom
• http://www.ids.ac.uk/eldis/pra/

Graduate School of Education, Harvard University, Cambridge, Massachusetts, USA
• http:/hugse l.harvard.edu/

Cornell University, Ithaca, New York, USA
• http://www.parnet.org/

Guelph University, Guelph, Canada
• http://tdg.res.uoguelph.ca/

InterAction, American Council for Voluntary International Action
• http://www.interaction.org/

Participatory Development Forum, Ottawa, Canada
• http://tdg.uoguelph.ca./~pi/index.html

United States Agency for International Development, Washington, D.C., USA
• http://www.info.usaid.gov/about/part_devtl

World Bank, Washington, D.C., USA
• http://www.worldbank.org/htmVhcovp/particip/partrepl.html
• http://www.worldbank.org/htmVedi/sourcebook/sbO303t.htm

About the Contributors

Edward T. Jackson is Director of the Centre for the Study of Training, Investment and Economic Restructuring and Associate Professor of Public Administration at Carleton University in Ottawa, Canada. He is also President of E.T. Jackson and Associates Ltd., a management consulting firm that has advised on development projects in fifty countries around the world. Dr. Jackson is co-editor of *Voices of Change: Participatory Research in the United States and Canada* (Bergin and Garvey/OISE Press, 1993) and *First Person Plural: A Community Development Approach to Social Change* (Black Rose, 1995).

Yusuf Kassam is a Toronto-based international development consultant specializing in education, training, rural development, and development management. Senior HRD Specialist with E.T. Jackson and Associates Ltd., Mr. Kassam is a former Professor of Adult Education at the University of Dar es Salaam in Tanzania and Director of Programs at the International Council for Adult Education. He is the co-editor of *Society for Participatory Research: An Emerging Alternative Methodology in Social Science Research* (Participatory Research in Asia, 1982), the author of *Illiterate No More: The Voices of New Literates from Tanzania* (Tanzania Publishing House, 1979), and *The Adult Education Revolution in Tanzania* (Shungwaya Publishers, 1978).

Marren Akatsa-Bukachi was a National Program Secretary of the Kenya YWCA in Nairobi. Educated at the University of Delhi, she previously worked in a senior capacity for the Kenyan Ministry of Culture and Social Services. Mrs. Akatsa-Bukachi was instrumental in developing an evaluation plan for the YWCA and working with grassroots women on projects that enhance their status.

Gary Anderson teaches methodology and program evaluation in the Department of Administration and Policy Studies in Education, McGill University, which he chaired until 1995. He is also President of Universalia, one of Canada's leading management consulting firms. His recent books include *Fundamentals of Educational Research* (Falmer, 1990) and (with his partner, Charles Lusthaus) *Institutional Assessment* (IDRC, 1995).

Kamla Bhasin, a social scientist by training, has been involved with issues related to development, education, gender, and media since 1972, when she joined a voluntary organization in Rajasthan, India. Since 1976, she has been working with the FAO's Freedom from Hunger Campaign/Action for Development in New Delhi, supporting innovative NGO initiatives, organizing training workshops and facilitating networking among NGOs, women's organizations, and people's organizations in South Asia.

Scott Clark is presently Principal Researcher, Criminal Law and Young Offenders Research Unit, Department of Justice of Canada, Ottawa. He also teaches anthropology and sociology at Carleton University, where he is an Adjunct Research Professor. Prior to his current position, he worked as an employee and consultant for First Nation communities and organizations in Canada. He received his Ph.D. in Social Anthropology from the University of Edinburgh.

John Cove is a Professor of Sociology and Anthropology at Carleton University. His primary field of interest is in Aboriginal rights movements. His research in Canada, Australia, and New Zealand has involved land claims, criminal justice issues, and the politics of research.

Philip Cox coordinated the process evaluation of the Nepal Health Development Project. He has been an evaluation and community development consultant with the Calgary firm PLAN:NET 2000 since 1990. In this role he has carried out participatory evaluation assignments for local and international clients, including the Mennonite Central Committee, Alberta Multiculturalism Commission, Canadian International Development Agency, and UNCHS (Habitat). He holds a B.A. in Political Science and is completing a Master's Degree in Environmental Design (Planning) at the University of Calgary. He is a member of the Canadian Evaluation Society.

Patricia Ellis is a Caribbean consultant with extensive experience in the areas of education and development. Among her interests are research and training, and she is well known for her expertise in using participatory methodology in conducting these activities. She has worked with women's organizations and with women at all levels of Caribbean society, and has also worked with women's groups in Nigeria. Dr. Ellis has carried out many studies examining women's condition and has conducted a wide range of training programs to empower, equip, and enable women to deal with their problems.

Marie-Thérèse Feuerstein, originally trained as a nurse/midwife, has worked for twenty years as a freelance consultant in health, community development, and adult education for UNDP, World Bank, and other UN and NGO development agencies. Author of *Partners in Evaluation*, reprinted eight times since 1987, Dr. Feuerstein has worked in Asia, Africa, and the Americas.

Jim Freedman is a Professor of Anthropology at the University of Western Ontario and operates a private firm that consults on international development for the United Nations, CIDA, and international NGOs. He has authored a number of books, monographs, and articles on topics ranging from the future of foreign aid to evaluation methodology to African religions and professional wrestling. His monograph, *Participatory Evaluation: Making Projects Work,* is published by the International Centre at the University of Calgary.

Sulley Gariba is a Ghanaian consultant specializing in rural development, water supply, institution building, evaluation, and cross-cultural training. His clients have included the World Bank, the German Technical Agency (GTZ), Partnership Africa-Canada, and the Canadian International Development Agency. He is President of G.A.S. Development Associates Limited, based in Accra, Ghana. Dr. Gariba has taught at the University of Development Studies in Tamale, Ghana, as well as at Carleton and Trent Universities.

Deborah Gilsig, a Universalia evaluation consultant, is particularly concerned with evaluation training and with research and data collection technology. She has been involved in the development of a variety of data collection approaches and is currently developing techniques for the third and fourth levels of training evaluation.

Budd L. Hall is a leader in the theory and practice of participatory research worldwide. A former Secretary-General of the International Council for Adult Education, Dr. Hall is Chair and Professor in the Department of Adult Education at the Ontario Institute for Studies in Education, Community Development and Counselling Psychology at the University of Toronto and a founder of the Institute's Transformative Learning Centre. He has published widely on participatory research, transformative learning, and environmental education and has worked in more than seventy nations around the world.

Andrew J. Livingstone is an Ottawa-based consultant with Cowater International specializing in the participatory and social dimensions of rural and urban water and sanitation. Formerly the manager of a major water project funded by CIDA and implemented by Wardrop Engineering and the Ghana Water and Sewerage Corporation in northern Ghana, Dr. Livingstone has also managed and advised projects in southern and eastern Africa and northern Canada. He is a member of the UN/WHO Collaborative Council Working Group on Operation and Maintenance and is active in the International Water Resources Association.

Bonnie B. Mullinix is Training and Program Officer with World Education Inc. in Boston. A specialist in training, small-enterprise development, and participatory evaluation, she currently supports projects in Kenya, Namibia, Mali, and Benin. Dr. Mullinix previously worked on adult education and literacy programs in Malawi and The Gambia, as well as with the Peace Corps. She holds a doctorate in international and nonformal education from the University of Massachusetts at Amherst.

Sheila A. Robinson coordinated the Nepal Health Development Project through the University of Calgary's International Centre (1989–1995). She holds a B.Sc. in Nursing, an M.A. in Development Studies, and a Ph.D. in Community Health Science. Her fifteen years' experience in international health and development spans fieldwork, research, teaching, supervision, project planning, management, and evaluation. She is an Adjunct Professor in the Department of Community Health Science and the Faculty of Nursing at the University of Calgary. Dr. Robinson served as President of the Canadian Society for International Health (1991–1994).

Elizabeth (Bessa) Whitmore is Associate Professor in the School of Social Work at Carleton University in Ottawa, Canada. Dr. Whitmore has taught and written widely on empowerment and evaluation and is presently preparing a book on the theory and practice of participatory evaluation. Her international work has involved projects in Mexico and Guyana and elsewhere in Central America and the Caribbean.

Index

aboriginal communities: guidance aids in Canada, 56–57; treaty rights in Australia, 38–39

accidental interviews, as information technique, 147

accountability: in cooperative development projects, 13–14; demanded by donor governments, 162; in result-based management systems, 50

accounting methods, use by Ghana's GWSC, 180

action anthropology, postwar advent of, 38

action groups. *See* AGs

actors, poor people as not qualifying, 26

advocate(s), anthropologists as, 39

African Medical Research Foundation (AMREF), 24–25

Agency for International Development (U.S.), 169

agriculture: land available for in Rose Hill, 210; status of in Ghana villages, 70, 73

AGs (action groups): as partners with people's organizations, 86, 87; realities and processes, 89, 90; self-evaluations, 90–94

"aid chain," participation at different points, 6–7

aid evaluation, local empowerment solutions, 3–4

Akatsa-Bukachi, Marren, 17

American Anthropologic Association (AAA), 40

analysis techniques: of community leadership status, 74; gender and social training, 53, 55, 110; of Rose Hill community project finances, 204–5

Anderson, Gary, 17, 58

antenatal care, in India, 102, 105, *table* 103

anthropology: ethical considerations in dealing with indigenous peoples, 36–48; and participatory action research, 9–10

antipoverty programs, as macro-level indicator, 59

appraisals, participatory, 27, 28, 55, 128–29, 146–47

Asian Drama (Myrdal), 26

aspirations, interplay with reality, 89

assets, economic, range of in a village, 73–74

Australia, aboriginal rights, 38–39

Australian Association for Applied Anthropology (AAAA), 40–41

awareness, public, evaluation in Ghana's GWSC project, *table* 190

bakery project, evaluation of in Rose Hill study, 205, 207, 210

Bangladesh, evaluations of BRDB programs, 108–20

Bangladesh Rural Advancement Committee (BRAC), 12, 116

Bangladesh Rural Development Board (BRDB), 109–10, 112, 119

banking: concepts taught in Nepalese villages, 138; corrupt officials in India, 100, 102

behavior, of the poor, 34

behavior, of the powerful: and participatory evaluation, 12–15; resistance to women's cooperatives, 113–14

beneficiary assessments: communication with project managers, 23–24; local program participants' perspectives and values, 5–6, 52

benefits: and costs of micro-level programs, 58; and costs of participatory evaluations, 165; results of Rose Hill program, 207–8, 210; of Shahapur Bittaheen Women's Cooperative Society, 112–17

betterment, personal, in areas of poverty, 34

Bhasin, Kamla, 8, 16

Bibi, Mosammat Jainab, description of her experience in a cooperative, 112–17

241